INVESTIGATIONS OF THE ART
OF THE INTERVIEW

INVESTIGATIONS AND THE ART OF THE INTERVIEW

FOURTH EDITION

Written by

INGE SEBYAN BLACK

LAWRENCE J. FENNELLY

Butterworth-Heinemann
An imprint of Elsevier

Library of Congress Cataloging-in-Publication Data
A catalog record for this book is available from the Library of Congress

British Library Cataloguing-in-Publication Data
A catalogue record for this book is available from the British Library

ISBN: 978-0-12-822192-1

For information on all Butterworth-Heinemann publications
visit our website at https://www.elsevier.com/books-and-journals

Publisher: Nikki Levy
Acquisitions Editor: Elizabeth Brown
Editorial Project Manager: Tracy Tufaga
Production Project Manager: Kiruthika Govindaraju
Cover designer: Mark Rogers

Typeset by SPi Global, India

Dedication

This book is dedicated to my daughters Brittany and Brooke and only son, Justin.

My beloved 22-year-old daughter, *Brittany Alexandra*, was tragically and abruptly killed by another motorist on June 6, 2012. Brittany is sadly missed by everyone who knew and loved her. Brittany will live in our hearts forever as she was filled with spirit, passion, wisdom, kindness, talent, and love. Her free spirit and radiance will forever be a shining light.

My daughter, *Brooke Samantha*, also decided to enter a male dominated industry as an electrician. She is driven, determined, passionate and a role model for other women.

Inge

I have nine beautiful grandchildren and wish to dedicate my contribution of this book to them: Bill, Maggie, Abbey, Emma, Coleman, Ben, Brian and twins, Megan & Claire. They are all are number one in my world. This generation should be called the achiever generation because what they have accomplished, in a short time, is beyond greatness.

Larry

Contents

Part 1

Introduction

1. Miranda warning and the equivalent across the globe

2. Glossary of terminology

3. Ethics

Part 2

The interview process

13. Communication for the investigation manager and key management skills

14. Initiating and prioritizing investigations

15. The rules of evidence

Part 3

Specific investigations and skills

16. Creating the report

17. Internal controls and investigations

18. Cargo theft investigative techniques

19. Cybercrimes and investigations

20. Investigations using open source intelligence (OSINT)

21. Fraud investigations

22. Workplace violence and harassment investigations

23. Skills of successful investigators

24. Lucky or skilled

Mission statement

Our goal is to help educate interviewers, even those who only occasionally participate in interviews. We encourage you to prepare for each interview as though it is the interview of your life, because maybe it will be. You might only have one chance to talk to your subject, so make it successful. We hope to help you learn to do that. Finally, reading this book should be ongoing throughout your career, as we have tried our best to provide you with as much information on these topics as possible.

Inge Sebyan Black
Lawrence J. Fennelly

Foreword

Being a specialized investigator with capabilities that are second to none is hard to come by. Inge is one of those few people who is second to none. When you study the methods and techniques used by investigators for intelligence gathering, interviewing, fraud investigations, and corporate due diligence as a few areas to consider, it is hard to know the best people to hire. Over the last 25–30 years, I have had the opportunity to learn specialized skills to accomplish investigations on a higher level. Being female in this industry has been an advantage and a privilege.

Then, years ago, I met Inge Sebyan Black. She was being honored for her history of accomplishments in the security industry. I listened to the description of her background and realized there is so much more that can be accomplished. Her specialties in both security and investigations were inspiring to me. The fact that she takes the time to write these incredibly informative books reminds me how much more we can achieve even when believe we have reached the top. She continues to evolve and remain relevant by challenging herself to learn and work in the information security/cyber security area. I am proud to be a colleague and a trusted friend of Inge's. You will learn more than you anticipated while reading this book.

Sandra Stibbards
Camelot Investigations

Preface

This wonderful book, *Investigations and the Art of the Interview,* is a classic and timeless reference work that belongs in every investigator's library. I am humbled and grateful to write this preface for Inge's book. Past editions have enriched my life and professional prowess. I am certain this new edition will do the same for you.

Over my 40-plus years of experience as a TV network investigative reporter, major-market radio talk show host, and private investigator, I have interviewed a remarkable cross section of society: presidents, senators, movie stars, NFL quarterbacks, Mafia hit men, Ku Klux Klansmen, skid-row drunks, Middle Eastern terrorists, captains of Industry, union leaders, professional deadbeats, illegal migrant workers, destitute welfare mothers, ordinary moms and pops, and criminals of every description. Most of these interview subjects had something to hide. My job was to ferret out their secrets to support TV news reports or courtroom litigation. I quickly learned that even the most cautious people will say damning things when skillfully questioned by a prepared and professional interviewer.

I learned how to do investigative interviews the hard way—through daily practice and lots of trial and error in newsrooms and on the streets, under the mentoring of tough-nosed editors and hard-boiled private eyes. I wish Inge's book had been available when I started my career, because it would have prevented many errors and humiliating embarrassments I experienced along the way. Believe me, there's nothing like bungling an interview on live TV to cut you down to size in a hurry!

I heartily recommend her book to both the novice and veteran interviewer. With the proliferation of pop psychology fads in our media and colleges, it is remarkably difficult to find solid information on interviewing techniques that is both time tested and reliable. The information revealed is worth its weight in gold, and no successful investigator can ever afford to stop learning.

I have learned repeatedly throughout my career that every investigation is only as good as the information it gathers and you can never ignore the human factor. Though an enormous number of facts can be determined through examination of written records and physical evidence, the information from human sources is always of critical importance to provide us with the full truth of events. Interviewing is a form of communication and evidence gathering. Getting accurate and truthful information out of people is always a challenge, even for the most highly trained investigative interviewer.

This book will help you learn how to develop and discover the human intelligence information that solves cases. Furthermore, learning investigative interviewing skills will help you in all aspects of your personal and professional life, because the techniques will help you distinguish fact from fiction and give you a competitive edge over others.

The job of an investigative interviewer is tough under the best of circumstances. The mission is to have a structured conversation that elicits information useful to establishing facts and determining culpability from interview subjects who are often evasive, reluctant, or hostile. It is an art to persuade any person to let us into his or her mind at the critical moments of an event so that we can get an insider's view of the action. The best investigative interviewers allow the person to talk about himself and describe a situation step by step from his own perspective and to talk about how he overcame obstacles along the way, all while guiding him into disclosing significant facts or admitting culpability he would otherwise conceal.

In my experience a good investigative interview yields information that can be divided into "hard" and "soft" categories. Hard information stated in an interview consists of the simple facts that often can be independently corroborated to help build a case. But interviews that generate only those facts usually lack richness and depth.

Often, more important is the "soft information" of human experience revealed during an interview, the complex tapestry of personal dramas, emotions, intentions, thoughts, reactions, values, and degrees of commitment or determination. It is the soft information that helps us establish motive and develops the color that provides us with a truer understanding of any event or situation. In trying to ascertain fact, there is no substitute for observing human behavior.

There is an old Chinese adage that a picture is worth a thousand words. That is true. But I learned in TV news that a videotape is worth a million words when it shows the body language of a smirk or arched eyebrow, the physical and verbal gyrations of an agonized confession, a vocal tone of arrogance or sarcasm, or the hysterical sobbing of an interviewee repenting their criminal deeds. There is no substitute for an effective investigative interview of a human being.

Many years ago, I investigated a powerful politician who was lining his pockets with graft and was introducing legislation that benefited his hidden personal financial interests. The documents I collected laid out the facts in great detail. But it was the TV investigative interview, in which the politician nonchalantly and flippantly admitted his misconduct without any visible remorse that told the full story and gave it life. His political career fizzled quickly after the TV audience saw and heard his performance.

So, what are the traits of truly great investigative interviewers? They have constant curiosity and an unquenchable thirst for knowledge. They prepare for an interview by researching in advance as much information as possible. They know what the answers to questions are likely to be before they are asked. They know that asking obviously well-informed questions helps create a sense of intimacy and often throws the people being questioned off balance by signaling that the interviewer is not to be taken lightly. They know how to quickly establish rapport and personal chemistry with the interview subject, then ask a blend of both open-ended and pointed questions with impeccable and precise timing while carefully listening to the responses to achieve successful results. They are excellent listeners of the spoken word and observers of unspoken body language. They can be simultaneously both gentle and tough questioners. They have a taste for going for the jugular while instinctively knowing when to back off or shift gears if the interview takes unexpected and useful turns. And they know how to keep their own emotions in check while hearing the most graphic and disturbing revelations.

Investigative interviewers usually make their biggest mistakes when they become impatient and try to speed up interviews to get key information. A skilled interviewer understands the value in taking plenty of time to listen and elicit information. Speeding up the process usually creates more problems than it solves, especially when interview subjects lose their comfort zone and begin to evade or clam up.

Skilled interviewers also know when to ask a pointed question and then shut up. Staying silent often causes an interview subject to fill in the uncomfortable gap by carrying on the conversation and inadvertently disclosing valuable information. Most people need some time to grapple with their thoughts and develop a response. Often a gem pops out of the interview subject's mouth just because the questioner was silent.

The best interviewers always invite the last word from those being questioned. They ask whether there is anything else that should be discussed or if there is any question the other person would like to ask. Sometimes an unexplored angle reveals the most useful information. These techniques and much more are explained in depth in *Investigations and the Art of the Interview*.

Investigative interviewing skills are not easy to acquire. It takes years of practice and experience to perfect them. As a veteran investigative journalist and private investigator, I say without reservation that this book will help you. Study it carefully and keep it handy for future reference. I am confident that the knowledge gained from studying *Investigations and the Art of the Interview* will greatly help shorten the learning curve for you to become a master of the art.

Good luck in your continuing search for truth and justice.

Pat Clawson

CNN and NBC News, Flint, MI, United States
CNN and NBC News, Washington, DC, United States

Note: Although we just recently lost Pat, I am grateful to my friend, and Pat's wife, Laurie Clawson and her support of Pat's writing and including this Preface.

About the authors

Inge Sebyan Black, CPP, CFE, CEM, is the CEO of Security Risk, LLC. She has spent over 42 years in corporate security management, specializing in workplace violence, risk assessments, investigations, and emergency management. Certified by FEMA and the State of MN as a Certified Emergency Manager, she also attended DOJ training in WMD/COBRA from an appointment by President Clinton. She has held her private investigator license in both the United States and Canada since 1997. Inge authored the book "The Art of Investigative Interviewing, third edition" and published chapters in over 10 books with such titles as: Security Management, Hiring the Right Fit, Officer Safety, Domestic Abuse, Rape on College Campuses, Workplace Violence, and others. Inge was presented with the Karen Marquez award in 2014 for her achievements in Physical Security. She was appointed Council Vice President for ASIS International Councils, overseeing ASIS Councils in 2018 and continues to serve as a CVP. In 2019 Inge entered the Information Security/cyber side of security and is currently working in Information Security/Cyber for a Fortune 100 Company.

Lawrence J. Fennelly, CPOI, CSSI, is an internationally recognized authority on crime prevention, security planning, and analysis and on the study of how environmental factors (CPTED), physical hardware, alarms, lighting, site design, management practices, litigation consultants, security policies and procedures, and guard management contribute to criminal victimization. In his security consultant experience, he has conducted surveys/audits of large and small complexes plus written a set of best practices. Mr. Fennelly is a Lifetime of the American Society for Industrial Security.

This association consists of about 34,000 members who are all in the security profession. He has been involved in several of their National Committees and lecturing for them. He is a past chair of the Crime Prevention & Loss Prevention Council and in 2015 the chair of the ASIS, School Safety & Security Council. Currently, he is the Chairman of the Board of Directors of IFPO.

Acknowledgments

I would like to express my thanks and love to the friends that have been on this journey with me for so many years, *Ann Shaw, Greg Carlson, Gail Essen, Debra Kuper, Laurie Broome, Pat Morris*, and *Mary* and *Gus Blanchard*, for their love and support. They constantly remind me of my strength while empowering, supporting, and encouraging me.

A special thanks to my mother, *Anna Marie*, for your love and support.

Inge Sebyan Black

Introduction

Inge Sebyan Black

This is the fourth edition of the *Art of Investigative Interviewing*, but it was more fitting to rename it, *"Investigations and the Art of the Interview,"* because the art is in the interview and I wanted to include the investigation process from the preparation through testifying in court. Chuck Yeschke, a friend and mentor, who authored the first and second editions, passed away in 2006. In 2012 I was asked write the third edition of *The Art of Investigative Interviewing*, without anyone knowing we had known each other for more than 30 years. I was honored and privileged to be asked to write the third edition, because of the connection I had to both Chuck and to the subject matter.

When I started my career in security management after my degrees in Police Science, Criminal Justice subsequently earning my Law Enforcement/POST license, most of my peers and definitely the majority of my predecessors had come from either a military background or a law enforcement background. The interviewing techniques used through the 1980s, which incorporated coercion and confrontation, are definitely different from the interview techniques used today. No matter the training or specific technique you have or will receive, your skills will continue to develop, and through continuous practice, your interviewing style will be unique to you.

My philosophy is to approach each interview with the knowledge that there is a high probability that you may only get one chance at interviewing your subject, so it is critical that you are fully prepared. Being prepared will make the difference between having a successful interview or an unsuccessful one.

I asked Larry Fennelly, my very dear friend, mentor, and the most dedicated person that I have ever met in my 42 years in security, to co-author this fourth edition alongside me. Our relationship started in 1982 when Larry asked me to join the Crime Prevention Council for ASIS International. We co-presented the first session of its kind in 1983, titled "Rape and Violent Crime." Since then, we have co-presented on many topics at ASIS International Annual Conference, now known as ASIS GSX.

In 1994 Larry asked me to write a chapter on domestic violence, turning into multiple editions over the last 30 years. I have also authored chapters in many of Larry's books since then. I have been so fortunate to have had the privilege of working with him, presenting with him, and writing with him. I will always aspire to being as good of a mentor and friend as Larry has been to me.

Our goal in writing this book is to pass along some of the skills we have learned through the many years. We hope this might be a helpful guide for new interviewers or those who only rarely conduct interviews but who need the information as much as skilled interviewers. Interviewers have to draw on elements from psychology, philosophy, and sociology and from their own personal empathy, respect, and compassion. We discuss all these elements throughout the book, along with the importance of preparation and determining the goal of each interview. We also discuss other factors that should be considered, such as the setting, location, and intensity of the interview.

Each interviewer brings unique skills to the task because of his or her training, personality, and experience. Interviewing is indeed an art because each of us brings our unique skill into each interview that we conduct.

PART 1

Introduction

Miranda warning and the equivalent across the globe

Introduction

Before we discuss interviewing, we must discuss the Miranda rights or equivalent in other jurisdictions. Police officers in many countries including the United States are required to give a person their Miranda rights *prior* to any interrogation or questioning of a person. Investigators in the private sector, such as corporation investigators and private investigators, are not required to give the Miranda prior to an interview.

There are 108 jurisdictions across the globe that have warnings similar to the Miranda warning used in the United States. Although the warnings across the globe vary, they include the right to remain silent and the right to legal counsel. Many countries also specify that a person arrested or detained has the right to be informed of the reasons for the arrest or detention or of the charges being brought. Additionally, in some countries, a person also has the right to have these rights explained in a language the person can understand. *Commonwealth countries have traditionally followed the English Judges' Rules developed in the early 20th century, and some continue to do so, while many Member States of the European Union (EU) have adopted an EU directive on the issue.*[1] *Points of variance among the countries concern the timing of the warning and whether the detainee is told that the fact of remaining silent will or will not be used in legal proceedings.*

Miranda v. Arizona 1966

Before a person in police custody or otherwise deprived of freedom "in any significant way" may be interviewed or interrogated, *Miranda* warnings must be given (*Miranda* v. *Arizona* [1966]). The exact wording

---

[1] https://www.loc.gov/law/help/miranda-warning-equivalents-abroad/index.php.

of the *Miranda* rights statement is not specified in the Supreme Court's historic decision. Instead, law enforcement agencies have created a basic set of simple statements that can be read to accused persons prior to any questioning. Here are paraphrased examples of the basic *Miranda* rights statements, along with related excerpts from the Supreme Court decision:

1. You have the right to remain silent.
2. Anything you say can be used against you in a court of law.
3. You have the right to have an attorney present now and during any future questioning.
4. If you cannot afford an attorney, one will be appointed to you free of charge if you wish.
5. Do you understand these rights?

These warnings have come to be known as the *Miranda warnings*, after the US Supreme Court case in which they were enumerated. The *Miranda* warnings apply *only* to "investigative custodial questioning aimed at eliciting evidence of a crime." Subjects in custody must understand what they are being told. The investigator is not permitted to bully a suspect into talking once they decide not to do so nor may the investigator attempt to dissuade a suspect from speaking with a lawyer. This ensures that subjects in custody know that they have the right to remain silent. After receiving the required warnings and expressing willingness to answer questions, a subject in custody may legally be interrogated. It is unnecessary to embellish the *Miranda* warnings or to add new warnings. Similarly, it is unnecessary to use the exact language contained in *Miranda*.

Canada, Canadian Charter of Rights and Freedoms, 1982

In Canada, equivalent rights exist pursuant to the Charter of Rights and Freedoms. Although not the exact wording with the right to silence, the Supreme Court has found the right protected as a principle of fundamental justice. The right to remain silent is implied in the Charter and varies from one police force to another.

To summarize the rights given by the Royal Canadian Mounted Police are as follows:

1. Right to silence
   a. The person does not have to say anything unless they wish.
   b. The person is not promised anything from what they say and not threatened if they chose not to talk.
   c. Anything a person states can be used as evidence.
2. Right to legal counsel
   a. The person has the right to retain and instruct the counsel of their choice immediately without delay.

b. Before answering any questions, they can contact their counsel or get free advice from Duty Counsel. If they want Legal Aid, they are provided with the number, along with a phone.

A detained person also has the right to be informed of why they are being questioned and to have the detention legally validated. If not legally detained, they can be released.

These warnings are given to criminal suspects in police custody before an interrogation begins.

Mexico

Under the Mexican Constitution a person suspected of a crime has the right to be notified, both at the time of arrest and when in court before a judge.

They are advised as follows:

1. They are told why they are arrested and the acts they are accused of committing.
2. They are told that they have the right to remain silent, and that if they chose to remain silent, it will not be held against them.
3. The person is told that they may have an attorney of their choice or one appointed by the government under circumstances.

Australia

There are no "Miranda" rights read to someone suspected of committing a crime in Australia; however, by law, suspects have the right to remain silent. Although Australia does not have a federal legislative bill of rights for those arrested or detained, the right to remain silent is recognized to be within the right to not self-incriminate. At the federal level the Crimes Act 1914 (Cth), with amendments made in 1991, does requires that a person arrested be informed of their right to talk with a friend, relative, or lawyer. It also stipulates that the investigator must advise the arrested person, before any questioning starts, that they have the right to remain silent and that anything they say or do can be used as evidence.

South Korea

South Korea has some rights similar to the Miranda through The Constitution of the Republic of Korea (South Korea). A suspect must be informed of the reason of their arrest and told that they have a right to counsel immediately. The prosecutor or senior judicial official must advise the arrested person, prior to any interrogation:

1. They have the right to remain silent, which will not be held against them.
2. If the suspect makes a statement waiving the right to refuse to make a statement, this may be used as evidence for being guilty.
3. The suspect has a right to counsel and the counsel can be present in the interrogation.

Protocol is if the suspect chooses to remain silent and chooses to have counsel, this shall be written down in their own handwriting. If the person is not able to write, their answer shall be written for them along with a required printed signature or seal.

Austria, Austrian Code of Criminal Procedures

Austrian Code of Criminal Procedure requires the accused person be informed of essential rights as soon as possible. The accused must be informed of the following:

1. Their right to remain silent or make a statement.
2. Their right to counsel (as long as there is no chance of evidence destruction).
3. The accused is informed that any statement can be used as evidence against him or her.

England and Wales

Rights for arrested persons follow the Codes of Practice, within the Police and Criminal Evidence Act 1984. When an arrest is made, the officer must

1. inform the person that they are under arrest
2. the reason for the arrest
3. that the person can remain silent, however it could harm their defense
4. they are advised that anything they say can be used against them.

There are circumstances that allow the court in England and Wales to draw adverse implications from the person's failure to say anything about their involvement in the criminal offense.

European Union

Right to information in criminal proceedings

Under Directive 2012/13 the EU has established common minimum standards on the rights of suspects. This is a Miranda-type warning.

The Directive requires Member States to follow national law in regard to accused persons as soon as possible:

1. Person is advised that they have the right to counsel.
2. Advised of free legal advice and conditions for such.
3. Advised of the reason of the arrest.
4. Advise of the right to interpretation and translation services.
5. The right to remain silent.

EU Members are required to provide this information orally or in writing and in a clear language that is understood by the accused. They also consider the needs of vulnerable persons.

The Directive also requires Member States to promptly provide a written Letter of Rights to accused persons. The accused are also given the chance to read the Letter of Rights and be in possession of them throughout their time of detention.

As indicated previously, many use similar language with variations.

To ensure that a confession holds up in court, follow proper procedures for interviewing the subject. If you are in the public sector, you must make it clear when a suspect is not under arrest and must document that the suspect is free to leave if he or she so desires. If the inquiry is held in an official location, such as a police station, it is imperative that interviewees comprehend that they are not being detained or in custody, if such is the case. Voluntary response is vital in these matters. To fight the admissibility of a confession in court, defense attorneys sometimes argue that psychological coercion was used to obtain the confession.

Some investigators earnestly urge the subject to grant permission for the interrogation; other investigators, directly or indirectly, strongly advise the subject not to grant permission. As you give the warnings, use a neutral tone and a matter-of-fact manner. This is not a time to caution, suggest, frighten, or admonish the person in custody.

Let's take a minute to examine the words *interview* and *interrogation*, because they will undoubtedly come up throughout this book and throughout your career as an investigative interviewer. An *interview* is a nonaccusatory question-and-answer session with anyone you are trying to obtain information from witnesses, suspects, or victims. If you recall, the successful interview is one that collects accurate and useful information. Some of the questions may be of an investigative nature, some to elicit behavioral responses. The interviewer is building rapport and maintaining a nonaccusatory tone and demeanor throughout the interview. The skilled interviewer will ask questions that produce a narrative answer rather than a yes-or-no response. Because of the nature of the questions, the interviewee will do most of the talking. The only information gathered should come from the interviewee.

An *interrogation* is often used to elicit the truth from a person the investigator believes has lied during an interview. There may come a point in the interview that it turns from an interview into an interrogation or the other way around. It will depend on the interviewee as to the information he gives up or the information he is hiding. An interviewer that is skilled will be able to take it from an interview to an interrogation and then back when necessary. It takes practice to be able to read a person and then determine your strategy. We will talk more about practice, preparation, and skill throughout the book.

When the *Miranda* warnings are required

In 1976 the Supreme Court removed the misconception that *Miranda* warnings must be given to anyone upon whom suspicion is "focused." Rather the Court said, the warnings are required only when the subject is in police custody.

In an earlier case the Court had defined "in police custody or otherwise deprived of freedom in any significant way" (the wording used in *Miranda v. Arizona* 1966). The Court said that the key elements are "the time of the interrogation, the number of officers involved, and the apparent formal arrest of the subject" (*Orozco v. Texas* 1969).

Regarding noncustodial interviewing within a police facility, the Supreme Court held that a noncustodial situation does not require the *Miranda* warnings simply because a reviewing court concludes that, even in the absence of any formal arrest or restraint of freedom of movement, the questioning took place in a "coercive environment" (*Oregon v. Mathiason* 1977). The Court considered the circumstances of the interrogation when it provided this opinion: Any interview of one suspected of a crime by a police officer will have coercive aspects to it, simply by virtue of the fact that the police officer is part of a law enforcement system that may ultimately cause the suspect to be charged with a crime. But police officers are not required to administer *Miranda* warnings to everyone whom they question. Nor is the requirement of warnings to be imposed simply because the questioning takes place in the station house, or because the questioned person is one whom the police suspect. *Miranda* warnings are required only where there has been such a restriction on a person's freedom as to render him "in custody." It was that sort of coercive environment to which *Miranda* by its terms was made applicable and to which it is limited.

Legally, *interrogation* is defined as asking a question, making a comment, displaying an object, or presenting a police report if this action calls for a response that may be incriminating. The subtle use of these actions makes them "functional equivalents" of direct questions asked during an interrogation (*Brewer* v. *Williams* 1977). This means that they, too, are bound by *Miranda*, but an exception can be found in *Rhode Island* v. *Innes* (1980).

If suspects who are not in custody freely consent to be interviewed or interrogated, there is no requirement that they be given the *Miranda* warnings. If an interviewee begins to confess without being interrogated, let him or her continue without interruption. When the confession has concluded, give the *Miranda* warnings to prevent any court from holding that custody began at the conclusion of the confession. Subjects in custody can waive their constitutional rights. This is usually done in writing and is signed, but oral waivers will suffice.

Police officers working private or part-time positions are bound by the *Miranda* ruling. If you are not conducting the investigation as a police officer, the *Miranda* decision does not affect you unless you are acting in cooperation with the police as a police agent. It's important to realize, however, that regardless of your role as an investigator, if you compel someone to confess, you are coercing a confession that will not hold up as legal evidence. Private security investigators generally do not have to administer *Miranda* warnings unless they have the authority to make an arrest.

Glossary of terminology

Introduction

What is an investigation? An investigation is a planned and organized determination of facts concerning specific events, occurrences, or conditions for a particular purpose. You need to answers the who, when, where, why (MOTIVE), and how.

An effective investigation report must be easy to read and follow, must be detailed enough so that someone unfamiliar with the case can understand what was done, documents the findings and facts of an investigation, demonstrates that all allegations were addressed, includes recommendations and a follow-up of corrective action taken, and is clearly written, without grammatical, spelling, and factual errors.

This glossary of investigative terms will aid you in the reading of this book and give you an understanding of terms and the contents of this book:

1. Interview (investigative)—A meeting in which a person is asked about personal views. General information gathering. A face-to-face meeting to gather evidence or information from a person. This type of interview uses a noncoercive approach and uses open-ended questions to encourage communication. This applies to all interviews regardless of whether the interviewee is a witness, victim, or suspect.
2. Interrogation—A meeting where a person is asked questions. Questioning a witness or suspect to obtain information about a crime.
3. Suspect—The person believed to have committed the offense.
4. Witness—Any person, other than the suspect, with information concerning the incident.
5. Relevance—Means that the information developed pertains to the subject of the investigation.
6. Subpoena—Is a legal process issued by a court directing a person to appear at a designated time and place for the purpose of testifying or producing documents or both.

7. Physical Surveillance—Focus is on the property or specific persons involved.
   Technical Surveillance—Focus is on the communications (cell phone, iPad, email, tape, and video).
8. Evidence—Is something that makes another thing evident (a sign, a statement, and an object). Types of evidence: oral evidence (court testimony), documentary evidence (written or taped testimony), and physical evidence.
9. Due diligence—Comes from common law and refers to the exercise of the amount of care appropriate to the circumstances.
10. Types of investigations:
    a. Open investigations—All interviews and facts are presented in the open.
    b. Covert investigations—The investigator tries to go unnoticed.
    c. Undercover investigations—When an investigator is placed into an environment with a hidden or masked persona in an effort to blend in, investigation from the inside.
11. There are FIVE attributes that characterize an effective and reliable investigation:
    a. objectivity
    b. thoroughness
    c. relevance
    d. accuracy
    e. timeliness
12. Age Discrimination in Employment Act
    The Age Discrimination in Employment Act bans discrimination on the basis of age against workers or applicants age 40 or older.
13. This act is actually an amendment to the Administrative Procedures Act and deals with the release and disclosure of certain kinds on information by the federal government.
    Many people think this is a new law, but it was actually passed in 1966. Only recently have the courts declared many of the documents to fall into the area of "Free for Disclosure."
14. (FOIA) Exceptions to the release of the information in place National Security concerns internal personnel rules and practices (the FBI and CIA have these in spades). Any information exempted by statute (again the list is long and distinguished) trade secrets, and confidential or financial information. The list of investigation records is long.
15. Fair Credit Reporting Act
    The federal Fair Credit Reporting Act (FCRA) is designed to promote accuracy, fairness, and privacy on information in the files of every "Consumer Reporting Agency" (CRA).

16. Americans with Disabilities Act of 1990
This act requires that public accommodations be made accessible and that public entities and utilities provide needed services for disabled persons.
17. Checking the Criminal Record "Much has changed because of case law" "Gregory versus Litton," No questions may be asked concerning prior arrest.
Questions MAY be asked about prior convictions. You can't categorically reject an applicant because of convictions. Whole man principle must apply.
18. Defamation
An untrue statement made by one person to another:
    a. Slander—An oral statement of untruth.
    b. Libel—A written statement of untruth.
19. Types of investigative functions:
    a. Application and/or background investigations.
    b. Incident investigations of suspected crimes or company policy violations.
    c. Administrative inquiries (this includes all other investigative areas).
20. During investigations, use caution to avoid the following:
Charges of invasion of privacy, incidents that could be embarrassing to the company, complaints to the FTO or other regulatory body, complaints to the EEOC, and allegations of unfair labor practices.
21. Preemployment investigations
Ninety-eight percent of all employment application falsifications fall into two general categories: willful omissions of material fact and misrepresentations of education or work experience.
22. Chain of Custody
Every person that touches a piece of evidence is a link in the chain. The longer the chain, the weaker it becomes. A detailed record on every person that handled the evidence (and who) must be kept to limit the contamination of the evidence.
23. National Crime Information Center (NCIC)
NCIC is the most widely used law enforcement computer system. Most major law enforcement agencies have NCIC connections.
24. CORI checks are part of a background check below that is a classic example:

(At St. John the Baptist Parish in Quincy, Massachusetts, they are committed to keeping our children safe and providing our parish family with the best information and resources available. Criminal Offender Record Information (CORI) annual background checks must be submitted each year for all clergy, religious, all paid parish staff (full or part time), and all parish volunteers who have any contact with children. St. John the Baptist is required to do this each year in March. However, it is necessary to bring a driver's license or other photo ID with you to complete this form).

We add these additional terms from the Office of the United States of Attorneys and the US Department of Justice for your review.[1]

Acquittal—Judgment that a criminal defendant has not been proven guilty beyond a reasonable doubt.

Affidavit—A written statement of facts confirmed by the oath of the party making it. Affidavits must be notarized or administered by an officer of the court with such authority.

Allegation—Something that someone says happened.

Arraignment—A proceeding in which an individual who is accused of committing a crime is brought into court, told of the charges, and asked to plead guilty or not guilty.

Arrest warrant—A written order directing the arrest of a party. Arrest warrants are issued by a judge after a showing of probable cause.

Beyond a reasonable doubt—Standard required to convict a criminal defendant of a crime. The prosecution must prove the guilt so that there is no reasonable doubt to the jury that the defendant is guilty.

Charge—The law that the police believe the defendant has broken.

Circumstantial evidence—All evidence that is not direct evidence (such as eyewitness testimony).

Complaint—A written statement by the plaintiff stating the wrongs allegedly committed by the defendant.

Conviction—A judgment of guilt against a criminal defendant.

Cross-examine—Questioning of a witness by the attorney for the other side.

Deposition—An oral statement made before an officer authorized by law to administer oaths. Such statements are often taken to examine potential witnesses, to obtain discovery, or to be used later in trial.

Evidence—Information presented in testimony or in documents that is used to persuade the fact finder (judge or jury) to decide the case for one side or the other.

Grand jury—A body of citizens who listen to evidence of criminal allegations, which are presented by the government, and determines whether there is probable cause to believe the offense was committed. As it is used in federal criminal cases, "the government" refers to the lawyers of the US Attorney's office who are prosecuting the case. Grand jury proceedings are closed to the public, and the person suspected of having committed the crime is not entitled to be present or have an attorney present. States are not required to use grand juries, but the federal government must do so under the Constitution.

---

[1] https://www.justice.gov/usao/justice-101/glossary.

Hearsay—Statements by a witness who did not see or hear the incident in question but learned about it through secondhand information such as another statement, a newspaper, or a document. Hearsay is usually not admissible as evidence in court, but there are many exceptions to that rule.

Interrogatories—Written questions asked to one party by an opposing party, who must answer them in writing under oath. Interrogatories are a part of discovery in a lawsuit.

Interview—A meeting with the police or prosecutor.

Jurisdiction—(1) The legal authority of a court to hear and decide a case. Concurrent jurisdiction exists when two courts have simultaneous responsibility for the same case. Some issues can be heard in both state and federal courts. The plaintiff initially decides where to bring the suit, but in some cases, the defendant can seek to change the court. (2) The geographic area over which the court has authority to decide cases. A federal court in one state, for example, can usually only decide a case that arose from actions in that state.

Misdemeanor—Usually a petty offense, a less serious crime than a felony, punishable by less than a year of confinement.

Mistrial—An invalid trial caused by fundamental error. When a mistrial is declared, the trial must start again, beginning with the selection of a new jury.

Modus operandi—Often shortened to as MO, referring to mode of operating.

Nolo contendere—No contest. Has the same effect as a plea of guilty as far as the criminal sentence is concerned, but the plea may not be considered an admission of guilt for any other purpose. Sometimes a guilty plea could later be used to show fault in a lawsuit, but the plea of nolo contendere forces the plaintiff in the lawsuit to prove that the defendant committed the crime.

Oath—A promise to tell the truth.

Plea—In a criminal case the defendant's statement pleading "guilty" or "not guilty" in answer to the charges in open court. A plea of nolo contendere or an Alford plea may also be made. A guilty plea allows the defendant to forego a trial.

Plea deal (or plea bargain or agreement)—Agreement between the defendant and prosecutor where the defendant pleads guilty in exchange for a concession by the prosecutor. It may include lesser charges, a dismissal of charges, or the prosecutor's recommendation to the judge of a more lenient sentence.

Pleadings—Written statements of the parties in a civil case of their positions. In federal courts, the principal pleadings are the complaint and the answer.

Search warrant—Orders that a specific location be searched for items, which if found, can be used in court as evidence. Search warrants require probable cause to be issued.

Sentence—The punishment ordered by a court for a defendant convicted of a crime. Federal courts look to the US Sentencing Commission Guidelines when deciding the proper punishment for a given crime.

Warrant—An arrest warrant is a written order directing the arrest of a party. A search warrant orders that a specific location be searched for items, which if found, can be used in court as evidence. Search warrants require probable cause to be issued.

Witness—A person called upon by either side in a lawsuit to give testimony before the court or jury.

Ethics

What is a code of ethics?

A code of ethics[1] is a guide of principles designed to help professionals conduct business honestly and with integrity. A code of ethics document may outline the mission and values of the business or organization, how professionals are supposed to approach problems, the ethical principles based on the organization's core values, and the standards to which the professional is held. A code of ethics also referred to as an "ethical code" may encompass areas such as business ethics, a code of professional practice, and an employee code of conduct.

Ethics is the study of the branch of philosophy that involves systematizing, defending, and recommending concepts of right and wrong conduct within a profession. Ethics deals with the examination of moral philosophy, combined with the duties and obligations within a certain profession. Ethical behavior results when the correct ethical decisions have been made and carried out.

Professional investigator code of ethics:

1. Respond to a client's professional needs.
2. Exhibit exemplary conduct.
3. Protect confidential information at all times.
4. Maintain a safe and secure workplace.
5. Dress to create professionalism.
6. Enforce all laws, rules, and regulations.
7. Encourage liaison with police officers.
8. Develop good rapport within the profession and obtain certifications.
9. Strive to attain professional competence.

---

[1] Code of Ethics, reviewed by Adam Hayes, Updated May 31, 2019, https://www.investopedia.com/terms/c/code-of-ethics.asp.

The code of ethics

Having a code of ethics helps guide us in decision-making. Being professional means more than this, but it is a necessary requirement.

Whether you conduct interviews for the government, the public sector, the private sector, or a corporation, it is likely that you will be guided by some form of a code of ethics. Common elements within a code of ethics are as follows:

- Work in accordance with local, state, provincial, or government laws.
- Work within company policies, if this applies.
- Be honest and impartial.
- Remain objective.
- Maintain the highest standard of morals and ethics.
- Have and maintain integrity.
- Provide truthful and accurate reports.
- Respect the inherent dignity of all people.
- Be diligent.
- Be ethical in soliciting business.
- Never disclose confidential information.
- Never knowingly cause harm.
- Accept no illegal or improper remuneration for services rendered.
- Refrain from representing competing or conflicting interests or the perception of conflicting interests.
- Support the purposes and objectives of the profession.
- Refrain from negative comment about other interviewers.

While researching ethics for investigators and security professionals, I found out that there are many codes of ethics. Some countries have their ethical standards, some states have their own, and then, there are professional organizations that have theirs. One particular ethical and behavioral standard that I felt was relevant and specifically addresses professional conduct of security professionals and investigators is described in the following section. As a matter of fact, this code was endorsed in the spring of 2013 by the Australasian Council of Security Professionals and provided to me by my co-council Ray Andersson, while serving together on the ASIS Crime Prevention Council in 2013.

Ethics and behavioral standards[2]

The Australasian Council of Security Professionals has created a code of conduct for the security profession: All security professionals and organizations must operate to the highest ethical values to engender trust

---

[2] Developed by Raymond Andersson, GAICD, AFAIM, RSecP, ICPS for the Australasian Council of Security Professionals (ASCP).

in all those they encounter in a professional capacity. Given the security industry's high profile, this Code of Ethical Conduct sets a standard that security professionals shall adhere to in their working habits and professional relationships. The values on which it is based apply to all situations in which security professionals participate and exercise their judgment. Registered security professionals are required to comply with the code in all of their professional activities. Failure to do so may be referred to the Security Professionals Registry—Australasia for disciplinary action.

Security professionals' code of conduct

The ASCP Code of Ethical Conduct requires that a security professional must operate to the highest ethical standards with all those they encounter in a professional capacity and shall

1. Act in the interests of the security of society and their client. A security professional shall
   a. Act honorably, responsibly, diligently, and lawfully and uphold the reputation, standing, and dignity of the security profession within society.
   b. Not act recklessly, maliciously, or in a manner that will negatively impact the reputation of other individuals or organizations.
   c. Act in the interests of the security of society and their client.
   d. Act honorably, responsibly, diligently, and lawfully and uphold the reputation, standing, and dignity of the company, employer, or client to which the security professional has a professional or legal association.
2. *Perform their duties in accordance with the law at all times.* A security profession shall
   a. Act in accordance with the laws of the jurisdiction(s) in which they are performing professional services.
   b. Hold paramount the health, safety, and security of others.
3. *Act and behave at all times with integrity.* A security professional shall
   a. Not abuse a professional position for personal gain and reject improper inducement.
   b. Avoid conflicts of interest.
   c. Avoid deceptive acts by actively taking steps to prevent corrupt practices or professional misconduct.
4. *Be diligent and competent in discharging their professional responsibilities.* A security professional shall
   a. Act for their employer or client in a reliable and trustworthy manner.
   b. Never knowingly mislead or allow others to be misled.
   c. Maintain currency in their security competencies through continued education and private research.

5. *Protect confidential information gained in the course of their professional activities and not disclose it to any unauthorized party nor use it for personal gain.* A security professional shall
  a. Protect client information in accordance with client information security policy.
  b. Apply effective physical, procedural, and IT controls to protect client or employer information in their care from unauthorized release.
  c. Implement and follow processes for the clearance of partners, employees, contractors, and other stakeholders in accordance with the classification of accessed client or employer information.
  d. Apply the need-to-know principle.
6. *Not maliciously damage the professional reputation or practice of colleagues, clients, or employers.* A security professional shall
  a. Refrain from unfounded criticism of work carried out by security professionals.
  b. Refrain from action deliberately designed to damage a colleague, client, or employer.
7. *Not knowingly undertake any action that brings the profession into disrepute.* A security professional shall
  a. Be objective and truthful in any statement made in their professional capacity.
  b. Act honorably, responsibly, diligently, and lawfully and uphold the reputation, standing, and dignity of the profession.
  c. Not engage in acts of collusion, corruption, or breaches of the law.
  d. Be a positive role model for others in the profession.[3]

It is appropriate that ethics is one of the first subjects we discuss in this book. Ethical issues surround every aspect of what investigators do. Supervisory and managerial roles amplify this further. Varied and changing employment relationships make the need for proper judgment even more challenging. Maintaining public trust is essential to protecting the public. This can only be obtained through ethical, professional conduct. Learning how to analyze ethical problems aids in ensuring ethical conduct. Growing ethical concerns include the proper handling of information and secondary employment. In this chapter, we discuss how ethics define our professionalism as investigative interviewers and why we need to understand and work within a set of principles.

For a certified fraud examiner, ethics training is required annually. Many positions involving interviewing, investigating, security, and fraud also require such training. There are reasons that annual ethics training is mandated and why it is critical. Ethics defines our professionalism as investigative interviewers and why we need to understand and work within a set of ethical principles.

---

[3] The Australasian Council of Security Professionals (ACSP).

Where there is not a code for private investigators, guidelines are set up by various professional departments, organizations, jurisdictions, or industries. Furthermore, regulatory agencies around the globe have developed a code of ethics and guidelines for practicing investigators such as the Association of Certified Fraud Examiners. These codes of ethics are established to promote and inspire confidence in our profession. *Truth, fairness,* and *honesty* are just some of the words we use when talking about ethics and principles.

It is essential, vital, and necessary to have ethical standards in our profession because potential consequences of interviews and interrogations are so great. If we want to be seen as a professional in the investigation industry, we need to maintain a set of principles. Ethics is something we hear about or talk about, but not everyone truly understands their ethical responsibility and the role ethics plays for those of us who conduct interviews.

Ethics is about human relationships and how we conduct ourselves, both in private and in groups. No matter whom we are interviewing or what the offense we are investigating, we must adhere to ethical standards. There is no absolute rule defining what is or is not ethical. In interviewing, your conscience will act as your guide to ethical behavior. Following ethical standards is inherently about right and wrong. You are either ethical or you are not.

Ethics is the inherent inner voice and the source of self-control in the absence of external compulsion. Ethics can be defined as the difference between knowing the right thing to do and knowing what you have a right to do. Ethics can be said to be based on the Golden Rule: "Do unto others as you would have them do unto you." Ethical behavior is judged by the way we act, the values that motivate us, the policies we have adopted, and the goals we seek to achieve. Every organization has an ethics strategy, whether explicit or implied. Each organization needs to have its specific ethical standards written down, describing its strategy. Every organization should have their "ethical standards" spelled out, in company policies, specifically detailing what is expected and what might be seen as unethical. In the absence of policy, procedures, or precedents, ethical effectiveness is based on organizational values that provide direction and consistency in decision-making.

The definition often used to describe ethics is, *moral principles* or *a system of moral principles.* Although the words *ethics* and *morals* may be quite different, depending on a particular class, group, or culture, they are both about values relating to human conduct with respect to right or wrong. Ethics may be defined individually, but as a professional, ethical behavior should be seen as vital. We all respond to moral dilemmas differently because we all have fundamental differences in our personal values. Ethics rely on personality traits such as values and attitude.

For an interviewer the line between ethical interview techniques and coercion can be a very fine line. We often look to others for moral guidance if we are in an unfamiliar situation. Ethics that are realistic and worth supporting are situational ethics; what is occurring at any given point determines what actions are effective, appropriate, and ethical. Values define who you are. All ethical decisions are determined by values that are clear and uncompromising statements about what is critically important. In organizations, clear values drive mission statements, strategic plans, and effective, result-oriented behavior.

Ethics come into play when external pressures push someone to act in a manner that is not consistent with his or her values. Only actions can be judged to be ethical or unethical. Ethics does not define what is acceptable about an action as much as they define what is *not* acceptable.

Ethics provides guidelines that outline what constitutes appropriate behavior. Once a clearly stated code of ethics is developed and made public, individuals are responsible for their own actions. The code of ethics supports the concept of dignity as the central element that drives human interaction in the workplace. Most organizational codes of ethics clearly demand that people treat each other with respect. When we show consideration for others, we are indicating that we hold them in high regard.

A code of ethics provides a commonly held set of guidelines that will provide a consistent, value-driven basis for judging what is right or wrong in any given situation and establishes the outer limits of acceptable behavior.

If a new code of ethics is going to be truly operational, people must have an opportunity to see where the ethics originate, what purpose they serve, and how they relate to each individual.

The phrase that I use to describe ethics is, *"ethics is when you do the right thing when no one else is looking."* Having a code of ethics will guide you as an interviewer to be respectful, honest, and reputable in your actions because the impact of your behavior can involve life-changing consequences.

Ethics from the top down

It is essential to have ethical leadership in any organization. Employees of organizations look to their leaders for ethical guidance and moral development. Ethical leadership can be very complex, and it goes much deeper than simply having strong morals or good character. An organization having ethical leadership sends a clear message about its ethics and values. This type of leadership also holds employees responsible and accountable for living up to these standards. This type of leadership makes the effort to find and develop the best people. To find the right people, consideration for ethics and character come into the selection and hiring process. Ethical leaders send the message that the organization has an ethical line and will reward good behavior and act decisively when moral and ethical lapses occur. These leaders have a deep sense of ethical principles, values, and character at the center of their leadership. These strengths are reinforced through training and communication. Conversations about ethics should routinely occur across all levels of business so that people can hold each other responsible and accountable. All employees should share in the responsibility for creating and maintaining an ethical culture. To accomplish this goal, leaders need to have a live conversation about whether they are living the values and bringing respect and compassion to their management of people. Leaders at the highest levels of their organization must clearly demonstrate their commitment to ethical behavior through their words and actions. Ethical leadership can be and should be incorporated into development programs for management. We can all be ethical leaders by looking at and reviewing our own behavior and values. We also need to make a commitment to accept responsibility for the effects of our actions on others and ourselves.

It is also essential to have a written code of conduct that clearly states what is and what is not acceptable. This code of conduct must be created from the bottom up, with input from employees at all levels. Ethical leaders need to put resources in place to let employees know what will and will not be tolerated, and that if an incident occurs, the organization will take strong action. There also needs to be a process in place for reporting any corrupt or unethical activities.

Ethical and unethical interviewing

Throughout recorded history, one of the great problems we have faced has been the development of a system by which truth may be made known. Solutions to this problem have ranged from such extremes as the torture chambers of the Middle Ages to the unhesitating acceptance of the word of a gentleman in the 18th century. Neither extreme meets the requirements of today. We respect human dignity too much to permit physical and psychological abuse of an individual in the search for truth. Yet, we recognize that many individuals will lie without hesitation, even under oath, if this will further their aims. The truth can be determined only after the evidence has been collected and analyzed. The public should not be misled into thinking that this is an automatic process. Investigative interviewers should use only the most ethical means available on behalf of society to obtain statements and the truth. There has been a critical analysis of various types of interview training in North America. Through the course of this analysis, new regulations have been formulated. Due to miscarriages of justice in some leading cases across the country, increased training of interviewers has occurred. Although each country has its own training programs, many programs have common features. The emphasis of an interview should also be on the search for the truth and on the collection of reliable information and, ultimately, a higher quality of information.

The interviewing tactics suggested in this book to encourage the cooperation of interviewees are ethical, as defined in this chapter. This book is partly intended to counteract the often illegal coercive tactics of the past and to promote perceptive interviewing. The following behaviors are considered unethical in North America but sadly are still used throughout the world:

- Using interrogation tactics instead of interviewing tactics.
- Treating each interviewee as though culpable, with little or no regard for the destructive public relations and psychological damage inflicted on interviewees who are blameless.
- Making threats.
- Making illegal promises.
- Using coercion.
- Using duress.
- Using force or the threat of force.
- Employing ruthless methods.
- Falsely imprisoning the interviewee.
- Not respecting the interviewee.
- Not maintaining the interviewee's dignity.

These and similar tactics have been used in the past in interviews with victims and witnesses as well as suspects. It is time for change. It is time that those involved in investigative interviewing be specifically taught what is ethical and what is unethical, beyond what is legal and what is illegal.

The conflicts of interest

As a professional, we must not engage in activities that may involve or create the perception of a conflict of interest. Conflict of interest can be defined as a situation in which one's external interests undermine or appear to undermine the investigators' ability to perform their legal, ethical, or professional duties. Conflict of interest might impair the investigators' judgment or create the impression that it does. Organizational conflict can be as complicated as personal conflict. We should always remain free of any interest or relationship that is connected to our clients.

There are many questions that you can ask yourself to avoid a conflict of interest:

- Do you have a personal relationship with the person you will be interviewing or another person who has an interest in the case?
- Do you have any financial relationship with the person you will be interviewing?
- Is this case somehow related to another organization you are working with?

- Do you have a professional relationship to another person or organization that is associated in any way to the case you are working on?
- Do you have any personal or professional bias that would make others question your ability to handle this case fairly and ethically?
- Would you personally benefit in any way from conducting interviews for this case?
- Have you had any direct knowledge of policies or practices that would affect the interviews you are about to do?
- Have you already formed an opinion on this case?

Ethics when using OSINT (open source intelligence)

As an investigator, it's important to remain professional and ethical throughout the life cycle of a case, including the preparation and research phase. While thorough research is critical, you will want to work within legal parameters of the local, state, federal, or jurisdiction that you are working. While researching information on social network sites, keep in mind that many of these sites make their users aware of searches that were done on them. While there are tools available to hide your identity online, you still need to work within the laws and maintain ethical behavior. Before all the privacy legislature, investigators were hired to, essentially, dig up any information possible. No one really questioned where the information came from, as long as it was confirmed to be true. In today's world, investigators do *not* have special privileges nor is it absolute that all of the information you find, can be legally used. New privilege and privacy legislation holds us accountable when digging up and sharing information. More information can be find in the privacy chapter. Keep in mind that not everything you do as an investigator, such as data analytics, recordings, reports, or notes, are protected by privilege. If your client is a lawyer, they can no longer look the other way regarding a private investigator's conduct.[4] Being unethical not only will affect you but also this case, future cases, and the clients that hired and trusted you to be professional.

Pretexting

Pretexting, also known as false motive or façade, is a social engineering tool involving someone lying to obtain information. Using a pretext can be seen as sneaky behavior and as a cover up to get information. This is a commonly known technique by many, however, what determines if the pretext being used is ethical or professional, is the type of information

---

[4] https://www.pinow.com/articles/2325/private-investigators-privilege-and-privacy-legislation.

being gathered. What makes this approach unethical and at times illegal is if the information being gathered is privileged.

Pretexting may be pretending to be someone you're not and can be used to confirm the identity of a person the investigator is talking to or to gather information, location, or data about another person. An investigator may pose as an authority figure (a law enforcement agent and impersonation and can be charged as a felony or misdemeanor depending on jurisdiction) or use a story, usually involving money due to the potential subject, to get the location, phone numbers, or employment of that subject.

In 1999 the Gramm-Leach-Bliley (GLB) Act banned the use of pretexting to gain financial data on individuals. The GLB Act specifically addresses pretexting as an illegal act but only specifically addresses pretexting as it pertains to financial information. The GLB Act applies to all organizations that handle financial data, including credit unions, tax preparers, banks, collection agencies, credit-reporting agencies, and real estate firms. The act does not apply to information that is on public record, such as bankruptcy, police records, real estate transactions, and property taxes. The distinction between whether a particular pretexting is legal or illegal is blurred with regard to telephone, cell phone, texting, email, or any other telecommunication records, since the laws regulating privacy from information gathering vary from state to state. Often investigators use pretexting to find a particular subject that they need to interview, or it may be used to determine a timeframe in which to conduct an interview.

The more important discussions to have and decisions to make with regard to pretexting are: professional responsibility and the concepts of right and wrong or ethical and unethical behavior and practices.

Ethical issues were raised by the Hewlett-Packard (HP) board of directors members' use of pretexting in 2010, during the investigation of corporate information leaks. Because HP was a publicly traded company, they had a financial obligation, under the Sarbanes-Oxley Act, to protect their information. Instead of reporting the leak of confidential information to the proper authorities, chairwoman Patricia Dunn hired a team of security experts to investigate board members and journalists, in an attempt to determine who leaked this confidential information. HP's choice to use pretexting included egocentrism and pressure to produce results. Additional concerns were: what is considered public domain (information gathered), expectations of privacy in the workplace, employee code of conduct, employee ethical behavior, ownership of records and the importance of continuous supervision of outsourced investigations.

Criminal charges and arrest warrants were filed against several of the board members and three outside investigators. One of the private investigators retained by HP, Bryan Wagner, was later charged by the federal government, with conspiracy and identity theft, for his role in obtaining social security numbers. Wagner pleaded guilty and received a 3-month sentence in 2012. In total, 24 individuals, including HP Board members, HP employees and journalists had their personal data compromised. Other records compiled were: 1,750 phone calls made on 157 cell phones and 413 landlines. There are *never* valid reasons to conduct unethical or illegal practices. This issue is an ethical concern. Ultimately the use of pretexting was ruled to be a nonissue and not illegal; however, this in itself does not mean that it was a good business decision. The fallout that came from this activity had negative repercussions for many members of the board; some resigned, including chairwoman Patricia Dunn, and others had their professional reputations questioned. The use of pretexting elicited debate over the legality and ethicality of pretexting. Private investigators need to know that if they engage in deception, otherwise known as pretexting, the Federal Trade Commission (FTC) can become involved. The FTC, mandated by Congress, has the obligation and authority to ensure that individuals are not subject to any deceptive business practices, including pretexting on the part of investigators.

When evaluating who owned specific records:

If the phone was purchased by the company and provided to the employee for official use. The company paid the monthly charges—subsequently there was no expectation of privacy because phone records are the property of the company.

If the phone is purchased by an individual who submits the bill for reimbursement to the company they are employed, they are afforded a reasonable expectation of privacy. In this case, pretexting may not be permitted (seek legal opinion.)

Records are owned by the owner of the phone.

This highlights the critical need for clear corporate policy detailing company reimbursement such as itemized receipts, individually owned property used for company business and employee acknowledgement by employee on acceptable use.

The advice from this author is to always consult with your Attorney or General Counsel on investigations involving company records, outsourcing investigations, or other matters that regulations waiver on privacy or legal regulations, before decisions are made.

A few examples of what one should never say in an e-mail:

- We were notified of an upcoming subpoena so clean up all files
- Don't share this with anyone
- I shouldn't have said this in an e-mail
- Get me a file deletion software.

Always remember:

- that e-mails are forever
- computer forensics can recover deleted emails and private files
- consider the legal, ethical implications before sending an email

- your email can be identified and discoverable in a legal proceeding
- only send after careful review

Liability for investigators

As we were putting this book together, ASIS was conducting a workshop entitled "Liability for Investigations." Their course identified 13 points, which we have listed below for your review. For additional information about this course we suggest you contact ASIS for future courses offered. They also offer an Advanced Investigation Program Workshop annually. Specific additional detail may be obtained from the ASIS Library O.P. Norton Information Resources Center, Internet address www.infoinc. com/product.html. In addition, ASIS offers an Advanced Investigation Program Workshop annually:

- Liability when conducting applicant background checks.
- Liability for not conducting applicant background checks.
- Detention and interrogation of employees.
- Search and seizure in the workplace.
- Undercover and surveillance operations.
- Employee discharge and failure to discharge.
- Discharge of employees for off-duty criminal conduct.
- Disclosure of evidence in worker's compensation and unemployment hearings.
- Release of adverse employee information.
- Misrepresentation and failure to warn about ex-employees.
- Filing of criminal charges.
- Discrimination-based investigations.
- Union and nonunion member investigations.

Civil liability

Public investigators[5] engaged in day-in-and-day-out activities are relatively free from civil actions because of governmental immunity. Civil action filings, if they occur at all, usually follow only extremely aggravated incidents. In this respect, governmental agencies are not as tempting a target as, for example, a utility company.

In the private sector, investigators are relatively vulnerable to civil actions as a result of exposure in their daily work, irrespective of culpability.

---

[5] The Process for Investigation, Elsevier Publishers, 2015, Charles A. Sennewald and John K. Tsukeyama, p. 11.

An investigator who interrogates an employee on documented evidence of dishonesty can easily expose the company to an unfair labor practice suit, slander or libel suit, extortion (e.g., promising a suspected employee he or she will not be referred to the police in exchange for an admission of culpability), or to charges of false imprisonment or malicious prosecution. Large companies are inviting targets—the bigger, the better.

4

Legal authority and misuse of authority

Introduction

Years ago a close friend Bill Ford of ours would lecture to law enforcement, District Attorney's, chief of police, etc., and he started out with a question, which was, "What two things are required to make a lawful Arrest?" I can tell you very, very few knew the answer, which is: *"Probable cause and the Authority to make the arrest." (William Ford, 1995)*

Security's place in the organization

The degree[1] and nature of the authority vested in security management and investigations become matters of the greatest importance when such a function is fully integrated into the organization. Any evaluation of the scope and authority required by security investigations to perform effectively must consider a variety of factors, both formal and informal, that exist in the structure. Here, we examine these factors.

Definition of authority

It is management's responsibility to establish the level of authority in which security management conducting such investigations may operate to accomplish its mission. Security management must have authority to conduct inspections of performance in many areas of the company. It must be in a position to evaluate performance and risk throughout the company.

---

[1] Gion Green, Robert Fischer Ph.D., Edward Halibozek MBA, *Introduction to Security*, 9th ed., Butterworth-Heinemann, 2020.

31

All such authority relationships, of course, should be clearly established by management and made with the assistance and guidance of a professional consultant. This trend has caused a growth in the number of security consultants, particularly independent consultants who do not have a vested interest in the outcome of their recommendations.

Determining costs and effectiveness is only the first step. Having done this, management will then have to face the important question of whether investigations, within security, can be truly and totally integrated into the organization. If, upon analysis, it is found that the existing structure would in some way suffer from the addition of new organizational functions, alternatives to the integrated proprietary security department must be sought. These alternatives usually consist only of the application and supervision of physical security measures. This inevitably results in the fragmentation of protective systems in the various areas requiring security. However, these alternatives are sometimes effective, especially in those firms whose overall risk and vulnerability are low. But as the crime rates continue to climb and as criminal methods of attack and the underground network of distribution continue to become more sophisticated, anything less than total integration will become increasingly inadequate.

Once management has recognized that existing problems, real or potential, make the introduction or enlargement of the security department a necessity for continued effective operation, it is obliged to exert every effort to create an atmosphere in which security can exert its full efforts to accomplish stated company objectives. Any equivocation by management at this point can only serve to weaken or ultimately undermine the security effectiveness that might be obtained by a clearer statement of total support and directives resulting in intracompany cooperation with security efforts.

Levels of authority

Obviously security managers operate at many mixtures of authority levels. Their functional authority may encompass a relatively limited area, prescribed by broad outlines of basic company policy. In matters of investigation, they may be limited to a staff function in which they may advise and recommend or even assist in conducting the investigation but not have direct control over or even assist in conducting the investigation, and they would not have direct control or command over the routines of employees.

It is customary for security managers to exercise line authority over preventive activities of the company. In this situation, they command their staff, who in turn command the employees in all matters over which security managers have jurisdiction. Security managers, of course, have full line authority over the conduct of their own departments, within which they too have staff personnel and those to whom they have delegated functional authority.

There are companies that will separate security, investigations, and audit, thus having to often conduct an investigation overlapping departments. This often occurs in fraud or workplace violence cases. More often the security department oversees investigations but is separate from audit.

Authority and neutrality in the investigative interview

Typically an authority figure functions as a representative of some organization or entity. As difficult as it may seem, an investigator is most successful when maintaining a middle ground, balancing on the tightrope of neutrality. An investigator's loyalty is to the organization she or he represents, but it can be extremely helpful to the success of an inquiry if this connection is obscured and not too clearly discernible.

It is critical when responding and investigating any harassment claim that the investigator is free from any conflict of interest and is neutral as this is a qualification of the investigator and will be part of all documentation that may be produced at some point.

Legal authority and power

In its simplest form, *power* is the ability to control, influence, or cause other to do what you want them to do.[2] Power can be expressed negatively or positively. *Authority* is the vested or conveyed right to exercise power over others. It is the right to command, to enforce laws, to exact obedience, to determine, or to judge, and its basis may be legal, traditional, or social. Investigators wield the authority granted them by virtue of their position, and they function on behalf of a segment of the community.[3] As with all positions of authority, an organization establishes guidelines that impact investigators' behavior. Each investigator then functions based on personal ethics, and no matter which organization investigators represent, they are personally responsible for how they command, determine avenues of inquiry, and judge outcomes. Because the misuse of their authority carries serious potential consequences, investigators have a great responsibility to exercise their power thoughtfully.

Some investigators wrongly consider power to be a permanent possession. In fact, legitimate power emanates from the role or position that the investigator holds. When used positively in an interview, authority promotes confidence and accomplishment, boosting the interviewee's self-esteem and encouraging his cooperation.

---

[2] Effective Uses of Power and Authority, 1980.
[3] Bennis et al., 1973, p. 62. The Leaning Ivory Tower.

The misuse of authority

Some interviewers exercise their authority aggressively all the time rather than assertively and only when necessary. These authoritarians demand absolute obedience without regard for the individual rights of others.[4] When crossed, they become intolerant. They threaten interviewees, describing the steps they will take if the interviewee does not cooperate. Arrogantly passing judgment, authoritarians humiliate interviewees, stripping them of their self-respect. They expect to be treated like gods, and they often are, because of the lack of awareness of their real selves. They are corrupt, prejudiced, sadistic opportunists exploiting their positions of power to try to earn the respect of their peers.

Authoritarians wield their power in such a way as to make interviewees feel helpless, impotent, and fearful, forcing them on the defensive.[5] The investigator's superior attitude tells interviewees that the investigator is not seeking a problem-solving relationship, that their help is not desired, and that it is likely that their power, status, or worth will be reduced if they cooperate with the investigation.[6] The result is resistance. If the investigator responds aggressively to resistance, someone may get hurt. The modulated use of power is the only legal and civilized tactic, but to respond constructively, you need to be keenly aware of what is happening in the interview. We all act in accordance with our own individual reasoning power; we tend to invent plausible explanations or rationalizations for our actions.[7] Often the individual interviewed uses rationalization to make themselves look better. If an interviewer uses power, the interviewee will likely become defensively. Avoid getting into any kind of power struggle as this does not encourage compliance and will only further alienate your subject.

The positive application of authority

The authoritarian interviewer's negative use of power arises from his feelings of insecurity and inadequacy. Proficient interviewers, on the other hand, use power in positive ways as they strive toward personal growth and self-affirmation. They are empowered with self-appreciation, vision, and purpose. Personal motivation is based on the principle that you are the end result of what you want to be. Success comes from inner strength, conscious willpower, and an unwavering determination to succeed. With these, you can develop courage, enthusiasm, confidence, and belief in your own ability.

---

[4] Ibid.
[5] Ibid, p. 252.
[6] Ibid, p. 492.
[7] Nierenberg, 1968.

When the needs of interview participants clash, develop a strategy to use to your advantage, applying referent power, the power of your position that symbolizes the organization you work for, in subtle ways. To argue with the interviewee is self-defeating. For interviewees, information is power. Faced with a threatening authoritarian, interviewees rarely see any constructive advantage to giving up what little power they retain. You should be willing to subtly and indirectly reach a point of agreement where some of the interviewee's needs are met. Interviewees may willingly provide information in return for assurances of confidentiality, protection, or some other concession.

Interviewees who have been pushed, pressured, bribed, or overpowered by parents or other authority figures may be guarded, extremely uncomfortable, or uncooperative during an interview. Don't take the interviewee's resistance personally. You may merely be a handy authority figure for the interviewee to lash out at. Try to subtly suggest that power returns to those who decide to comply.

The interviewing techniques suggested in this book are intended to encourage your use of positive authority in everything you do—from the tone of your voice to the way you actively listen. Although you may to some degree be insecure and self-consciousness in your behavior, your human interaction skills will improve with practice. It is too easy to use harsh, abrasive methods. If you strengthen your willpower, you will not be easily drawn into destructive behavior.

Neutrality

True professionals never collect evidence to suit some preconceived notion of who is culpable. To be a successful interviewer, you should approach all investigations (and all interviewees) with a floating-point strategy and an open mind. As we discuss in the evidence chapter, all evidence must be reviewed on an impartial and fair basis, ultimately heading to logical conclusion.

You should always inspire the interviewee's compliance by reinforcing the fact that you are neutral and have already determined conclusions. Being judgmental will not allow your interviewee to freely talk to you and may hinder a successful interview. You might even give the impression that you are ever so slightly leaning toward the interviewee's side. Treating interviewees respectfully, no matter what we think or know they did, is still the right thing to do. Remember that when you begin your interview, select your first words carefully. It takes but a few moments, a few words, and a few nonverbal signals to reveal your relative position—that is, your opinion of the interviewee. Do not conduct the interview in an accusatory way; instead, keep yourself open, positive, and neutral. Do not reveal any suspicions you might have of the interviewee's truthfulness or innocence until and if the time is right to do so. Especially when you want someone to undergo a detection-of-deception exam or other test, it is important to adopt a neutral, wait-and-see stance. The tension associated with the test may be enough to interfere with the interviewee's clear thinking, causing him to refuse to cooperate. Don't make matters worse by taking on an accusatory attitude.

While remaining neutral and objective in your methods, do not give interviewees a way of relieving tensions easily except through verbal expression. You will want the interviewee to stay focused, giving the facts as they fit the case and not dwell on their anxiety or emotional state. Often the interviewees anxiety can get cloud the facts, sometimes distorting them. It is your job to be in control of the interview, focusing on the facts and controlling any emotional responses.

Do not allow the interviewee's mood to determine your mood or composure. Be prepared to put up with a certain amount of verbal abuse from rebellious interviewees. Your neutral stance in explaining how the interviewee can assist in your inquiry is vital to your success.

Signaling your neutrality

Interviewees can pick up on subtle signals that belie your claims of neutrality. It is nearly impossible for interviewers to eliminate the effects of prejudice, hate, and other emotions on their behavior. However, investigators can control the expression of their personal views and values to avoid destroying their chances of obtaining an interviewee's compliance.

Presenting a neutral facade is a difficult task. Regardless of the hat you wear, interviewees may suspect some hidden objective or ulterior motive. Hence, you should do your best to avoid displaying negative signals during an interview. Many comments can be negative or positive in character, depending on how they are voiced. Saying "Uh-huh" or "Right" with the wrong intonation might stop the flow of information. Your tone of voice may signal that you are biased and not neutral, causing a breakdown in communication.

Your tone of voice, facial expressions, language, and timing must all be congruent with your claim of neutrality. If by force, volume, or tone of voice you emphasize certain consequences, the interviewee will quickly decide that you're hoping to hear a particular response. Consequences imply an either—or situation, such as "If you don't do such and such, then...." If you repeatedly call attention to a particular set of consequences or if you react to an interviewee's focus on the positive consequences by quickly switching to a discussion of the negative consequences, the interviewee may question your neutrality.

Making an accusation

Why would an interviewee talk openly with an investigator who seems judgmental, critical, or skeptical? You will find that it is difficult to keep your personal views and your suspicions hidden, but doing so is vital to the progress of your inquiry. Don't be too quick to provide an opinion regarding the interviewee's veracity. Don't make your suspicions known until you are reasonably certain of your facts. Interviewees who sense that you have prematurely concluded that they're lying will become defensive. When you have been convinced, after analyzing all the evidence, then your personal views may be more evident. Reserve your opinion until then.

Liability for investigators

As we were putting this book together, ASIS was conducting a workshop entitled "Liability for Investigations." Their course identified 13 points, which we have listed in the succeeding text for your review. For additional information about this course, we suggest you contact ASIS for the date and time of their next program. Specific additional detail may be obtained from the ASIS Library O.P. Norton Information Resources Center, Internet address www.infoinc.com/product.html. In addition, ASIS offers an advanced investigation program workshop annually. Below are examples for which investigators could be held liable:

* Liability when conducting applicant background checks.
* Liability for not conducting applicant background checks.
* Detention and interrogation of employees.
* Search and seizure in the workplace.
* Undercover and surveillance operations.
* Employee discharge and failure to discharge.
* Discharge of employees for off-duty criminal conduct.
* Disclosure of evidence in worker's compensation and unemployment hearings.
* Release of adverse employee information.
* Misrepresentation and failure to warn about ex-employees.
* Filing of criminal charges.
* Discrimination-based investigations.
* Union and nonunion member investigations.

Anyone can be sued for anything. However, many investigators who cross the invisible line may face liability.

Here are several situations that might cause liability concerns:

* Conducting applicant background checks.
* Not conducting applicant background checks.

- Detaining and interrogating employees.
- Search and seizure in the workplace.
- Undercover and surveillance operations.
- Employee discharge and failure to discharge.
- Disclosing evidence in worker's compensation and unemployment hearings.
- Obtaining information illegally.
- Misrepresentation and failure to warn about ex-employees.
- Filing criminal charges.
- Discrimination-based investigations.
- Union and nonunion member investigations.
- False acquisition based on sloppy investigation.
- Misuse of wiretap.
- Abuse of authority.
- Abuse of power.
- Filing or claiming false charges.
- Failure to follow legal process to get IP address.
- Suing for fraud.
- Being an unlicensed investigator and providing a service.
- Carrying a gun to work.
- Withholding evidence.
- Spreading unfounded slander.
- Releasing confidential information.

Testifying in court

Introduction

Testifying in court is like firing your weapon in the line of duty—it's unlikely you'll ever have to do it, but if you do, you'd better be accurate! There is always the possibility that you, as a security supervisor/manager, will have to testify in a court of law. Court appearances can be intimidating and frightening to those who have little or no experience in testifying. This chapter will do more than just alleviate fear of testifying. It will prepare the security supervisor/manager to present his or her testimony in a confident and professional manner.

Testifying in courtrooms

At times you may be required to testify in court as a result of some incident at work. The following are some helpful hints to assist you:

- Being nervous is nothing new. Lawyers are even nervous. Go to court early before you are to testify.
- Observe where everyone is sitting and where you testify. At this point do not talk, laugh, or whisper or cause any disturbance.
- When called upon, say Good Morning to the judge before you sit down, smile, and make eye contact with the jurors when you answer the lawyer's questions.
- Remember, it's the jury not the judge that is going to decide on the outcome of the case.
- If you can, leave after you testify.
- Be aware of the fact that the jury may observe your behavior in the hallway and elevator.
- Finally, remember these six points:
  1. Tell the truth and do not exaggerate.
  2. Look the jurors in the eye; making eye contact is important.

3. Lawyers ask questions, you answer to the jury.
4. Give full and complete answers.
5. During cross-examination, give short, truthful answers.
6. Sit comfortably in the witness chair and avoid hand motion. Try locking your fingers together as if in prayer.

Grand jury versus trial jury

The grand jury,[1] the initial step in the trial process, decides whether to prosecute based on the strength of the evidence offered by the prosecutor. This evidence may include oral testimony of a security officer. The grand jury environment is ordinarily a relaxed and informal setting in which the prosecutor presents the case to a jury, usually consisting of between 6 and 24 jurors.

Grand jury proceedings are conducted in secret and are closed to the defense counsel, press, and the public. Nevertheless, the grand jurors get an immediate impression of the professional training, skills, and abilities of the testifying officer and his or her agency.

Since testimony presented in front of trial (petit) juries is done in open forum, the press and public can closely scrutinize a testifying officer's professional conduct. Testimony should be presented in a confident and professional manner. Trial juries consist of 6 or 12 jurors who consider your testimony, the oral testimony of other witnesses, and physical evidence to decide on the guilt or innocence of the accused.

Expert witness versus regular witness

An expert witness is considered to be one who is qualified to speak with authority by reason of his or her special or unique training, skills, or familiarity with a particular subject. An expert witness is allowed to render opinions and draw conclusions (in contrast, witnesses not qualified as experts are generally not allowed such latitude). A person becomes qualified as an expert witness by demonstrating to the judge, or sometimes the jury, that he or she has the required education, knowledge, training, and/or experience to qualify as an expert in the subject matter under consideration.

Most police and security officers do not qualify as expert witnesses as their duties are usually more general in nature. In most cases an investigating security officer can testify only to that information of which he or she has personal knowledge. For example, while the case may have involved questioned documents, the officer can only testify as to what he or

---

[1] Security Supervisor and Management, Elsevier Publishers, Sandi J. Davies, and Chris Hertig editors, 3 edition.

she knows about the documents and cannot testify as to the authenticity of the documents themselves. The document examiner in the case would be the expert witness.

Preparation for court

Probably the most important part of being a successful and confident witness in court is your preparation before testifying. The first step in this preparation is to realize that you may be called on to testify on any official act you perform in your job as a security supervisor/manager. Preparation actually begins at the scene of a crime or when conducting the initial investigation. Officers should consider every call, complaint, and investigation as possible material for a future court case. In every case and in every investigation, think ahead about the possibility of having to testify to all your actions in that particular case.

The easiest way to do this is to picture the judge, jury, and/or defense counsel looking over your shoulder as you perform your duties and ask yourself such questions as: "How will I explain this on the stand?," "What if they ask me about this?," and "Can I explain this action in court?"

Review your case in detail before going to trial. You may have forgotten just enough to present some inaccurate information and put reasonable doubt in the mind of the jury. If you are going to testify concerning a situation that happened months or even years earlier, you will have to refresh your memory. Refer to the notes you took at the scene of the incident.

Review any reports you wrote regarding the incident. Talking with co-workers who may have knowledge of the situation may help you to recall forgotten details. But do not try to develop a common story. Remember your testimony must state what you recall, not what somebody else told you.

Let's take a quick look at notes as they may be of assistance to you in court. Officers who perform their job professionally are well aware of the necessity to take good field notes, maintain good field notebooks, and prepare well-written and accurate reports in all cases. Field notes and the notebooks in which they are kept represent the basic source of information drawn on when writing the incident, offensive, or investigative report. They are very valuable and of great assistance when the officer testifies in court.

Field notes should begin with the officer's assignment to a case and continue until the case is closed. The time and place to get factual data and information is at the scene during the initial investigation. Anything omitted or overlooked is either lost or must be ascertained later. That is usually a difficult, time-consuming task that often leaves out important facts that may be crucial testimony or evidence in court.

If you pictured the judge, jury, and/or defense counsel watching over your shoulder during the investigation and listening to your interviews, you will find that your notes, which may be introduced as evidence in a trial, and your reports (written from your notes) will be more complete, thorough, and accurate. Your self-confidence will be evident to the judge and jury, and you will actually feel better.

If documents, photographs, records, etc. are going to be introduced into evidence in your case, gain some familiarity with them. You don't need to be an expert, but you should become generally familiar with their use, purpose, and how they are used in the normal course of business.

Look for discrepancies between the field notes and the report and be ready to explain these differences. This comparison between field notes and reports will take place and could destroy your credibility.

Speaking and acting with confidence in court

It is said that an audience remembers 7% of what you say, 38% of how you sound, and 55% of how you look. A jury, like any other audience, is made up of real people. It can and will have feelings about you as a person, not only as a witness. They may like or dislike you, respect and admire you, or look at you as an incompetent idiot. Juries, like other audiences, are not easily deceived. If what the jurors see and hear is believable, they will believe it. You can win their trust, respect, and admiration by appearing confident, self-assured, and by telling the truth. Even before getting into court, there are some things you should do that will assist you in presenting a winning case.

Following these guidelines will help you to develop that feeling of self-confidence that can help your case:

1. Know which courtroom you'll be testifying in. If you are unfamiliar with the particular courthouse or courtroom, check it out before the trial so you will appear to know your way around.
2. Know who the major players are the prosecutor, defense counsel, and judge. Learn something about them if possible; the more you know about them, the more comfortable and confident you'll be.
3. Do not discuss anything about the case in public or where your conversation may be overheard. You just don't know who could be a juror or defense witness!
4. Treat people as if they are the judge, defense counsel, defense witness, or juror in your case going to trial. Your professionalism, politeness, and courtesy will be noted and remembered—especially by those who do see you in court as a witness.
5. Do not discuss your personal life, official business, biases, prejudices, likes and dislikes, or controversial subjects in public for the same reasons in the preceding text. You might create a poor impression on a judge, juror, defense counsel, or witness.

6. Always be on time for your case. Know what time you will be expected to be called.
7. Dress appropriately at all times. Look businesslike and official. If in uniform, it should be clean, neat, and complete. (If you don't know, check in advance if you need to leave your weapon off.) If not in uniform, a neat and clean sport coat and slacks are as appropriate as a business suit (male and female officers alike).
8. Try to avoid the defense counsel and any defense witnesses before the trial. You should assume that they will try to take advantage of you and get you to say something about the case. If you do say something, look for it to appear later, in a way to discredit you and your testimony.

Giving your testimony

Hopefully, you have prepared yourself mentally, emotionally, and physically for testifying by now. You've got the butterflies under control; you know your case (without memorizing it), and you feel confident. So, let's go to court and see how to give your testimony in a winning way:

1. First, in your mind, review and practice everything we've discussed so far.
2. Avoid undignified behavior, such as loud laughter, telling jokes, from the moment you enter the courthouse or courtroom. Normally, smoking and chewing gum are permitted in the hallways of courthouses, but not in courtrooms.
3. Stand upright and erect when taking the oath—it shows confidence in yourself and in your knowledge of the case in which you'll be testifying.
4. Control signs of nervousness. There is no reason to be scared or nervous if you've done your homework by reviewing the case carefully and preparing yourself.
5. When you take the oath, you swear that you will tell the truth. DO IT!
6. Speak directly to the members of the jury if it is a jury trial, otherwise, speak directly to the judge. Speak loudly enough so the juror furthest from you can hear you without difficulty.
7. Speak in your own words and do not use slang or police type jargon.
8. Listen carefully to each question and make sure you understand it before you start to answer. Have the question repeated if necessary.
9. Be alert for any question that will lead you to make conclusions (remember, only expert witnesses can give opinions and draw conclusions).

10. Try to answer with a simple "yes" or "no" if possible. Avoid saying "I think," "I believe," and "to the best of my recollection" types of answers. You should be testifying only to the facts as you know them.
11. Answer only the question asked and then stop. Do not volunteer any information as your answer may become legally objectionable under the technical rules of evidence. Do not exaggerate anything.
12. Sometimes, you just have to answer "I don't know." There's nothing wrong with this; just minimize doing it.
13. If you find that you gave a wrong or unclear answer to a question, correct it immediately yourself by asking the judge if you can do so.
14. Refrain from showing or indicating emotions such as happiness, joy, disgust, or disappointment about anything that occurs in the courtroom or during the trial.
15. Always be polite and maintain your composure. Do not be argumentative or sarcastic or get involved in verbal fisticuffs with counsel.
16. Finally the officer who presents honest testimony and maintains a professional bearing during testimony has nothing to fear during cross-examination.

6

Public versus private investigative interviews

Introduction

Whether from the public or private sector, first-class investigators resemble each other more than they differ. For clarity, *public* investigators are official law enforcement agents, such as federal, state, or local police officers, and *private* investigators are licensed private detectives, private investigators, asset protection, security management, or loss prevention specialists. Investigators, whether public or private, are successful because they share well-practiced skills. This chapter reviews some distinctions between the kinds of crimes public and private detectives investigate (with particular attention to white-collar crime) and the procedures they follow.

In the United States, if you are in the private sector, you are not required to read the Miranda warning before questioning a suspect. We also have no time restrictions when talking to employees about company business. We also have access to employees' company computers, company cell phones, or any other equipment that is owned by the company, *without* a search warrant.

The fundamental difference between public and private investigations is the *objective*. In the public sector the objective is to serve the interests of society. The primary objective of the investigative process in the private sector is to serve the interests of the organization, company, or client that employs the investigator. What might serve the best interests of society may differ from what might be in the best interests of the organization or client. In the private sector, my primary concern as a private investigator might be recovering an asset or obtaining a statement. Since I would be working for a client, my tasks or project will be defined by the client. In the public sector the main concern is prosecution. In the public sector the investigator knows that the victim is society, whereas the private investigator's victim could be the shareholders of a company or an organization.

Various perceptions and objectives have a direct impact on the strategies and character of the investigation process. This leads to other differences in the interviewing process as well, such as choices and decisions based on whether this is a private investigation or a public one. The public investigator represents the sovereignty of government, the authority of which is vested in laws, both constitutional and statutory. The source of funding is ultimately through taxation, whereas the private investigator is hired by management. Although state, federal, and corporate laws must be followed, there are plenty of differences, including limitations on government records, authority, detention, interview process, Miranda warning, and arrest.

Advantage of being a notary public in private sector

In the private sector, one investigative interviewing tool to consider is obtaining authorization as a notary. The ability to interview a subject, take their statement, and notarize the statement, eliminates the consequences of what could happen if the interviewee refuses to meet with you again. I learned this early on in my career when investigating a sexual harassment and assault case at a corporation between a supervisor and his subordinate. The key witness, who could substantiate the victim's story, agreed to talk with me and provided information that would support the victim's story. The witness opened up and gave pertinent details of what he knew and saw. I returned to my client's corporate office and meet with the witness. He refused to sign or notarize the statement he'd made. He stated that after he spoke to me the first time, he realized that since he still worked at the company, he couldn't risk his job and refused to sign his statement. Of course, this adversely affected the victim's case, and we had to look at alternatives to help support and win the case. Obtaining notary status is helpful in that the interviewee's statement, and signature is captured the first time and possibly the only time they might agree to meet with you. This also eliminates, in most cases, the need to have a notary with you as a witness. Meeting and interviewing someone that first time might very well be the last time. If you are with a law enforcement agency, you will likely find it easier to see and interview someone multiple times, but in the private sector, this is not always the case. In many of my interviews, once I completed the interview, the interviewee suddenly realized that they said something they shouldn't have said. They realize their statement or comments might affect a relationship, a job, or his family or might have other consequences. Interviewees will likely realize that they should *not* have talked to you or, at the least, should not have divulged information. They have second thoughts, and when you go back to have them sign the statement, they suddenly can't recall what they said.

Another case involved three males, who had assaulted another man in a parking ramp. The perpetrators bribed and threatened approximately six witnesses. I interviewed all the witnesses, who ultimately lied on the witness stand in court. However, I had taken all of their statements by hand and notarized them, and the case was won based on their signed and notarized statements. I am always prepared for the reality that I may have just one shot at interviewing someone. Always be prepared that you may only have one shot at interviewing someone. Being prepared means doing your research/due diligence, preparing the questions, determining when and where you will conduct the interview and walk through scenarios of how best to ensure that it is notarize. You also need to have a plan to stay safe.

As a notary, you interview, questioning and obtaining answers pertinent to the case, and write (in complete, clear, detailed sentences) both the stated question and answers as given to you. Once the interviewee has completed stating all the information he has, you will read the statement to the interviewee and verbally verify what they told you. If the statement is correct, the interviewee needs to sign (with their legal name) and date the document, at which time you will notarize it, along with validation (State photo ID) of their identity. This eliminates the need to return to the interviewee with a notary to have a notarized signature.

In the United States, a Notary Public is an official appointed by state government, authorized to perform legal formalities, including witnessing the signing of important documents. Their role is to deter fraud by verifying the signer's identity through valid identification, such as driver's license or passport, and to verify the signer is signing without duress. You can often find a Notary at a bank, a law firm, real estate company, or in any capacity within many businesses. In 32 states, the main requirements are filling out a form and paying a fee, whereas other states have restrictions on applicants with criminal histories. In 18 states, applicants have to take a course, pass an exam, or both. These are just a few examples of how becoming a notary may vary by locale.

Notaries in the United States, unlike in foreign countries, are not attorneys nor judges. In Canada, being a notary varies among provinces and territories, and the process can take years. For example, in Quebec and Manitoba, only individuals with law degrees can apply to be notaries. In British Columbia an applicant only has to have taken a university course. In Ontario, they allow both lawyers and nonlawyers to serve as notary public, but if you are not a lawyer, there is a 3-year term appointment, and application is through the attorney general's office.

Reporting and classifying crime

Before we continue, let's take a brief look at how crime is reported and classified. We will look at the United States, Canada, and the United Nations—affiliated European Institute for Crime Prevention and Control.

The Criminal Code of Canada sets out three main offense classifications, which are as follows:

1. Purely summary conviction offenses. These offenses are the most minor.
2. Purely indictable offense, the most serious offenses. The majority of criminal charges in Canada are hybrid offenses such as DUI and assault charges.
3. Hybrid offenses, more serious than the most minor, follow the summary conviction offenses. These proceed summarily (less serious) or by indictment (more serious), depending on the classification the prosecutor chooses.

Canada has a Uniform Crime Reporting Survey (UCR) that was designed to measure the incidence of crime in Canada and its characteristics. This survey is used by federal and provincial policy makers. The Canadian Centre for Justice Statistics (CCJS) collects police-reported crime statistics through the Uniform Crime Reporting Survey.

In Europe, there are several agencies that collect crime data:

- European Institute for Crime Prevention and Control, affiliated with the United Nations (HEUNI), located in Finland.
- The United Nations Office on Drugs and Crime (UNODC), located in Vienna, Austria, collects data on crime and provides analysis to the international community. The UNODC works on developing standards for national crime and criminal justice information systems and for victimization surveys. Through collecting periodic reports on selected crime issues, they can provide in-depth analysis on issues that are global and regional. Another initiative is Data for Africa, which collects and analyzes data and trends in drugs, crime, and victimization in African countries.
- The United Nations Survey on Crime Trends and Operations Criminal Justice Systems (abbreviated as UN-CTS) collect basic information on recorded crime and on resources of criminal justice systems in member regions such as Europe and North America.

In the United States, city, county, and state law enforcement agencies keep track of the yearly incidence of various crimes in their jurisdictions. Compiled by volume and frequency, these statistics are sent to the Federal Bureau of Investigation (FBI), which issues the annual *Uniform Crime Report*. The FBI classifies the most serious crimes, such as murder, rape, and robbery, as *Part I offenses*. These crimes, which are the most likely to be reported to the police, serve as the major index of crime in the United States. The crimes listed as *Part II offenses* are considered less serious—that is, less harmful to individuals and less damaging to society. The FBI considers fraud and embezzlement to be Part II offenses. The federal guidelines define fraud as "fraudulent conversion and obtaining money or property by false pretenses (confidence games and bad checks, except forgeries and counterfeiting, are included)" and embezzlement as "the misappropriation or misapplication of money or property entrusted to one's care, custody, or control." Fraud and embezzlement cost US businesses billions of dollars each year. To control their losses, many companies have established their own security or loss prevention staffs to investigate these crimes. More often than not the police are never notified when these crimes occur.

Offense definitions

This section is reprinted, with permission, from Appendix II—Offenses in Uniform Crime Reporting, from Crime in the US 2004, Department of Justice, FBI. The Uniform Crime Reporting (UCR) Program divides offenses into two groups: Part I and Part II crimes. Each month, participating law enforcement agencies submit information on the number of Part I offenses that become known to them; those offenses cleared by arrest or exceptional means; and the age, sex, and race of persons arrested for each of the offenses. Contributors provide only arrest data for Part II offenses.

The UCR Program collects data about Part I offenses to measure the level and scope of crime occurring throughout the nation. The program's founders chose these offenses because they are serious crimes, they occur with regularity in all areas of the country, and they are likely to be reported to police.

The Part I offenses are as follows:

- *Criminal homicide.* (a) Murder and nonnegligent manslaughter—the willful (nonnegligent) killing of one human being by another. Deaths caused by negligence, attempts to kill, assaults to kill, suicides, and accidental deaths are excluded. The program classifies justifiable homicides separately and limits the definition to (1) the killing of a felon by a law enforcement officer in the line of duty or (2) the killing of a felon, during the commission of a felony, by a private citizen. (b) Manslaughter by negligence—the killing of another person through gross negligence. Deaths of persons due to their own negligence, accidental deaths not resulting from gross negligence, and traffic fatalities are not included in the category of manslaughter by negligence.
- *Forcible rape.* The carnal knowledge of a female, forcibly and against her will. Rapes by force and attempts or assaults to rape, regardless of the age of the victim, are included. Statutory offenses (no force used—victim under age of consent) are excluded.
- *Robbery.* The taking or attempting to take anything of value from the care, custody, or control of a person or persons by force or threat of force or violence and/or by putting the victim in fear.

- *Aggravated assault.* An unlawful attack by one person upon another for the purpose of inflicting severe or aggravated bodily injury. This type of assault usually is accompanied by the use of a weapon or by means likely to produce death or great bodily harm. Simple assaults are excluded.
- *Burglary (breaking or entering).* The unlawful entry of a structure to commit a felony or a theft. Attempted forcible entry is included.
- *Larceny; theft (except motor vehicle theft).* The unlawful taking, carrying, leading, or riding away of property from the possession or constructive possession of another. Examples are thefts of bicycles, motor vehicle parts, and accessories; shoplifting; pocket picking; or the stealing of any property or article that is not taken by force and violence or by fraud. Attempted larcenies are included. Embezzlement, confidence games, forgery, check fraud, etc. are excluded.
- *Motor vehicle theft.* The theft or attempted theft of a motor vehicle. A motor vehicle is self-propelled and runs on land surface and not on rails. Motorboats, construction equipment, airplanes, and farming equipment are specifically excluded from this category.
- *Arson.* Any willful or malicious burning or attempt to burn, with or without intent to defraud, a dwelling house, public building, motor vehicle or aircraft, personal property of another, etc.

The Part II offenses, for which only arrest data are collected, are as follows:

- *Other assaults (simple).* Assaults and attempted assaults where no weapon was used or no serious or aggravated injury resulted to the victim. Stalking, intimidation, coercion, and hazing are included.
- *Forgery and counterfeiting.* The altering, copying, or imitating of something, without authority or right, with the intent to deceive or defraud by passing the copy or thing altered or imitated as that which is original or genuine, or the selling, buying, or possession of an altered, copied, or imitated thing with the intent to deceive or defraud. Attempts are included.
- *Fraud.* The intentional perversion of the truth for the purpose of inducing another person or other entity in reliance upon it to part with something of value or to surrender a legal right. Fraudulent conversion and obtaining of money or property by false pretenses. Confidence games and bad checks, except forgeries and counterfeiting, are included.
- *Embezzlement.* The unlawful misappropriation or misapplication by an offender to his/her own use or purpose of money, property, or some other thing of value entrusted to his/her care, custody, or control.
- *Stolen property—buying, receiving, and possessing.* Buying, receiving, possessing, selling, concealing, or transporting any property with the knowledge that it has been unlawfully taken, as by burglary, embezzlement, fraud, larceny, robbery, etc. Attempts are included.

- *Vandalism.* To willfully or maliciously destroy, injure, disfigure, or deface any public or private property, real or personal, without the consent of the owner or person having custody or control by cutting, tearing, breaking, marking, painting, drawing, covering with filth, or any other such means as may be specified by local law. Attempts are included.
- *Weapons—carrying, possessing, etc.* The violation of laws or ordinances prohibiting the manufacture, sale, purchase, transportation, possession, concealment, or use of firearms, cutting instruments, explosives, incendiary devices, or other deadly weapons. Attempts are included.
- *Prostitution and commercialized vice.* The unlawful promotion of or participation in sexual activities for profit, including attempts. To solicit customers or transport persons for prostitution purposes; to own, manage, or operate a dwelling or other establishment for the purpose of providing a place where prostitution is performed; or to otherwise assist or promote prostitution.
- *Sex offenses (except forcible rape, prostitution, and commercialized vice).* Offenses against chastity, common decency, morals, and the like. Incest, indecent exposure, and statutory rape are included. Attempts are included.
- *Drug abuse violations.* The violation of laws prohibiting the production, distribution, and/or use of certain controlled substances. The unlawful cultivation, manufacture, distribution, sale, purchase, use, possession, transportation, or importation of any controlled drug or narcotic substance. Arrests for violations of state and local laws, specifically those relating to the unlawful possession, sale, use, growing, manufacturing, and making of narcotic drugs. The following drug categories are specified: opium or cocaine and their derivatives (morphine, heroin, and codeine), marijuana, synthetic narcotics such as manufactured narcotics that can cause true addiction (demerol and methadone), and dangerous nonnarcotic drugs (barbiturates and benzedrine).
- *Gambling.* To unlawfully bet or wager money or something else of value; assist, promote, or operate a game of chance for money or some other stake; possess or transmit wagering information; manufacture, sell, purchase, possess, or transport gambling equipment, devices, or goods; or tamper with the outcome of a sporting event or contest to gain a gambling advantage.
- *Offenses against the family and children.* Unlawful nonviolent acts by a family member (or legal guardian) that threaten the physical, mental, or economic well-being or morals of another family member and that are not classifiable as other offenses, such as assault or sex offenses. Attempts are included.

- *Driving under the influence.* Driving or operating a motor vehicle or common carrier while mentally or physically impaired as the result of consuming an alcoholic beverage or using a drug or narcotic.
- *Liquor laws.* The violation of state or local laws or ordinances prohibiting the manufacture, sale, purchase, transportation, possession, or use of alcoholic beverages, not including driving under the influence and drunkenness. Federal violations are excluded.
- *Drunkenness.* To drink alcoholic beverages to the extent that one's mental faculties and physical coordination are substantially impaired. Driving under the influence is excluded.
- *Disorderly conduct.* Any behavior that tends to disturb the public peace or decorum, scandalize the community, or shock the public sense of morality.
- *Vagrancy.* The violation of a court order, regulation, ordinance, or law requiring the withdrawal of persons from the streets or other specified areas, prohibiting persons from remaining in an area or place in an idle or aimless manner, or prohibiting persons from going from place to place without visible means of support.
- *All other offenses.* All violations of state or local laws not specifically identified as Part I or Part II offenses, except traffic violations.
- *Suspicion.* Arrested for no specific offense and released without formal charges being placed.
- *Curfew and loitering laws (persons under age 18).* Violations by juveniles of local curfew or loitering ordinances.

According to the 2011 *Crime in the US* report, the estimated number of violent crimes reported to law enforcement (1,203,564) decreased for the fifth year in a row, whereas the estimated number of property crimes reported to law enforcement (9,063,173) decreased for the ninth year in a row.[1]

Violent crime

The South, the most populous region in the country, accounted for 41.3% of all violent crimes (lesser volumes of 22.9% were tallied in the West, 19.5% in the Midwest, and 16.2% in the Northeast).

- Aggravated assaults accounted for the highest number of estimated violent crimes reported to law enforcement at 62.4%.
- Firearms were used in 67.8% of the nation's murders, 41.3% of robberies, and 21.2% of aggravated assaults. (Data on weapons used during forcible rapes is not collected.)

---

[1] FBI website, www.fbi.gov, March 1, 2013.

- In 2011 64.8% of murder offenses, 41.2% of forcible rape offenses, 28.7% of robbery offenses, and 56.9% of aggravated assault offenses were "cleared"—either by the arrest of the subject or because law enforcement encountered a circumstance beyond its control that prohibited an arrest after the subject was identified (i.e., death of the subject).

Property crime and internal theft

Property crimes that are crimes against property, in the United States, are typically referred to criminal offenses such as burglary, larceny, fraud, embezzlement, forgery, car theft, and arson. Another property crime offense, shoplifting, is a form of larceny. The property crime offense list is vast and can also be described as crimes against property/material-based items. Data show that 43.2% of the estimated property crimes occurred in the South (followed by the West with 22.8%, the Midwest with 21.1%, and the Northeast with 13.0%).

- Larceny-theft accounted for 68% of all property crimes in 2011.
- Property crimes resulted in estimated losses of $156.6 billion.
- Also cleared were 21.5% of larceny-theft offenses, 12.7% of burglary offenses, 11.9% of motor vehicle theft offenses, and 18.8% of arson offenses.

The FBI's Uniform Crime Reporting (UCR) program is one of two statistical programs administered by the Department of Justice that measure the magnitude, nature, and impact of crime. The other is the National Crime Victimization Survey (NCVS), conducted by the Bureau of Justice Statistics.

The programs were designed to complement each other, providing valuable information about aspects of the nation's crime problem, but due to methodology and crime coverage differences, users should not compare crime trends between the two programs. The UCR program provides a reliable set of criminal justice statistics for law enforcement administration, operation, and management as well as to indicate fluctuations in the level of crime. The NCVS provides previously unavailable information about victims, offenders, and crime, including crimes not reported to police. Additional information about the differences between the two programs can be found in the "Nation's Two Crime Measures" section of *Crime in the United States*.

Looking ahead to 2013 and beyond, the UCR program is working to complete the automation of its data collection system, which will result in improved data collection efforts with new offense categories and revised offense definitions as well as a faster turnaround time to analyze and publish the data. In addition, beginning with the 2013 data, the new definition of rape will take effect; the FBI is developing options for law enforcement agencies to meet this requirement, which will be built into the new data collection system.

UCR's *Law Enforcement Officers Killed and Assaulted, 2011* and *Hate Crimes Statistics, 2011*

Investigations in the public and private spheres

Traditionally, private investigators have dealt with fraud and embezzlement, whereas the police have handled the violent crimes of murder, rape, and assault. Until just recently, law enforcement officers were not properly trained to investigate sophisticated white-collar crimes. Rather, police training was reactive in nature, emphasizing how to diffuse violent situations, how to perform first aid, how to shoot straight, and such topics. The subtle aspects of human interaction, the gentle art of communication, and their usefulness in investigative interviewing were all but ignored.

Property protection—line of defense

- Perimeter is your first line of defense. It is either man-made or natural.
- The building complex is your second line of defense.
- Inner defenses, alarmed areas, and secured safes or secured and locked containers.

Protected by

- Security, safety audits, and risk assessments.
- Covered by insurance. Supervised by other devices.

External theft

- Robbery—armed or unarmed.
- Shoplifting.
- The professional theft to the unprofessional.
- Burglary.
- Checks and credit/debit cards.

Controlled by

- Digital surveillance.
- Sales personnel.
- Security personnel.

Today, businesses call on private investigators to look into various offenses committed against companies or their employees. Many large businesses have trained investigators on staff to investigate crimes ranging from stalking to theft. Typically, if a Part I offense has occurred, the internal investigation is turned over to the appropriate police agency. However, if the incident can be investigated by internal security personnel, it is. Few companies want the embarrassment of a public disclosure of their problems. In addition, many businesses do not think law enforcement agencies can properly investigate so-called white-collar crimes or cyber incidents.

Private sector

In the private sector, private detectives and security personnel for corporations might investigate an incident, even though no civil or criminal matter is pending. The investigation might be aimed specifically at providing information to help management make administrative decisions regarding the violation of company rules or procedures. Often the evidence collected never reaches the outside world or the civil or criminal courts. The decision to reveal or not reveal the evidence to the public depends on what's ultimately best for the company.

In Chapter 17, we examine internal controls and investigations from the corporate perspective and the role in which you could likely find yourself should you be working on an internal investigation in the private sector.

Police agencies investigate few embezzlement cases. The vast majority of such cases are handled by private investigators. Why aren't police agencies involved in the investigation of more white-collar crimes?

Based on our many years of experience, businesses, banks in particular, do not want their internal matters revealed to the public. Reports of internal theft lead to bad press. That is, if internal losses become public knowledge, the bank's image as a safe place to deposit money will suffer.

At one time the FBI investigated all internal and other bank thefts, and technically it still retains jurisdiction. But today the FBI does not investigate cases involving losses of only a few thousand dollars. The bureau has shifted its priorities, leaving local police agencies to investigate most cases of fraud and embezzlement. Unfortunately, local police agencies are generally not properly trained in these investigations, and even if they were, most bank managers would still prefer to handle the matter privately.

The collection of evidence

Whether the investigator is a police detective, a loss prevention officer of a large corporation, or a private investigator hired to look into a particular incident, he or she must operate within predefined parameters in conducting an investigation and collecting evidence. Police investigators must work within federal and state laws intended to protect society from unreasonable police behavior. In addition, they work within the bureaucracy and operating procedures of their respective agencies.

Private investigators have a wider choice of investigative methods because there are fewer laws governing their actions. A company's internal investigators may take investigative liberties that might seem unreasonable, but their actions do not affect society generally. Still, their behavior is limited and controlled by company policy and the fear of possible civil suits. Company control of an investigator's behavior generally cannot influence the inquiry to such an extent that it causes the investigator to violate personal ethics and professional responsibilities. If this happens, there is a question of integrity.

Regardless of whether an offense is investigated by public or private detectives, the evidence needed to prosecute the case is the same. If a piece of evidence is to be of value to a company (or, for that matter, to society), the methods used to collect and preserve it must meet the highest standards imposed by the courts. This is true even when the collected evidence serves only to justify an employee's dismissal rather than prosecution in court. The case may turn ugly if the fired employee sues the company for wrongful termination and the company must produce the evidence on which it based the termination. If evidence collection and preservation fall short of acceptable standards, the company may be in deep trouble financially. In the public sector, of course, if a police investigator does not properly collect and preserve evidence, the prosecution's case may dissolve, allowing the guilty party to go free.

Testimonial evidence

Obviously the main topic of this book is the collection of testimonial evidence through investigative interviewing. Most, if not all, of the offenses cataloged in the FBI's *Uniform Crime Report* require investigative interviewing of victims, witnesses, and suspects. Most of the evidence presented during the prosecution of Part I and Part II offenses was obtained in an interview or interrogation.

There are legal means available to assist both public and private investigators in searching out all forms of evidence that will reveal the truth. Subpoenas, for example, help investigators collect evidence without resorting to illegal methods.

As this book points out, the investigator's major job is to persuade the interviewee to cooperate long enough to reveal truthful information about the crime under investigation. To this end, investigators of all kinds must cultivate professional attitudes and techniques that promote communication and cooperation. Most interviewees will acquiesce to requests for information, but they need encouragement from the investigator. There is always some resistance to an investigator's inquiries. Some people believe that the degree of resistance depends on the nature of the offense under investigation. My thought is that the degree of resistance is a reflection of the interviewee's personality, the interviewer's attitude, and the qualities the interviewer brings to bear on the interview.

Are people more likely to refuse to cooperate with a private investigation than with a police investigation? Certainly, people perceive less of a threat from private investigations. Most consider losing a job to be less damaging than being fined or going to jail. Employees are expected to cooperate in reasonable inquiries undertaken by company management. The refusal to cooperate in an investigation is often regarded by management as insubordination and sufficient cause for dismissal. But it does not prove that the employee is guilty.

Occasionally the greater threat of a police investigation works to obscure rather than reveal the truth. Because of the fear that a police interview can inspire, interviewees feel pressured to provide answers that they sense the investigator wants—and thus lead the police to a wrongful arrest. It can be difficult for police investigators to discover the truth while simultaneously protecting the rights of the alleged victims and the accused. There is a need for comprehensive training in interviewing at the beginning and throughout a police officer's career.

PART 2

The interview process

Preparation: Preparing for successful interview

Investigative interviewing is about having a conversation that results in information. This information, or fact-finding, is your goal. Successfully reaching your goal will result in solving your case. You might think that success comes only from a confession, but there is so much more that comes from fruitful conversations. Having a conversation might sound easy, but as an investigator or interviewer, you must be *prepared* for this conversation. Preparation is the single most important aspect of a successful interview. Even if you have a natural ability to interview, you still have to prepare. Preparation involves attitude, psychology, intuition, flexibility, curiosity, imagination, and research. This chapter takes you through each of these factors, the role each plays in every interview, and how you can use them successfully.

Attitude

Why do we talk about attitude if we are interviewing a suspect, witness, or victim? If you want information from an interviewee, you need to know what attitude you should have with that person to obtain the response or information that you are seeking.

If the response you seek in an interview is full and open cooperation, you must maintain a positive attitude toward each and every interviewee. Each of us has a history filled with experience, which creates bias and prejudices. That experience will determine the preconceived opinions and perceptions with which we go into each interview. I encourage you to be honest with yourself and understand how and why you have formed your specific opinions, so that you can conduct each interview in a fair and impartial way, treating each interviewee with a level of respect. In addition, understand how your discriminatory actions affect others.

Showing respect means remaining calm, actively listening, and maintaining a positive attitude. By having confidence in your skills and ability, you will display that you are self-assured. A positive attitude, persistence, and general determination are the attributes that lead to successful interviews. Interviewees are more likely to comply with an interviewer with a friend attitude. A positive attitude is always effective, no matter what your objective. Perceptive interviewees can sense your attitude as it is expressed through the formulation and presentation of your questions and by the way you listen to the responses. They are keenly aware of verbal and nonverbal signals expressing negative attitudes. If you ridicule or degrade interviewees, you will only promote antagonism. Characteristics of a positive attitude are warmth, empathy, acceptance, caring, and respect. You should learn to have and project these qualities because they will help you become a proficient interviewer.

These are three important qualities to incorporate into your positive attitude:

- *Congruence.* To be in congruence with yourself means to be aware of and comfortable with your feelings and to be able to communicate constructively with interviewees in a way that expresses your humanity. To be in congruence with the interviewee means to recognize and accept the human qualities, needs, and goals that we all share.

- *Unconditional positive regard.* Just as a parent expresses unconditional love for a child, you should strive to display a positive regard for interviewees, without reservations or judgments. Regardless of the inquiry and even when dealing with unsavory interviewees, treat everyone as a valuable human being. Develop a genuine liking for people, and be tolerant of human weakness. When you're dealing with interviewees you consider repugnant, do not show how you really feel. When your inner feelings are critical of the interviewee's behavior, put on a convincing show of acceptance of or tolerance for their behavior. This show is intended to encourage interviewees to let down their guard when talking with you. As I said earlier, identifying your prejudices and biases will help you understand the people you interview and avoid prejudging them.

- *Empathy.* Empathy is the ability to identify with someone else, to understand their thoughts and feelings from their perspective. Pay attention as interviewees express themselves verbally and nonverbally so that you can pick up on their messages. Interviewees often express some deep emotional hurt that influenced their behavior in some way. By comprehending those hurts and putting them into your own words, you show that you are deeply tuned in, and this expresses closeness and caring.

Controlling your negative feelings throughout an investigation and with interviewees will be invaluable. Avoid being condescending or patronizing. These feelings will only cause antagonist behavior. Keep in mind, your goal is to get information that will help solve a case. Obtaining the facts and not being judgmental will affect the outcome. If you have negative feelings, you can change them if you really desire to change. As a professional, you can make a commitment to modify your attitudes and thus change your behavior to become a more effective interviewer. To change your attitudes, you must first change your feelings or your thinking. Authoritarianism, which breeds resentment, retaliation, and reluctance or refusal to cooperate, is based on your biases and prejudices.

A significant challenge is to become aware of your own strengths and limitations. The more aware you are of your good and bad qualities as an investigator, the more likely it is that you will make changes to improve yourself. Having a positive attitude is the first important step you will take to prepare for interviews.

Psychology

Psychology plays an integral role in an interview. We need to prepare psychologically for each interview, and we need to understand psychology to help interpret and assess the interview as the interviewee speaks and reacts.

Let's start by talking about how to prepare psychologically. We discussed attitude in the previous section; part of our attitude is to enter the interview with an open mind. We also discussed being accepting and nonjudgmental, even when we are interacting with people we consider suspects. We have to understand the psychology of human needs and understand how remaining positive will go a long way toward achieving our success.

The effective interviewer sets the stage for eliciting accurate information by knowing, accepting, and attempting to satisfy the emotional needs that motivate all human activity. We have to be aware of the subliminal messages we are sending and the ones we are receiving. As stated earlier, communication is the way you get information, but communication is an extremely complex process in which psychology plays a role. We will get information only if we communicate effectively, form a rapport with the interviewee, and understand the psychology behind why the interviewee will give us information. Having knowledge of the psychology of interviewing will make you a more effective interviewer.

The fundamentals of human personality are needs, emotions, thinking, and the ability to relate thoughts and feelings. Our actions are a result and composite of all these elements. Humans function mostly on feelings and not logic. But most of all, it is the satisfaction of meeting essential and predictable needs that motivates every type of human behavior. Individuals try to satisfy their needs by maintaining physical comfort, avoiding the unsafe, attempting to gain understanding, detesting anonymity, desiring to be free from boredom, fearing the unknown, and hating disorder. Underlying each interview action is a desire to satisfy one of the basic human needs: food, water, and shelter.

Intuition

The heart has reasons of which reason has no knowledge—Pascal Imagination, knowledge, and awareness combine to produce intuition. Intuition has many other names: instinct, perception, gut feeling, hunch, sixth sense, third ear, reading between the lines, and quick insight. Intuition is the power of knowing through the senses, without recourse to inference or reasoning. As Edward Sapir (1884–1939), an American anthropologist who laid the foundation for modern linguistics, wrote: "We respond to gestures with an extreme alertness and, one might say, in accordance with an elaborate code that is written nowhere, known by none, and understood by all."[1] Most people possess a remarkable sensitivity to others, but their intuition remains dormant in the subconscious because it is never brought into play. The seeds of intuition are probably within you to be discovered, nurtured, and enhanced.

Although some people disregard intuition and consider its use unscholarly, I believe it is a valuable asset in interviewing. Keen intuition is spontaneous, accurate, and helpful, although difficult to explain. In an interview, allow your intuitive judgment to help you select the investigative pathways you will pursue. Let your intuition direct the interview and guide your responses. When you interact with interviewees, be alert to hints of facts and feelings revealed by a slip of the tongue, but conceal your interest. Subtle behavioral cues, words, gestures, and body language can direct you if you listen to your intuition. This is not to imply that you shouldn't plan your approach. Rather a good balance is required. Acquiring a mental warehouse of information about human behavior is a must. As Alexander Pope so aptly said, "The proper study of mankind is man." With that study comes greater success. Try to achieve a careful balance of the scientific and the intuitive so that you can avoid rigid procedures in your interviews. Listen to your intuition during an interview and allow it to guide you through sensitive issues. If you don't, you will be unprepared for the spontaneous developments that occur in most interviews. As the Greek philosopher Heraclitus proclaimed around 500 BC, "If you expect not the unexpected, ye shall not find the truth." Since seeking truth is your primary objective, you must expect the unexpected.

---

[1] Sapir, 1949, pp. 533–543.

Trust yourself to understand what your intuition senses. Seemingly insignificant nonverbal messages may help you develop the information you need. Bodily tension, flushing, excitability, frustration, ambiguousness, depression, and sadness can either confirm or contradict the interviewee's words. Actively listen by drawing on your knowledge and your experiences stored in your subconscious. The subtleties of the interviewee's behavior can influence your judgment. Therefore, concentrate on using your intuition, knowledge, and experience to capture every subtlety you sense.

At first, you may not understand the apparently arbitrary techniques used by skilled interviewers. They frequently cannot explain the role of intuition in their interviewing process. Still, proficient interviewers confidently nurture their intuitive judgments and act on them. They sense the interviewee's tenseness and spontaneously select the words or actions that will encourage truthful responses. If you want to follow their example, you will have to learn how to trust your intuition. This will come through practice and experience. You will find that your total sensing of the situation, along with your common sense, is more trustworthy than your intellect.

In almost all worthwhile endeavors, the degree of your success is directly related to the effort you make. This applies equally to using intuition. Initially, rely on your self-confidence to implement your intuitive judgments, and be prepared to learn from your success or failure. Work not only through the various steps of interviewing, following the generally accepted concepts, but also on developing techniques that capitalize on your intuitive talents. Use your intuition positively to read the interviewee's psychological movements, feelings, private logic or rationale, and any other signs that will help you achieve your goal.

The intuition of interviewees

Interviewees, too, are intuitive, and it would be foolhardy to ignore their ability to sense your judgments. In fact, through their exercise of their intuition, perhaps to achieve less-than-positive ends, they may have become quite skillful. Keenly alert to your signals, they respond positively or negatively to what they sense about you and your presentation. They may scrutinize your every move and gesture, the delivery of your questions, and your reactions to their answers.

Therefore ask yourself these questions:

- Have I fully researched everything possible prior to the interview?
- Do I convey a positive, self-confident, calm composure?
- Was my approach nondefensive?
- Do I keep an open mind during the interview?
- Do I demonstrate that I care about the interviewee, and am I respectful?

- Do I understand that displaying an accepting attitude toward all interviewees does not mean that I condone antisocial behavior and does not compromise my personal values?
- Do I understand that interviewees are secretly searching for a signal from me that it is indeed okay to be open and reveal the information?
- Do I consciously provide positive signals so that interviewees can count on my acceptance and fairness?
- Do I understand that I may subconsciously project my bias during interviews, triggering hostile feelings, threatening rapport, and therefore ending the interview?

Flexibility

Flexibility implies that you have the ability to change gears when and if needed in the process of interviewing. This quality is extremely important because no two interviews will ever be the same and there are no scripts for interviews. During interviewing, you need to adapt to changes in questioning, strategies, tone, or behavior. To obtain the cooperation of some interviewees, you might need to temporarily modify your methods and thinking. You might have to do or say things that you normally find objectionable.

For example, if you are neutral when interacting with the interviewee, I suggest figuratively leaning in favor of the interviewee by giving the impression that if you were in a similar circumstance, you might have done something similar to what the interviewee did, even though you know that you would never engage in that particular behavior. Treat everyone that you interview, even those you suspect of involvement in the matter under investigation, with professionalism and neutrality. Your professional, calm, nonjudgmental methods signal to victims, witnesses, and suspects that they can safely trust you.

Regardless of the style or styles of interviewing you have learned or may use, keep an open mind and stay ready to adjust your style. Without losing sight of your objective, try several methods of questioning with uncooperative interviewees. This is where the art of interviewing enters the picture.

Curiosity

Curiosity or inquisitiveness is a trait that can be very helpful throughout the investigative process and during the interview process. Certainly, as investigators, we are driven by wanting the answers and the truth.

We are also suspicious by nature. However, questions full of genuine curiosity rather than accusatory suspicion will further your investigation.

Imagination

Imagination has a part to play in training interviewers and in preparing for and conducting actual interviews. An excellent method for developing practical interviewing skills is to pool your ideas with one or more other imaginative interviewers. Group role playing can be used to test the ideas you generate. This approach allows less imaginative and less assertive interviewers to benefit from their more skilled peers. As general preparation for interviewing, strive to broaden your knowledge and awareness of other people to improve your ability to imagine the unimaginable.

Part of a successful interviewing venture is to try to consider why *you* might have done the crime in question. Imagine the motivation of the person you are interviewing while you conduct the interview. Don't be surprised by any basis for the event under investigation—people justify, blame, and rationalize in ways that sometimes lack logic. Imagination is a special quality not shared by all investigators. Those who possess it naturally are fortunate, for it is questionable whether imagination can be taught.

Research

We can never say enough about the importance of research in preparing for an interview. Never before have we had such a powerful research tool as the Internet. The Internet has changed the way we prepare and the extent of that preparation. Before we conduct the interview, we can gather a wealth of information to prepare for everything from the interview location to the questions we ask. Thoroughly research the background of each interviewee. It is critical to bring all important documents with you to the interview. You want to be fully prepared for whatever possibilities arise. As a corporate and private investigator, the one critical lesson we learned early on was that we might get only one chance to interview a person. This is one particular lesson we will talk about in other chapters because I think it is worth discussing.

There are many reasons you might have only one shot at your interview, but here are a few:

- Immediately after the interview, the interviewee is remorseful as to what they just told you.
- The interviewee suddenly wants to stop being cooperative.

- The interviewee is still employed at the business you are investigating, and he has changed his mind as to how involved he wants to get.
- The interviewee realizes that she just said something to implicate herself.
- After the interview, someone talked to the interviewee and made him see things differently than previously stated.
- The interviewee has had a change of heart toward either the suspect or the victim.
- The interviewee has been asked not to cooperate with any investigation or with one particular side of the investigation.
- The interviewee doesn't want to commit to any investigation.

Being prepared for all of these possibilities will determine the level of success of your interview.

Style

Someone said once that the hardest thing about conducting an interview is the conducting of an interview. It takes practice, practice, and more practice before you can develop a style. Using psychology, attitude, intuition, and the other qualities we've discussed, you will develop your own personal style.

In preparation, consider the following questions and pointers. In the chapters ahead, these specific questions will be addressed:

- What is your purpose in conducting this interview?
- Determine whether this will be an interview or an interrogation.
- What interview techniques will you utilize?
- What qualities should you as the interviewer have to get the optimum results?
- Be confident in verbal and nonverbal indicators.
- What indicators will you use for assessing verbal behavior and evaluating nonverbal behavior?
- Are there special circumstances that need to be addressed for this interview?
- What types of questions will you use for this interview?
- In regard to the interview, know your local, state, and federal laws and the companies involved, if this is a corporate internal investigation.
- Where will your interview be conducted? If you are able to decide on a setting, have you prepared accordingly?

8

Seeking the truth

Introduction

Truthfulness

Truthfulness, also known as honesty and sincerity, is signaled by an acute memory, a perceptive recounting of facts, and a flowing narration. Truthful interviewees display a consistent recollection of details and attempt to dig up related specifics, often offering more information than they are asked for. With encouragement, they remember facts they thought they had forgotten. They will allow the interviewer to see their mental wheels moving in search of additional details. With the truthful, you might witness a furrowed brow, squinted eyes, and a contemplative silence. They are open and relaxed in their manner of speech, though they may be somewhat uneasy. In addition, they clearly explain the sequence of events, wanting to be correct.

The fundamentals of human personality are needs, emotions, thinking, and the ability to relate thoughts and feelings.[1] Our actions are a result and composite of all of these elements. But most of all, it is the satisfaction of essential and predictable needs that motivates every type of human behavior. Individuals try to satisfy their needs by maintaining physical comfort, avoiding the unsafe, attempting to gain understanding, detesting anonymity, desiring to be free from boredom, fearing the unknown, and hating disorder. Because social needs are comparatively unsatisfied, they have become a primary motivator for behavior. Interviewees desperately seek approval and reassurance that they are in control. Interviewees who feel threatened, inferior, or ridiculous will try to increase feelings of security, acceptance, and self-regard. Everyone experiences feelings of inferiority from time to time. You may succeed in gaining the cooperation of interviewees if you nourish them with

---

[1] Maslow and Lowery, 1998, Changing Minds.org "The hierarchical effect". March 17, 2013.

69

feelings of security, friendship, and dignity and encourage them as they strive to satisfy their needs.

As we strive, directly or indirectly, to satisfy our needs, we have urges to behave in ways that will help or hinder our striving. Complications may develop as we seek to satisfy our needs. Either we modify our behavior to overcome the obstacles that are blocking the satisfaction of our needs, or we become frustrated at our failures. Frustration may provoke the emotional reactions of aggression, regression, and fixation and assorted defense mechanisms.

Dealing with false confessions

As[2] noted at the beginning of this chapter, the goal of ethical interviewing, questioning, and interrogation is to elicit the truth, and the truth can include statements that are either inculpatory confessions of guilt or exculpatory denial of involvement in a crime. Whenever an investigator has interrogated a suspect and a confession of guilt has been obtained, that investigator needs to take some additional steps to ensure that the confession can be verified as truthful before it goes to court. These additional steps are required because, although the investigator has not used any illegal or unethical techniques, the court will still consider whether the accused, for some reason, has confessed to a crime they did not commit. A skilled defense lawyer will often present arguments alleging that psychological stresses of guilt or hopelessness from exposure to overwhelming evidence have been used to persuade a suspect to confess to a crime they did not commit. In such cases, it is helpful for the court to hear any additional statements made by the accused, such as those that reveal that the suspect had direct knowledge of the criminal event that could only be known to the criminal responsible.

In police investigations, there are many details of the criminal event that will be known to the police through their examination of the crime scene or through the interview with witnesses or victims. These details can include the actual way the crime was committed, such as the sequence of events, the tools used in the crime, or the means of entry, path of entry/exit, along with other obscure facts that could only be known by the actual perpetrator. There are opportunities in a crime scene examination for the investigator to observe one or more unique facts that can be withheld as "hold-back evidence." This holdback evidence is not made part of reports or media release and is kept exclusively to test for false confessions. Confessing to the crime is one thing, but confessing to the crime and revealing intimate details are much more compelling to the court. Regardless of the effort and

---

[2] https://pressbooks.bccampus.ca/criminalinvestigation/chapter/chapter-9-interviewing-questioning-and-interrogation/.

care that investigators take to not end up with a false confession, they still occur, and there are some more common scenarios where false confessions happen. It is important for an investigator to consider these possibilities when a confession is obtained. These situations are as follows:

1. *The confessor was enlisted to take the blame*—On occasions where persons are part of organized crime, a person of lower status within the group is assigned or sacrificed to take the blame for a crime in place of a person of higher status. These organizational pawns are usually persons with a more minor criminal history or are a young offender, as they are likely to receive a lesser sentence for the offense.

2. *The sacrificial confessor*—Like the confessor enlisted in an organized criminal organization, there is another type of sacrificial confessor, the type who steps forward to take the blame to protect a friend or loved one. These are voluntary confessors, but their false confession can be exposed by questioning the confessor about the holdback details of the event.

3. *The mentally ill false confessor*—This type of false confessor is encountered when there is significant media attention surrounding a crime. As Pickersgill, 2015, noted, an innocent person may voluntarily provide a false confession because of a pathological need for notoriety or the need to self-punish due to guilt over an unrelated past offense. Additionally, those suffering from psychosis, endogenous depression, and Munchausen syndrome may falsely confess to a crime they did not commit. As with other false confessors, these people can be discovered using holdback detail questioning.

4. *Are voluntary confessions obtainable on a systemic basis?*[3] A confession to the police is not admissible unless, as a due process matter, it is given voluntarily. According to the Court in *Mincey* v. *Arizona*, a confession is not voluntary unless it is the product of "a rational intellect and a free will." If given after the police have taken the suspect into custody, a confession is not admissible unless the police administered Miranda warnings and obtained a "voluntary, knowing, and intelligent waiver."

Critics[4] argue that various features of the Reid interrogation method may lead certain innocent suspects to confess. For example, one critique argues that "the guilt-presumptive nature" of the Reid method "creates a slippery slope for innocent suspects because it may set in motion a sequence of reciprocal observations and reactions between the suspect and

---

[3] *Colorado* v. *Spring*, 107S. Ct. 851, 853 (1987). See *Miranda* v. *Arizona*, 384 U.S. 436, 475 (1966). If the interrogation continues without the presence of an attorney and a statement is taken, a heavy burden rests on the government to demonstrate.

[4] Interrogation techniques, by James Orlando, Associate Attorney.

interrogator that serve to confirm the interrogator's belief in the suspect's guilt" (Moore and Fitzsimmons, 2011, p. 513). According to some critics of the Reid technique, aspects of Reid-style interrogation that may lead to false confessions include the following:

1. Misclassification (the police attributing deception to truthful suspects).
2. Coercion (including psychological manipulation).
3. Contamination (such as when police present nonpublic information to a suspect and the suspect incorporates that information in his or her confession) (Gudjonsson, 2012, p. 695; discussing Leo and Drizin, 2010, among other studies).

Reid and Associates, Inc. disputes the contention that their methods lead to false confessions. They argue the following:

> False confessions are not caused by the application of the Reid Technique…[but instead] are usually caused by interrogators engaging in improper behavior that is outside of the parameters of the Reid Technique…such as threatening inevitable consequences; making a promise of leniency in return for the confession; denying a subject their rights; conducting an excessively long interrogation; etc.

The company also cites court cases upholding their methods or denying the admission of expert testimony that would link those methods to false confessions (e.g., *U.S.* v. *Jacques*, 784 F.Supp.2d 59, D. Mass, 2011).

Voluntary confessions

If you are a private investigator, a corporate investigator, or a security manager, you will want to get a written confession after a suspect makes a verbal confession. This written confession will be a statement detailing all the facts of the case that the interviewee can recall. If you work for a law enforcement agency or a federal agency, you are required to give a suspect a *Miranda warning*.[5] The confession must still be voluntary but obtained after the suspect was given a *Miranda* warning or the confession will be rejected as evidence at a trial or administrative hearing. Before a person in police custody or otherwise deprived of freedom "in any significant way" may be interviewed or interrogated, *Miranda* warnings must be given (*Miranda* v. *Arizona* [1966]).

Some investigators earnestly urge the subject to grant permission for the interrogation; other investigators, directly or indirectly, strongly advise the subject not to grant permission. As you give the warnings, use a neutral tone and a matter-of-fact manner. This is not a time to caution, suggest, frighten, or admonish the person in custody.

---

[5] http://usgovinfo.about.com/cs/mirandarights/a/miranda_2.htm.

Let's take a minute to examine the words *interview* and *interrogation*, because they will undoubtedly come up throughout this book and throughout your career as an investigative interviewer. An *interview* is a nonaccusatory question-and-answer session with anyone you are trying to obtain information from—witnesses, suspects, or victims. If you recall, the successful interview is one that collects accurate and useful information. Some of the questions may be of an investigative nature and some to elicit behavioral responses. The interviewer is building rapport and maintaining a nonaccusatory tone and demeanor throughout the interview. The skilled interviewer will ask questions that produce a narrative answer rather than a yes-or-no response. Because of the nature of the questions, the interviewee will do most of the talking. The only information gathered should come from the interviewee.

An *interrogation* is often used to elicit the truth from a person the investigator believes has lied during an interview. There may come a point in the interview that it turns from an interview into an interrogation or the other way around. It will depend on the interviewee as to the information he gives up or the information he is hiding. An interviewer that is skilled will be able to take it from an interview to an interrogation and then back when necessary. It takes practice to be able to read a person and then determine your strategy. We will talk more about practice, preparation, and skill throughout the book.

Legal tactics used in seeking a confession

Be fair and practical in interrogating or interviewing anyone, particularly suspects in custody. It is vital to avoid saying or doing anything that might cause an innocent person to confess. Do not use coercion, intimidation, threats, promises, or duress to force a confession; such action is neither legal nor acceptable. Intimidation reaps resentment, not truthful cooperation. Different parts of the world have different ethical standards and techniques; not all techniques used in some countries would be considered fair and professional in North America. Such tactics are self-defeating and inappropriate.

The following legal tactics can be used during an interrogation:

- Exhibit confidence in the subject's culpability.
- Present circumstantial evidence to persuade the subject to tell the truth.
- Observe the subject's behavior for indications of deception.
- Empathize with and help the subject rationalize his or her actions and save face.
- Minimize the significance of the matter under investigation.

- Offer nonjudgmental acceptance of the subject's behavior.
- Point out the futility of not telling the truth.
- Follow your senses and intuition.

Trickery and deceit are often used in interrogations. The US Supreme Court gave recognition to the necessity of these tactics in *Frazier* v. *Cupp* (1969). The Court held: "The fact that the police misrepresented the statements that [a suspected accomplice] had made is, while relevant, insufficient in our view to make this otherwise voluntary confession inadmissible. These cases must be decided by viewing the totality of the circumstances."

References

Gudjonsson, G.H., 2012. False confessions and correcting injustices. New Engl. Law. Rev. 46 (Summer), 689.

Leo, R.A., Drizin, S.A., 2010. The three errors: pathways to false confession and wrongful conviction. In: Lassiter, G.D., Meissner, C.A. (Eds.), Police Interrogations and False Confessions: Current Research, Practice and Policy Recommendations. Univ. of San Francisco Law Research Paper No. 2012–04. American Psychological Association, 23pp.

Moore, T.E., Fitzsimmons, C.L., 2011. Justice imperiled: false confessions and the Reid technique. Crim. Law Q. 57, 509. Available at: http://www.cbc.ca/thenational/includes/pdf/CLQ-2.pdf.

9

Overview of the interview and interrogation process

Rapport is the understanding between individuals created by genuine interest and concern. **Karen M. Hess and Wayne W. Bennett, Criminal Investigation (1991)**

Introduction

An interview is a free flowing discussion used to gather information and even to confirm information.

The role of the interview

Interviews are part of the investigative process. An investigation is a systematic and thorough examination or inquiry into something or someone that involves the collection of facts and information and the recording of that examination in a report.[1] Investigations can involve the police or private security regarding administrative incidents (policy and/or procedural infractions) and/or criminal matters.

Interviews will review information that will often be vital to the investigation of an incident or crime. The most effective tool for gathering information about an incident is interviewing people.[2] Therefore any information gained from an interview, typically in the form of statements, will be considered evidence. This may form a type of evidence known as testimonial evidence or, if involving a written statement, documented evidence. The detailed explanation of types of evidence is not important at this stage; what is important for the protection officer is to understand that when interviewing someone,

---

[1] ASIS International. (2006). Protection of Assets Manual, Chapter 1, Part 1, p. 8.
[2] ibid.

even if it appears casual and unofficial, it will produce a statement, either verbal or written, and this statement could become important evidence. That is why it is important to understand the procedures that should be followed when interviewing someone and obtaining their statement.

What is the difference between an interview and an interrogation? An *interview* is a nonaccusatory question-and-answer session with anyone you are trying to obtain information from either witnesses, suspects, or victims. A successful interview is one that collects accurate and useful information. Some of the questions may be of an investigative nature and some to elicit behavioral responses. The interviewer is building rapport and maintaining a nonaccusatory tone and demeanor throughout the interview. The skilled interviewer will ask questions that produce a narrative answer rather than a yes-or-no response. Because of the nature of the questions, the interviewee will do most of the talking. The only information gathered should come from the interviewee.

An interrogation is often used to elicit the truth from a person the investigator believes has lied during an interview. There may come a point in the interview that it turns from an interview into an interrogation or the other way around. It will depend on the interviewee as to the information he gives up or the information he is hiding. An interviewer that is skilled will be able to take it from an interview to an interrogation and then back when necessary. It takes practice to be able to read a person and then determine your strategy. We will talk more about practice, preparation, and skill throughout the book.

Typically, interviews involve witnesses or victims, and an interrogation is an interview of a suspect. The goal of an interrogation is not only to seek the facts of what happened but also to obtain a confession. It is not likely that a protection officer will be required to conduct an interrogation as part of their duties, and only trained investigators skilled in the techniques of interviewing should conduct interrogations. Trained interviewers and interrogators spend years learning and practicing to become skilled in this art and science.

Interrogations

The interrogation is an accusation interaction with an individual; remember it must be conducted in a controlled environment designed to provide the suspect to confess and tell the truth.

Nine steps of interrogation

The Reid technique's nine steps of interrogation are as follows[3]:

---

[3] Zulawski, David E.; Wicklander, Douglas E. (2001). Practical Aspects of Interview and Interrogation. Ann Arbor: CRC Press. ISBN 978-0-8493-0101-8.

1. **Direct confrontation.** Advise the suspect that the evidence has led the police to the individual as a suspect. Offer the person an early opportunity to explain why the offense took place.
2. Try to shift the blame away from the suspect to some other person or set of circumstances that prompted the suspect to commit the crime. That is, develop themes containing reasons that will psychologically justify or excuse the crime. Themes may be developed or changed to find one to which the accused is most responsive.
3. Try to minimize the frequency of suspect denials.
4. At this point the accused will often give a reason why he or she did not or could not commit the crime. Try to use this to move toward the acknowledgement of what they did.
5. Reinforce sincerity to ensure that the suspect is receptive.
6. The suspect will become quieter and listen. Move the theme of the discussion toward offering alternatives. If the suspect cries at this point, infer guilt.
7. Pose the "alternative question," giving two choices for what happened—one more socially acceptable than the other. The suspect is expected to choose the easier option, but whichever alternative the suspect chooses, guilt is admitted. As stated earlier, there is always a third option that is to maintain that they did not commit the crime.
8. Lead the suspect to repeat the admission of guilt in front of witnesses and develop corroborating information to establish the validity of the confession.
9. Document the suspect's admission or confession and have him or her prepare a recorded statement (audio, video, or written).

Do's and don'ts of interrogation

Following is a list of other do's and don'ts that can be helpful to the security interrogator[4]:

- Do use silence as a weapon. Ask a direct question and then wait for the response. The silence may seem like a long time, but it is thundering in the mind and ears of the accused, to whom it seems like an eternity.
- Do keep questions short.
- Do ask only one question at a time.
- Do question the answers.
- Do guard yourself against giving away information.
- Don't make promises of any kind.

---

[4] The Process of Investigation, Charles A. Sennewald and John K. Tsukayama, Fourth edition, 2015, p. 109.

- Don't lose your patience or persistence—any anxiety you feel is much amplified in the subject.
- Don't threaten an accused with discharge, police involvement, or violence.
- Don't show surprise at any answers.
- Don't use profanity. Some still believe the only way to communicate with tough employees or outsiders are to speak "their" language. Don't lower yourself to them; rather, raise them up to you.
- Don't be a big shot. Arrogance and pomposity close communication lines, which defeats the interrogator's purpose.
- Don't lie. It may be unwise to tell all, but what you do tell must be truthful.
- Don't ever lose your temper. If you lose your temper, you "got the stress" and lose the interrogation. The subject will do and say things, both intentionally and by chance, that can make you angry. Resist this urge and remain the clinical professional.

Understanding people is another important aspect of interviews and statements. Many studies have been conducted on human behavior and crime. Investigators have learned from the research about how to effectively interact with individuals to facilitate useful communications, which in turn can produce valuable information for the investigation. The protection officer can also benefit from understanding human behavior.

The power of communication

Interviewing someone involves communication in two ways:

1. verbally
2. nonverbally

Verbal communication is the most commonly understood form of interview and statement. The interviewer speaks, and the interviewee responds or vice versa. This seems simple; however, in many situations, the interviewer seeks to obtain information from people who are reluctant to speak or cooperate. We will illustrate reasons why building rapport and understanding human behavior and psychology assist the interviewer.

Research has shown that people form their basic impressions of one another during the first few minutes of an interview.[5] Therefore it is very important for the interviewer to always think about how they are presenting themselves to the other person. If the officer does not initially conduct himself or herself in a professional manner, this may create a negative relationship with the interviewee. A negative mood will be counterproductive in an interview.

---

[5] Quinn and Zunin, 1972.

The art of building rapport

The interviewing process is not limited to the criminal justice and security arena. Interviews are conducted in virtually every area of human endeavor. Human resource specialists conduct interviews routinely; supervisors conduct them routinely as they conduct performance plans and handle disciplinary problems. Doctors, lawyers, admission coordinators, and pastors all perform interviews as one of their many job responsibilities. During any interview, no matter who the interviewer happens to be, or for whatever reason the interview is being conducted, the interviewer needs to build rapport, along with being proficient in active listening. Interviews are not normal social encounters in which two people exchange ideas and experiences on an equal footing. In an investigative interview the interviewee should do most of the talking, while the investigator acts as a catalyst, a persuader, and a simulator of thoughts. The interviewer promotes an unspoken chemistry that produces cooperation. He or she asks appropriate questions to probe for facts, anecdotes, and feelings from the interviewee. To prepare for your role as interviewer catalyst, look at each inquiry with clear thinking as you plan your approach. Detach yourself from the emotional content of the interview, adopt a positive attitude, and be flexible. In your role as an investigator, its critical to develop your skills in both building rapport and active listening.

One example of a successful interview, using both rapport and active listening, led to the 2010 conviction of sex killer Russell Williams, former CFB Trenton, Ontario commander. This interview was conducted by a skilled, veteran investigator, OPP Det. Sgt. Jim Smyth.[6] Det. Smyth used a variety of skills, such as using the first name of the interviewee to eliminate special status, remained calm throughout the interview, used friendly tone, and thanked him for cooperating and closely watching all the nonverbal body language, all skills requiring building rapport and psychology. The technique used in this case was nonconfrontational in nature. This was an interview that was fascinating to watch and will be praised for many years. I recommend viewing the 10-h interrogation, which can be viewed on Canadian Broadcast Radio.[7]

Mutual confidence and trust are important if you expect truthfulness, but when you are interviewing a suspect or witness, you will have to work to earn both. Your goal is to determine the truth in an investigation; the interviewee's goal might be to protect himself from a variety of consequences. You can overcome this obstacle and encourage interviewees to provide information by building *rapport*. If you can plan, organize, and

---

[6] https://www.ctvnews.ca/a-deeper-look-into-the-interrogation-of-russell-williams-1.565832.
[7] Canadian Broadcast Radio, Russell Williams, 2010, https://www.youtube.com/watch?v=lj7QRP37Wn0.

evoke cooperation in social situations, you probably possess basic qualities of leadership and can establish rapport, inspire confidence, elicit information, and keep interviews under control.

Rapport can be described as a good feeling or warmth that exists between people and is characterized by an interpersonal relationship that is cooperative. In an interview, rapport is like an electric current that flows between participants. It is based on how they communicate rather than on what they say, and it requires practiced effort. Rapport involves building a degree of comfortableness together and a level of trust in one another. It is basic goodwill that permits nondefensive behavior. To develop rapport is to create a feeling within yourself and the interviewee of alertness, well-being, and even excitement. Rapport is a psychological closeness established in the very beginning of an interview, when you blend your verbal and nonverbal actions with those of the interviewee. The first few minutes are crucial because people determine their basic impressions of one another during the first few minutes of an interview. Rapport is important in an interview because the degree of rapport you establish determines the degree of compliance you obtain from the interviewee.

Investigators who succeed in establishing rapport with interviewees demonstrate their empathy with them and generally obtain their truthful cooperation. They feel less inhibited in asking questions, even questions about sensitive or personal matters, and interviewees are less resistant about answering. The development of rapport does not require that the interviewer becomes emotionally involved or that the interviewer's commitment, persistence, or objectivity be eroded. You are not trying to become the interviewee's best buddy. You are trying to solve the case. You want the interviewee to buy into your friendliness only long enough so that you can obtain the information you need. When all is said and done, no one will misunderstand your behavior.

Active listening, discussed throughout this chapter, is an important technique for building rapport, but there are others. Rapport can be developed through small talk, a good orientation, and through a very warm, friendly manner. To achieve rapport with the interviewee, try to find an area of common interest. There is usually something that you can find that could help identify with the interviewee. You can call attention to similarities in such subtle ways as by complimenting the person (thus showing that you have similar tastes). You can also build rapport by enhancing the interviewee's self-image. If your inquiry is handled in a professional way so that cooperation will benefit the interviewee's self-image, he or she will feel honored to cooperate and will later be proud of assisting "the authorities." Attempt to make your inquiry relevant to the interviewee's life and concerns. Your attitude is communicated by the ways you listen and ask questions. People find it flattering to be asked for their opinions. In an interview, this technique compliments the interviewee's views and may strengthen rapport. Expressions of genuine interest and empathy, positive recognition, easy eye contact, and appropriate positive silences also help build and maintain rapport. These are techniques that you can practice and become very natural at doing.

At the beginning of an interaction, the interviewee may display signs of uneasiness. Even truthful interviewees may have some anxiety over whether you will be fair and unbiased in your methods and judgment. As rapport develops, you may notice a distinct sigh of relief, signaling a lessening of the interviewee's distress and the building of trust. From that point onward the interview may take on a more relaxed character.

You need to be alert to whether the interviewee is truly listening. Just because interviewees are silent and appear to be listening does not mean that they are truly receptive to what you are saying. They may be lost in an emotional maze of fear. Periodically ask questions designed to test whether the interviewee is listening. A blank, unresponsive stare may signal distress, unclear thinking, or an unbalanced mental process.

Control your emotions without losing your enthusiasm. Keep your thoughts collected and composed; think your comments through carefully before presenting them to the interviewee. Refuse to become ruffled, and keep your goal clearly in mind. The use of sarcasm, ridicule, or cynicism only creates tension instead of building rapport and gaining cooperation from the interviewee. Generally speaking, people resist being thought of as inferior and might be reluctant to establish rapport with or to be persuaded by anyone who tries, either consciously or unconsciously, to make them feel that way. Instead, help the interviewee rationalize and save face. Other actions that tend to block rapport are making negative comments, engaging in monologs, second-guessing the interviewee, displaying a condescending attitude, and trying to hurry through the interview.

Through participant role reversal an interviewee may skillfully unseat you and take over the role of leader in the interview. An inexperienced interviewer may not see the signals of this switchover and may discover too late that he or she has given up command of the interview, answering rather than asking questions. This role reversal is embarrassing only if it continues. Proficient interviewers realize when role reversal is taking place and immediately regain control without making it too obvious or causing conflict. Entering into a power struggle with interviewees can create alienation instead of rapport.

When you're ending an unsuccessful interview, do nothing to create hard feelings. Even when hostile interviewees refuse to answer your questions, don't hold a grudge; don't show disgust, frustration, or anger; and don't allow yourself to vent your displeasure. Don't allow your pride to cause you to blame interviewees for their lack of cooperation. Instead, lay a positive foundation for future interviews. Aim to have all interviewees leave with a positive feeling, allowing them to believe that they experienced a meaningful and valuable interaction.

The interviewer's success depends on the interviewee talking to them, and building rapport is the catalyst to this communication. This means the interviewer will attempt to establish a bond between them that is a connection where the interviewee perceives the interviewer to be a caring, impartial, and concerned individual. Here are some recommendations:

1. **Be empathetic**—show the person you understand and care about how they feel. This helps the interviewee accept and feel comfortable with the interviewer and will facilitate open and honest communication.
2. **Eliminate your prejudices**—try to detach yourself from any personal prejudices or bias you may have against the interviewees.
   - **Actions**—detach yourself from what the accused may have done, no matter how bad it was.
   - **Race**—do not discriminate against the person based on race or ancestry.
   - **History**—show the person that you are not prejudging based on past history.
   Try to be nonjudgmental and do not place immediate blame.
3. **Be patient**—show the person you can wait to listen and understand their story of what happened and why. This is a sign of a very good listener when they can show they are patient. This is a sign to the interviewee of tolerance, acceptance, and understanding.
4. **Reflect feedback**—repeat back to the interviewee statements, facts, and comments they have related. The interviewer should be reflecting back to the interviewee their words and feeling, which lets them know you are listening and cares about what they have to say.
5. **Do not interrupt**—it is rude to interrupt, just like in any communication or conversation, so do not interrupt the interviewee when they are relating their story to you. Allow them to finish what they are saying.
6. **Concentrate**—interviewing someone requires complete concentration on what they are saying and how they are saying it. Concentration can best be equated to playing a game of chess; the interviewer not only needs to concentrate on what is currently being said but also must think ahead to expect what the interviewee might (or should) say.

Why would concentration be important and matter when the interviewee is telling the story and relating the facts as they know it? This is because the interviewee will sometimes not tell the truth and attempt to deceive the interviewer, for a variety of reasons. This is why the interviewer needs to concentrate on what is said and follow the story and attempt to detect deception. Detecting deception is explained in more detail later.

"Nonverbal communication" is a type of communication between persons that involves written statements (discussed later) and bodily movements that are considered a form of communication. This is important for an interviewer to understand because how a person (this includes the interviewer, too) projects themselves can inadvertently give significant information about their state of mind. For example, someone who shows by their nervous voice tone, shaking hands, and darting eyes that they are anxious and afraid should be recognized by the interviewer so that they can try to calm the interviewee and make them feel more relaxed. This helps toward developing rapport between the interviewer and interviewee. Additionally, changes in behavior and body movements can indicate stress. Stress is an important indicator for an interviewer. This can be the stress of the interview itself or from a specific and directed question such as "Did you take the money?" A guilty person may show signs of "fight-or-flight syndrome." Fight or flight is an instinctual phenomenon, based on when humans relied on this instinct to help them either run from danger (flight) or face it (fight). It actually is a manifestation of bodily reactions to stress that humans will experience even nowadays when confronted with stress. Asking a question that may compel the interviewee to lie will often cause this type of stress. A well-trained interviewer can act as a human polygraph (lie detector) when someone attempts to deceive by telling a lie or not revealing information. Many of these telltale signals come from nonverbal and verbal responses to stress and are evident in clusters of observed body movements and reactions. As mentioned, it can take many years of training and experience for a skilled interviewer to recognize these signals of deception, and further specialized training is recommended before anyone attempts to seek or analyze verbal and nonverbal behavior in an interview. Nonetheless, here are some examples of verbal and nonverbal behavior when subjected to stress:

- Changes in voice and speech patterns, such as changes in the types of words used.
- Changes in the rate and volume of speech (louder, softer, faster, or slower). Tension will often cause speech to become more rapid and stammered, sometimes two to three times the normal speed.
- Burst of anger (threats to sue you, complaints of how the interviewee has been handled, and comments about your incompetence).
- Pausing, stalling, or delaying tactics (the interviewee suddenly needs to leave for an appointment, long pauses to try to think of an answer, changing the topic in an attempt to delay the interview, suddenly wants a lawyer).
- Nervous or false laughter (this is a form of energy release when someone is under stress).
- Sudden shifts in body movement not normally displayed by the interviewee during the interview (some examples include shifting body position, pacing, jumping out of chair, waving hands and arms, shaking, kicking legs and feet, coughing, and yawning). These are also forms of energy release when someone is feeling stressed.

It is vital for the protection officer to understand that nonverbal indicators need to be analyzed by a trained investigator and interviewer. It is important to understand as a protection officer (interviewer) you will outwardly display your feelings by how you present yourself. Therefore be careful and aware about how you may appear to the interviewee.

Before your interview, consider these steps:

1. **Prepare yourself, physically and mentally.** Consider your attitude and your appearance. Remember to stay confident and focused.
2. **If possible, try to use a suitable location for the interview.** The interview location should be private and quiet to avoid distractions. Anyone hearing the interviewee's account could contaminate the interview.
3. **Ask open-ended questions.** Questions that are closed-ended will solicit a "yes" or "no" response. Open-ended questions will encourage the interviewee providing longer answers and possibly more of a narrative response. Examples are as follows:
   - "Please tell me everything that happened."
   - "In detail, can you please explain what occurred here today?"
   - "Please describe everything you saw regarding what happened here."
4. **Record the interview (for private sector, follow state regulations on recording laws).** Although it is common to write detailed notes from interviews, if you are in a jurisdiction that legally permits audio- or videotape the interview—this is the best method of maintaining an accurate account of what exactly is stated.
   - When taking a statement, the best method is to obtain a "pure version" statement.
   - Pure version statements allow the interviewee to provide their version of an account in a narrative format without any prompting from the interviewer other than a request, similar to "Please write in detail everything that happened from the time you left your house to the time the police arrived at the scene."
   - If the person responds with "What exactly do you want me to say?" The protection officer's response should be "Please explain in as much detail as possible everything that happened from the time you left your house to the time the police arrived at the scene."
   - The pure version statement remains the best method to obtain the interviewee's account of what happened. This statement becomes the basis for further questions that can be asked by the investigator to complete a detailed account of what occurred.
   - Be careful what questions you ask. It is part of the psychology of interviewing that an interviewer needs to consider the questions they ask an interviewee—the famed investigator, Avinoam Sapir, who discovered through his extensive research the process known as "Statement Analysis," has aptly said: "Specific questions are not designed to obtain information. Specific questions are designed to

detect deception. The most serious disadvantage of questions is that one can ask only about what is already known. What is not known would not be explored and therefore would remain unknown." It is also from an interviewer's questions that an interviewee can learn how much the interviewer already knows (or doesn't know) about the incident.

5. **Remember the elements for useful statements**[8]:
   - Identify who wrote the statement (interviewee's name and identification information).
   - Date, time, and location of the interview.
   - Indicate if the statement is voluntary.
   - Signed by the interviewee.

Other guidelines for written statements[9]:

- Use lined paper and write margin to margin.
- The text should flow into additional pages (if necessary).
- If corrections are required, draw a line through the sentence or word and sign your initials on the change.
- Sign your initials next to the last word on a page and where the page number is written: (Example: "Page 1 of 3" INITIALS).
- Ensure the interviewee understands what is written (if the statement is written for them)—have the interviewee read back what is written.
- Include a sentence acknowledging the statement is voluntary, without the influence of drugs or alcohol, and is the account of the interviewee.

Interviewing the victim

Victims[10] are difficult to interview because they are reacting emotionally to their plight. The intensity of the emotion tends to be a delayed reaction, peaking after the reality of the incident sets in and then tending to dissipate with the passage of time. And the emotional reaction should be predictable. A female employee who received an obscene phone call will be frightened; an employee whose new automobile was broken into and damaged while in the company parking lot will be angry (with the culprit and the company); the employee who cashed her paycheck only to have the cash stolen from her purse before the end of the day will be frantic or depressed.

---

[8] Sennewald and Tsukayama, 2006. The process of investigation: Concepts and strategies for investigations in the workplace (3rd ed.). Elsevier/Butterworth-Heinemann.

[9] Ibid.

[10] The Process of Investigation, Charles A. Sennewald and John K. Tsukayama, Fourth edition, 2015, p. 98.

If an interviewer is with the victim at the peaking of emotion, the victim should not be pushed for information. Instead the interviewer could get the victim a cup of coffee or let him or her light up a cigarette or whatever, biding for time. If time runs out because the shift is over and the victim must catch a bus or carpool with others, the interview can be put off until the next day.

Forcing the interview is no more or less than victimizing the victim again. It builds resentment against the investigator or firm. On the other hand, to show concern for and sensitivity to a victim, after getting the basic facts and advising the individual that the interview can wait until he or she feels better the following day, develops good will. (It is necessary to emphasize "after getting the basic facts" because the victims of certain crimes must immediately share basic information.)

The interview's ultimate objective is to gather all the facts, every fact possible; details are important. Take, for example, interviewing a witness/ victim who is the recipient of an indecent phone call from an unknown suspect pretending to be doing a lingerie survey for a well-known local department store. The receiver of the call, when asked to describe what happened, will tell a "story." The "story" (not meant as a fabrication, but rather the retelling or recalling of the incident) will invariably leave out pertinent details. Following would be a typical retelling of the incident:

> This morning, I got a call from a man from your company who said his name was Mr. Barkins, and he said he was doing a survey for the lingerie department. He asked if I would answer questions to the survey, and I would then receive a certificate worth $25 to buy merchandise in your store. I said fine. He then asked my lingerie color preference, then my bra size, slip size, and panty size. I felt uncomfortable but answered. He then asked if I wore the brief panties or regular cut. I said brief. He then asked if I shaved to wear the briefs. I didn't think that was right, so I just said no. Then he asked me if I didn't shave, did hair show. I was so shocked I couldn't think of an appropriate answer, and then he asked me a filthy question, to which I slammed down the phone. That's what happened, from beginning to end.

After using open questions to elicit some additional facts, the interviewer must then develop unstated details. Examples are as follows:

- Does your telephone system have caller ID or a last caller dial-back capability?
- What time exactly did the caller call? Fix the time by association with her schedule or routine.
- What was she doing when the phone rang? Watching a favorite TV program? Still having coffee? Husband just left for work? and so forth.
- Did he use the store's name first, or at first identify himself by name, claiming he was with the store?
- Did he say he was Mr. Jones, or did he use a first name also?
- Was the phone connection clear? Was it a cell phone call?
- How old a man did he sound like?

- Did you hear any sounds in the background such as a radio or TV, phones ringing, sounds of traffic, voices, or were there no sounds whatsoever?
- Did he sound like an educated man in terms of his choice of words, diction, delivery, or sentence structure? (Qualify the answer by asking her to compare to husband, family, or friends.)
- Was there any distinguishable accent?
- Was there any other characteristic in his manner of speaking, for example, fast, slow, lisping, stuttering, preceding questions with "ah," and so on?
- Did he make any reference as to how or why he called you? For example, did he say the local credit bureau provided your name as a good customer in the community?
- Is your telephone number listed in the directory?
- If your phone number is listed, how is it listed, under your own name?
- Did he ever refer to you by your first name, if it's not listed?
- Are you well known in the community by virtue of your personal, social, or political activities?
- Is it generally known in your neighborhood that you are alone during the morning?
- Did the caller sound like anyone, even vaguely, you have met or known?
- Would you be able to recognize the caller's voice if you heard it again?

Obviously the answers to these questions and more give the investigator details. And in that detail can be the key to the identity of the caller, if not in this incident, then in another. It is important that only one question at a time is asked, and if the answer is appropriate and intelligent, determine if that answer deserves another question.

Sometimes, however, investigators deny themselves every detail by having, for example, the wrong person conduct the interview. Consider the female employee who received an obscene phone call. If a male investigator were conducting that interview, some of the language during that conversation, language that could tie in with a past or future case, might not surface. A female investigator would probably obtain the entire conversation, word for word. Ideally, then, a female investigator would do the follow-up interviewing on sex-related offenses involving female victims. That is also true in situations where children are witnesses. As a rule, small children will confide in a female more readily than in a male, and older people feel more at ease with investigators closer to their own age.

Further reading

Davies, S.J., Fennelly, L.J., 2020. The Professional Protection Officer, second ed. Elsevier, Cambridge, MA.

10

Interviewing techniques

Introduction

Interviewing is best done face to face. In the complex interaction that takes place during an interview, observations are made by both participants as they check and recheck each other's verbal and nonverbal behavior. There is a mutual analysis: the interviewee is scrutinizing the investigator for signs of believability while being observed for patterns of deception. Seasoned interviewers know that luck is merely what is left over after careful planning and preparation. They develop a plan for each interview but remain flexible when applying it. They help interviewees rationalize and save face, thus encouraging their cooperation.

It is worth remembering, that when someone is being interviewed, they are likely going to undergo stress, even if in minimal amounts. As difficult as it may be for you, finding a way to portray yourself as kind and gentle, may pay off at some point during the investigation/interview. It is important to be empathetic, while remaining curious, and to interview with purpose. Your questions need to be objective, thorough, relevant, and accurate. Proficient interviewers have a keen sense of observation, resourcefulness, and persistence as well as a tireless capacity for work. They also use common sense. Acting stern, imperious, or harsh will not help your interview. Be guided by your intuition, not guesses or speculations, but be sure your intuition is based on your direct observation and immediate experience. Be prepared to interview without conveying pressure or suggestion and encourage the interviewee to provide a narrative account of their statement. Ask the interviewee to recall everything related to this particular case, observed or known. It is always better to interview witnesses as soon as possible after an incident, so that they can give a more accurate report.

Interviewing and interviewing techniques have changed tremendously over the past 10 years, specifically in regard to the way witnesses and suspects are interviewed. Years ago, interviews were often times confrontational, whereas now, our goal should be cooperation, producing a meaningful interview.

Unobtrusively direct the interview, deciding when to listen, when to talk, what to observe, and so on. In so doing, observe, evaluate, and assess the interviewees, including what they say both verbally and nonverbally, how they say what they say, and what they fail to say. The plausibility of a witness's observation is critical to the overall investigation; therefore consider the ability of each interviewee to see and hear what was reportedly observed. With overly talkative interviewees who ramble or with those who tend to wander from the topic, gently and empathically guide them back, redirecting them through leading questions to a discussion of the issue at hand.

Interviewees provide opinions wherever and whenever they can; it is your job to distinguish true factual information from opinionated, emotional comments. Separate observations from interpretations and facts from feelings. If you notice interviewees interpreting facts rather than presenting observed details, avoid being judgmental and pouncing on them. Without pressure or suggestion, encourage them to provide a narrative of their observations regarding the investigative problem. Avoid knowingly bringing into your inquiry any biases or prejudices that might lead to misguided observations and improper evaluation.

Question formulation

Interviewers succeed when they convince their subjects to provide truthful information. It's not a matter of *telling* but rather of *selling*. Well-crafted questions can sell the interviewee on the idea of telling the truth. You need to be a persuader of sorts, using properly phrased questions in a setting and under circumstances that persuade the interviewee to answer honestly. Questions encourage compliance when their design is simple. Make them more specific and complex only after evaluating the interviewee's responses. Aristotle said, "Think as wise men do, but speak as the common people do." Ask questions spontaneously to express ideas in a natural and subconscious manner. Trust yourself to ask properly worded questions while encouraging the subject to cooperate. When appropriate, make your questions specific, definite, and concrete. Vague, general questions permit interviewees to wiggle and squirm away from your desired goal.

Choose your words with care. Words represent partial images, not the total picture. Avoid legal-sounding terms like *homicide, assault,* and *embezzlement.* Misused, these words tend to make interviewees unnecessarily defensive. Interviewees welcome the opportunity to respond to questions for which they know the answers, and they feel freer to talk when the topic is familiar. Interview suspects tend to avoid answering questions that make them appear dumb, foolish, or uninformed. When embarrassed or upset over a question, interviewees avoid eye contact and may display signs of distress. Some people appear shifty-eyed when they are lying, are planning to lie, or have been asked to reveal private information about themselves.

Question presentation

A question is a direct or implied request for the interviewee to think about a particular matter. Comments based on assumptions can be regarded as questions if they invite the interviewee to respond. Rather than rely on many questions, allow the interviewee to speak freely. Some interviewees elaborate more readily when asked fewer questions. Once an interviewee decides to talk, you often need only guide the discussion with timely encouragement. Your assumptions, behavior, and method of questioning will, to some extent, determine the interviewee's response and willingness to cooperate. Even your vocabulary could cause embarrassment or fright. Interviewees who lose face because they don't understand your words may become disturbed or insulted, they may feel naked and vulnerable, and they may become judgmental and skeptical (Berne, 1974[1]). Often, ones resentment may cause them to fail to think clearly, to refuse to cooperate, or even to lie. On the other hand, some interviewees will be extremely cooperative in trying to answer all questions, even with an interviewer who asks poorly phrased questions based on crude, biased assumptions. By initiating the question-answer pattern, you tell interviewees as plainly as if put into words that you are the authority and the expert and that only you know what is important and relevant. This may humiliate some interviewees who regard such a pattern as a third-degree tactic. Therefore phrase your questions carefully and be sensitive enough to realize when not to ask questions. Noticing the sincerity of your tone of questioning and how you avoid asking abrasive, leading questions, interviewees will feel less need to be defensive.

Question objectively. Avoid giving the impression that you have taken sides in the investigation. This may be difficult for interviewers who represent certain organizations, such as law enforcement agencies. Avoid looking surprised or shocked at any statement an interviewee makes.

Regard the interview as a conversation, not a cross-examination. "Do not grill the interviewee as a prosecuting attorney might do. Ask questions in a conversational manner, because your purpose is to hold a conversation with someone who has knowledge or has experienced something that you want to know about. Holding a conversation implies a certain amount of give and take during the interview. Your goal is to ask questions that are productive, yielding information. Try to avoid making statements that do not illicit an answer.

---

[1] The Adams County Sun & Berne Daily Witness (Berne, Ind.) 1974 to 1976, Cognitive Psychology 7 (4), October 1975, pp. 560–572, Elsevier Pub.

Never ask questions in a belligerent, demeaning, or sarcastic manner. Questions that begin "Isn't it true that you..." tend to be abrasive and promote defensiveness. Pushing interviewees into a corner where they will have to defend themselves is self-defeating. Do not embarrass interviewees by asking questions that they cannot answer. This will only make them uneasy and will create unnecessary tension. Similarly, asking questions accusingly, suspiciously, or abruptly or asking "trick questions" may arouse fear and defensiveness and will not promote cooperation. All of these tactics are counterproductive.

To emphasize your genuine interest in the details the interviewee has provided and to promote a positive view of your thoroughness, review all details during questioning. This will allow coverage of more specific areas of interest as the need arises. Make it appear that some details are not as clear as they could be or claim to have missed some meaningful information.

Types of questions

Two main types of questions are generally used in interviews: closed questions and open questions. The objective of the inquiry determines the use of closed or open questions. Fewer tactical restrictions apply to using open questions. By tactical restrictions, I mean strategic limitations that might hamper your progress in calling for the truth. Open questions allow for various angles or degrees of considered approach. They can be calculated to emphasize points of the inquiry using various levels of review and encouragement.

Closed questions

Closed, or closed-ended, questions are specific, offering a limited number of possible responses. Yes-or-no questions and multiple-choice questions are types of closed questions. These types of questions are also risky because they don't allow the interviewee to communicate freely. Oftentimes, closed-ended questions are counterproductive and limit rapport building. If used, ask them at the beginning of an interview to encourage affirmative responses and to put interviewees more at ease. Used later in the interview, closed questions will limit your efforts to reveal information.

The yes-no or either-or option of some closed questions limits the scope of responses and options. This can be useful when you want to maintain maximum control over the interview and thereby save some time. They are also handy when dealing with reluctant interviewees who will not give detailed responses. To gain information, narrow [closed] questions have the advantage of eliciting details. Open-ended questions rely on the [interviewee's] ability to recall. However, the unrestricted use of closed questions will hamper your efforts. "Narrow questions can inhibit the development of rapport.... The misuse of narrow questions involves detailed probing before the [interviewee] is ready. People will be willing to provide details, particularly about sensitive subjects, only if they feel comfortable in doing so. Therefore, probing too soon, without first having developed a rapport, may cause the interviewee to feel improperly invaded."[2]

Open questions

Open, or open-ended, questions start with *who, where, what, when, how,* or *why.* They cannot be answered yes or no, and they require the suspect to think clearly. Although they create the most distress, they also reveal the greatest amount of information. These questions are also the most productive ones. Open questions help interviews flow. Most open questions ask *what, why,* or *how.*

To learn the cause, reasons, or purpose, ask the question *why. Why* questions search out the facts of a situation and probe areas not commonly touched by more complicated questions. There are times, however, when the *why* question creates a threatening situation in which interviewees become defensive. Faced with the question "Why?" they may feel rejected, misunderstood, or imposed upon. They may withdraw, prevaricate, or hit back with silence that may confuse or frustrate you. Questions beginning with *why* may provoke undue stress because they generate too much challenge. Interviewees generally cannot answer the question "Why?" regarding subconscious thinking or behavior. Answering reveals too much of the self, and self-disclosure makes people uncomfortable.

Open questions can help you accomplish several goals:

- Discover the interviewee's priorities, attitudes, needs, values, aims, and aspirations.
- Determine the interviewee's frame of reference and viewpoints.
- Establish empathic understanding and rapport.
- Engage in active listening, stroking, positive regard, and recognition.
- Allow and encourage interviewees to express their feelings and reveal facts without feeling threatened.
- Promote catharsis or expression of the interviewee's emotions.

Several different types of open questions can be used effectively during an interview. Anticipating the impact of each question that you ask will help you formulate them. Open question types are discussed in the following sections.

---

[2] Binder and Price, 1977, pp. 44–45.

Reflective questions

Reflective questions mirror the subject's comments. They are used to handle objections. You might begin, "Let me see if I've got this straight…" or "So, what you're saying is…." Once you've responded to the interviewee's concerns, repeat the question that triggered the objection. By removing the obstacle to cooperation, you help the interviewee feel more comfortable responding to your subsequent questions.

Directive questions

Directive questions are used to direct the interviewee's attention to areas of agreement with the investigator. Interviewees want to know the benefits to themselves of cooperation. A directive question answers this concern: "You do want to get to the bottom of this, don't you?"

Pointed questions

Pointed, or *direct*, *questions* are detailed and specific in nature, pointing directly at the goal. Pointed questions are complex and persuasive. They are designed to rouse the interviewee to action. Most of the questions asked in forensic interviews are pointed questions. By asking exactly what is desired, you show interviewees that you believe they are ready, willing, and able to respond. This method, which is based on the self-fulfilling prophecy, works most of the time.

Pointed questions might stimulate the physical expression of the interviewee's stress, but they need not be offensive or accusatory. On the contrary, they should be thoughtfully developed and subtly applied to avoid invoking stress and making the subject defensive. You can gently stimulate the interviewee's thinking with pointed, creative questions. For example, if you believe that the interviewee accidentally set a fire, you might ask, "On the day of the fire, how often did you smoke in the break room?"

Indirect questions

Pointed questions are not always appropriate. *Indirect questions* provoke less stress, less fear, and hence less defensiveness on the part of the interviewee. They help subjects save face and rationalize their behavior by giving them "a universal blessing." For example, you might say, "I've talked to many of the other employees, and they believe that… What do you think?" Indirect questions of this nature can help interviewees express their hidden selves, their thoughts and feelings, and so on. Indirect questions are often used at the beginning of an interview and as a change of pace during the course of the discussion. They can also be used as diversion questions (see the discussion that follows).

Self-appraisal questions

Self-appraisal questions ask the interviewee to evaluate or judge himself. They help the investigator develop a hypothesis about the *who, how,* and *why* of a crime or another incident. Through self-appraisal questions the interviewer gains a deeper understanding of the interviewee's needs and probes his opinion, revealing possible evasiveness and distress. It is almost impossible for a deceptive or evasive interviewee to be consistent in answering self-appraisal questions. To respond deceptively the interviewee must first think of an answer, decide that the answer would not sound good, and then make up a new story and tell it convincingly.

Diversion questions

Diversion questions focus on something or someone near and dear to the interviewee. They have two purposes: (1) They lessen tension by distracting the interviewee from a tension-producing issue, and (2) they restore rapport between the subject and the investigator with a direct or indirect compliment. Diversion questions are useful when dealing with highly emotional interviewees. For example, the investigator might say in a matter-of-fact tone, "Now, let's put that aside for a minute. I want to cover another point with you about your view of how the company can improve the security. As I mentioned, part of why I'm interviewing several people is to accomplish two things. First, I would like to get that missing money back, and second, I want to prevent this from happening again. Let me ask you, how can such a loss be prevented in the future?" The rambling nature of the question provides time for the interviewee to calm down if the interviewer had pushed some emotional buttons in previous questions.

Leading questions

Leading questions include some assumption on the part of the investigator. For example, the statement "From what I hear you say, you must have had a rough time in that job last summer" contains an assumption and invites the interviewee to elaborate or explain. Leading questions containing implicit messages can be used to maintain moderate emotional tension in the interview, but they need not be abrasive if thoughtfully constructed. Leading questions can guide the interviewee toward greater cooperation with your investigation. They reflect your assumption that the interviewee can provide useful information. Leading questions can convey the interviewer's acceptance of the individual, thereby enhancing rapport.

Leading questions are usually thought to produce invalid, unreliable answers. This is true when they are carelessly used. Novice investigators sometimes have trouble using leading questions because their tone of voice and related nonverbal signals are not well controlled. Consequently, interviewees may feel condemned when faced with carelessly presented leading questions. Ulterior motives are typically built into leading questions. Use leading questions with the ulterior motive of stimulating conversation and encouraging the interviewee to reveal the truth.

Techniques for effective questioning

The following guidelines will help you formulate effective interview questions:

- Avoid the third degree.
- Use closed questions when appropriate.
- Use open questions when appropriate.
- Keep your questions simple.
- Avoid ambiguously worded questions.
- Use leading questions properly.
- Ask self-appraisal questions.
- Have the gall to ask tough questions.
- Encourage cooperation.
- Mentally assume an affirmative answer.
- Pursue unanswered questions.
- Identify and challenge deception.
- Handle trial balloons calmly.
- Assume more information is available.

Having the gall to ask

Investigators sometimes have problems asking tough or embarrassing questions, and they may even avoid asking these questions to save themselves from embarrassment. There is no doubt it takes a certain amount of gall to ask someone if he stole the money or killed the wife. Conducting an investigative interview requires that you be brave enough to ask questions that would be rude and intrusive in other situations. As a skilled interviewer, you will know when and how to ask the hard questions.

Encouraging cooperation

If an interviewee has a role in an investigation, it is one of assisting the investigator by providing information that she alone may have. Encourage interviewees to provide information even when they might not understand what their role is in the investigation. The investigator collects information picked up by the interviewee who may have seen or heard something of value to the inquiry. Intentionally, altering your verbal and nonverbal communication in a positive manner may stimulate your interviewee to be cooperative and truthful. Encourage her to feel that co-operation enhances her sense of usefulness.

When interviewees try to argue that they should not comply, they are indicating that they are at least considering compliance or they wouldn't argue the point. Even interviewees who show up for a scheduled inter-view and sit quietly without responding to questions signal that they are considering compliance. Assume that reluctant interviewees have some degree of resentment, and ask questions designed to uncover that hidden resentment. An interviewer's concerned attempts to convey compassion to a victim may be enough to encourage someone to share needed infor-mation. That someone may be the interviewee's friend or relative who learns of the attempt at compassion.

Refusal tends to be the most resistant response from uncooperative interviewees. The interviewee may decide to cooperate in the future. If interviewees sense that they can leave if they choose, they often start trust-ing the interviewer. Their freedom to leave tends to release any fear that might hinder compliance.

Although most interviewees feel a personal obligation to answer truth-fully, that obligation is lessened when the investigator is obviously unskilled in formulating questions. If the interviewee's expectations conflict with the investigator's questioning style, the interviewee may feel frustrated or an-noyed. Rapport needs to be a developed to encourage cooperation.

Interviewee reluctance or hostility may indicate avoidance of the topic under investigation, fear of retaliation, or maybe personal involvement in the delinquency. Your task is to guide the subject toward cooperation, convincing her to cooperate. If and when the interviewee feels a sense of obligation, she will provide you with information. If necessary, help the interviewee create a temporary new identity that will allow her to move from limited compliance to more complete cooperation. Such tactics are not negative if your intentions are basically helpful and honorable.

You can encourage cooperation by beginning the interview with simple closed questions that invite a positive response before asking more com-plex, specific, open questions. By conveying the impression that you need and expect additional facts, you can subtly encourage the interviewee to reveal more information. If you can do so without creating unnecessary tension, imply that you have already obtained considerable information against which you will check the interviewee's responses.

Mentally assuming an affirmative answer

Uncooperative interviewees are willing to terminate an interview as soon as comfortably possible, particularly if they sense that you doubt your own abilities to obtain information. All they need is some encouragement in the form of negatively phrased questions, such as "You wouldn't happen to know anything about the fire, would you?" Investigators typically shake their head from side to side when asking questions such as this one.

To avoid receiving negative responses that lead you to a dead end, mentally assume an affirmative answer to a closed question, and ask the next logical question instead. For example, don't ask, "Have you seen or talked with Sam Smith recently?" The interviewee could define recently as "within the last several hours" and could answer no, closing off further discussion. Instead, assume that the interviewee *has* seen Smith recently and ask, "When was the last time you saw or talked with Sam Smith?"

This second question, an open question, cannot be answered yes or no. The interviewee must give a complete response if he answers at all. The response you receive will determine the direction of subsequent questions. For example, if the interviewee responds, "I spoke with Sam two days ago," you might ask, "What was Sam wearing when you last saw him? What kind of car was he driving? Who was he hanging around with?" These questions will help you determine Smith's appearance, his means of transportation, and his current associates.

Pursuing unanswered questions

There are many reasons why an interviewee might fail to answer a question or might provide an incomplete or nonsensical response. Perhaps the interviewee is preoccupied or distracted and did not hear the question correctly, or perhaps, he is too overwhelmed by emotion to answer. If your question was poorly worded, the interviewee might not have understood what you were asking. Be patient. Give the interviewee time to think without challenging him. Then, ask the question again, varying the wording if appropriate. Never ignore an unanswered question to go on to another topic. To go on and leave questions unanswered will only cause you eventual frustration.

Of course the interviewee might ignore a question because she has something to hide. Always maintain a certain amount of unexpressed skepticism. When repeating a question, be alert for possible signals of deception. Be aware of patterns indicating that the truth is emerging. By not answering an innocent interviewee might hope to avoid discussion of a difficult topic. You can reduce tension by repeating or rewording your question. When the interview touches on sensitive or threatening topics, you may need to restate a question to find a more acceptable form. Some words trigger mental images that may be emotionally painful to the interviewee, causing her to block out certain thoughts. Whether you repeat or reword a question depends on the circumstances and how you evaluate your progress in the interview.

There are times when it is useful to ask a mild, modified version of an emotionally loaded question before asking the main question. This warns the interviewee of the emotional question to follow, helping the interviewee prepare for it. At other times, it is necessary to spring emotion-laden questions on the interviewee to reveal any hidden tension.

Never demand an answer to a question. Don't point out that the interviewee failed to answer. Instead, reword your question and try again. Some interviewees will try to provoke you into challenging them, so they will feel justified in storming out of the interview room. Even victims and witnesses of a crime may feel insulted if challenged by a demand to answer a question. By calmly repeating your questions, you signal persistence, patience, and humanity, which strengthen the bonds of interpersonal communication.

Identifying and challenging deception

Although we cannot claim King Solomon's special wisdom, we can at least use our talents as observers to uncover the truth. We can watch for behavioral patterns that indicate possible deception.

A lead-in that introduces a change of topic—for example, "Now I'm going to ask you a few questions about the day the money was missing"—causes some interviewees to nonverbally signal their intent to deceive. They may fidget in their chair, cross their legs or arms, or break eye contact. Any such sign of uneasiness should cause you to question mentally the truthfulness of the answers that follow.

Do not immediately confront or challenge interviewees who display signs of uneasiness prior to or while answering announced questions. To challenge indicates that you have concluded that the topic of the question is bothersome or that the interviewee intends to lie. Instead, ask your question, and note the interviewee's uneasiness for review later. Look for patterns of evasiveness that may indicate deception. When a clear pattern of evasiveness becomes evident, gradually challenge the interviewee. Isolated signs of evasiveness, although important, are not enough to warrant a challenge.

Some degree of unprovoked anxiety may be useful in an interview. *Unprovoked anxiety* means an uneasiness brought to the interview and not caused by the investigator as some planned effort. That anxiety may be caused by the interviewee's knowledge of someone's personal responsibility. When you sense unprovoked anxiety, you can use it as the basis for displaying your humanity and showing you are okay to talk to. You can enhance tension through your use of questions or by commenting about the interviewee's defense mechanisms or sensitivity to certain events. However, insensitive confrontation over conflicting details in the interviewee's story could cause undue tension, evasiveness, and defensiveness, resulting in an unproductive interview.

Handling trial balloons

Interviewees sometimes ask *trial balloon questions*. For example, a subject might ask, "Let's say I did take the money—what would happen to me?" or "What usually happens to a person who steals merchandise?" These *what-if* questions may indicate that the interviewee is on the brink of reporting some significant fact.

When the interviewee floats a trial balloon, avoid pouncing on it as an admission of guilt. Instead, calmly respond to the inquiry, and subtly ask questions that encourage the interviewee to tell the truth. What-if questions are used to test the water, so to speak, to see if it is safe. They signal the need for continued patience and persistence; they do not indicate that it is time to charge ahead destructively.

Terminating the interview

Always assume that more information is forthcoming and that you need only ask appropriate questions and give adequate encouragement. Even when it seems you have reached the termination point when it seems as though, all questions have been asked and answered continue to assume that the interviewee has more to tell you. You might ask, "What else can you tell me about what happened?" or "What else should I know about this matter?"

At some point, of course, you will need to terminate the interview. You can do this several ways. Even if you have no intention of questioning the subject again, you might announce that a second interview is possible. Or you might make arrangements for a second interview and give yourself time to further prepare. Finally, you might lead into a confrontation by announcing that you believe there are inconsistencies that must be resolved or by specifically accusing the interviewee of the crime. Your next step would be to attempt to gain a confession or an admission of guilt. In most instances, you will probably end the interview and not need to speak with that person again.

Conclusion

On a final note, take the recent interview of the 2013 Boston Marathon bomber. The second bomber had been captured and was interviewed for the first time. Reports stated that he had been shot in the throat and couldn't speak. Assume that you are instructed to conduct the interview and you need to be prepared and ready for a series of questions that you need to address immediately, knowing that he will likely stop talking once he is given his Miranda warning. Remember that the right questions could prevent future mass casualties and mass destruction.

11

Interviewing the victim

Introduction

Victims[1] are difficult to interview because they are reacting emotionally to their plight. The intensity of the emotion tends to be a delayed reaction, peaking after the reality of the incident sets in and then tending to dissipate with the passage of time. And the emotional reaction should be predictable. A female employee who received an obscene phone call will be frightened; an employee whose new automobile was broken into and damaged while in the company parking lot will be angry (with the culprit and the company); the employee who cashed her paycheck only to have the cash stolen from her purse before the end of the day will be frantic or depressed.

If an interviewer is with the victim at the peaking of emotion, the victim should not be pushed for information. Instead the interviewer could get the victim a cup of coffee or let him or her light up a cigarette or whatever, biding for time. If time runs out because the shift is over and the victim must catch a bus or carpool with others, the interview can be put off until the next day.

Forcing the interview is no more or less than victimizing the victim again. It builds resentment against the investigator or firm. On the other hand, to show concern for and sensitivity to a victim, after getting the basic facts and advising the individual that the interview can wait until he or she feels better the following day, develops good will. (It is necessary to emphasize "after getting the basic facts" because the victims of certain crimes must immediately share basic information.)

The interview's ultimate objective is to gather all the facts, every fact possible; details are important. Take, for example, interviewing a witness/victim who is the recipient of an indecent phone call from an unknown suspect pretending to be doing a lingerie survey for a well-known local

---

[1] The Process of Investigation, Charles A. Sennewald and John K. Tsukayama, Fourth edition, 2015, p. 98.

department store. The receiver of the call, when asked to describe what happened, will tell a "story." The "story" (not meant as a fabrication, but rather the retelling or recalling of the incident) will invariably leave out pertinent details. Following would be a typical retelling of the incident:

> This morning, I got a call from a man from your company who said his name was Mr. Barkins, and he said he was doing a survey for the lingerie department. He asked if I would answer questions to the survey, and I would then receive a certificate worth $25 to buy merchandise in your store. I said fine. He then asked my lingerie color preference, then my bra size, slip size, and panty size. I felt uncomfortable but answered. He then asked if I wore the brief panties or regular cut. I said brief. He then asked if I shaved to wear the briefs. I didn't think that was right, so I just said no. Then he asked me if I didn't shave, did hair show. I was so shocked I couldn't think of an appropriate answer, and then he asked me a filthy question, to which I slammed down the phone. That's what happened, from beginning to end.

After using open questions to elicit some additional facts, the interviewer must then develop unstated details. Examples are as follows:

- Does your telephone system have caller ID or a last caller dial-back capability?
- What time exactly did the caller call? Fix the time by association with her schedule or routine.
- What was she doing when the phone rang? Watching a favorite TV program? Still having coffee?
- Husband just left for work? And so forth.
- Did he use the store's name first, or at first identify himself by name, claiming he was with the store?
- Did he say he was Mr. Barkins, or did he use a first name also?
- Was the phone connection clear? Was it a cell phone call?
- How old a man did he sound like?
- Did you hear any sounds in the background such as a radio or TV, phones ringing, sounds of traffic, voices, or no sounds whatsoever?
- Did he sound like an educated man in terms of his choice of words, diction, delivery, or sentence structure? (Qualify the answer by asking her to compare to husband, family, or friends.)
- Was there any distinguishable accent?
- Was there any other characteristic in his manner of speaking, for example, fast, slow, lisping, stuttering, preceding questions with "ah," and so on?
- Did he make any reference as to how or why he called you? For example, did he say the local credit bureau provided your name as a good customer in the community?
- Is your telephone number listed in the directory?
- Have you made any lingerie or other intimate apparel purchases anywhere lately?

- If your phone number is listed, how is it listed, under your own name or your husband's?
- Did he ever refer to you by your first name, if it's not listed?
- Are you well known in the community by virtue of your personal, social, or political activities, or is your husband so known?
- Is it generally known in your neighborhood that you are alone during the morning?
- Did the caller sound like anyone, even vaguely, you have met or known?
- Would you be able to recognize the caller's voice if you heard it again?

Obviously the answers to these questions, and more, give the investigator details. And in that detail can be the key to the identity of the caller, if not in this incident, then in another. It is important that only one question at a time is asked, and if the answer is appropriate and intelligent, determine if that answer deserves another question.

Sometimes, however, investigators deny themselves every detail by having, for example, the wrong person conduct the interview. Consider the female employee who received an obscene phone call. If a male investigator were conducting that interview, some of the language during that conversation, language that could tie in with a past or future case, might not surface. A female investigator would probably obtain the entire conversation, word for word. Ideally, then, a female investigator would do the follow-up interviewing on sex-related offenses involving female victims. That is also true in situations where children are witnesses. As a rule, small children will confide in a female more readily than in a male, and older people feel more at ease with investigators closer to their own age.

Reid technique

The Reid technique involves three components—factual analysis, interviewing, and interrogation. Following is a brief summary of these components; more information is available on the company's website.

Reid and Associates, Inc. disputes the contention that their methods lead to false confessions. They argue the following:

> False confessions are not caused by the application of the Reid Technique...[but instead] are usually caused by interrogators engaging in improper behavior that is outside of the parameters of the Reid Technique...such as threatening inevitable consequences; making a promise of leniency in return for the confession; denying a subject their rights; conducting an excessively long interrogation; etc.

The company also cites court cases upholding their methods or denying the admission of expert testimony that would link those methods to false confessions (e.g., *U.S.* v. *Jacques*, 784 F.Supp.2d 59, D. Mass, 2011).

Legal tactics used in seeking a confession

Be fair and practical in interrogating or interviewing anyone, particularly suspects in custody. It is vital to avoid saying or doing anything that might cause an innocent person to confess. Do not use coercion, intimidation, threats, promises, or duress to force a confession; such action is neither legal nor acceptable. Intimidation reaps resentment, not truthful cooperation. Different parts of the world have different ethical standards and techniques; not all techniques used in some countries would be considered fair and professional in North America. Such tactics are self-defeating and inappropriate.

The behavior analysis interview

Through our contact over the last 50 years with many different investigators across the country, we realize that the terms interviewing and interrogation do not have a universal meaning. As a general observation, many investigators consider an interview as an information-gathering session with a victim or witness (someone who is not a suspect). An interrogation, on the other hand, is frequently considered an accusatory question and answer session held with a suspect.

Throughout this text, when we use the word "interview," we are referring to a nonaccusatory question and answer session with a witness, victim, or a suspect. In addition to standard investigative questions, we advocate the asking of structured "behavior provoking" questions to elicit behavior symptoms of truth or deception from the person being interviewed. This structured procedure is referred to as a behavior analysis interview or BAI.

An interrogation, on the other hand, is an accusatory process—accusatory only in the sense that the investigator tells the suspect that there is no doubt as to his guilt. The interrogation is in the form of a monolog presented by the investigator, rather than a question-and-answer format. The actual demeanor of the investigator during the course of an interrogation is understanding, patient, and nondemeaning. The following chart lists some of the differences between an interview and an interrogation (Fig. 11.1).

A behavior analysis interview (BAI) consists of a fairly structured nonaccusatory question-and-answer session with the suspect. During the 30–40 min interview, the investigator begins by asking background questions such as the suspect's address, age, marital status, and occupation. In addition to establishing personal information about the suspect, these questions also permit the investigator to evaluate the suspect's "normal" verbal and nonverbal behavior such as the latency of the suspect's response to

Interview	Interrogation

1. Nonaccusatory
2. Dialog—question and answer format
3. Goals
   a. Elicit investigative and
     behavioral information
   b. Assess the subject's truthfulness
   c. Profile the subject for possible
     interrogation
4. Note-taking following each response
	1. Accusatory
	2. Monolog—discourage the suspect from talking
	until ready to tell the truth
	
	3. Goals
	   a. Elicit the truth
	   b. Obtain a court-admissible confession if it is
	     believed that the suspect is guilty
	4. No note-taking until after the the suspect has told
	the truth

FIG. 11.1 The interview and interrogation formula.

questions, the nature and degree of eye contact, and general demeanor and posture. After the suspect's normal behavior has been established, the investigator asks "behavior-provoking" questions that are designed to elicit different verbal and nonverbal responses from truthful and deceptive suspects. Interspersed with behavior-provoking questions are investigative questions that evaluate the suspect's alibi, reported opportunity and access to commit the crime, explanation for incriminating evidence, etc. Regardless of the probable guilt of the suspect, the investigator does not accuse the suspect of lying during a behavior analysis interview.

The BAI serves several important functions. Primarily, it provides objective criteria to render an opinion about the suspect's truthfulness through evaluating responses to the behavior-provoking and investigative questions. In addition, the BAI facilitates the eventual interrogation of guilty suspects. This is done by establishing a working rapport with the suspect during the nonaccusatory BAI and developing insight about the suspect and his crime to facilitate the formulation of an interrogation strategy. The latter procedure is referred to as "profiling" the suspect for interrogation.

Deception in the interview

The interviewer's goal

Success in influencing the behavior of interviewees lies in convincing them to answer questions honestly—and that begins with your attempt to understand and, to some extent, satisfy the needs underlying their behavior. The anticipation and satisfaction of needs are central to successful interviewing. When we think of our basic universal needs as humans, we are most often talking about security, freedom, understanding, and affection. If you fail to anticipate the interviewee's needs, tension will develop, and unless the interviewee's basic needs are fulfilled, the interview will be little more than a waste of time. Building a relationship with the person you are interviewing will determine your success. There are many skills that a seasoned investigator uses to exhibit understanding and acceptance of the interviewee's needs. By attempting to gain a deeper understanding of those needs, the investigator uncovers possible evasiveness and distress. Keep in mind that our ultimate goal is to obtain truthful statements that will ultimately lead to successful resolution of a case.

Pressures, loyalties, obligations, needs, and restrictions frequently cause interviewees to be uncomfortable and stressed. Gaining their cooperation requires active listening, kindness, consideration, and respect. These traits are not easy to portray in many instances.

Whether using the *Reid model*, the *Wicklander-Zulawski model*, the *PEACE model*, or other techniques, the interviewer should leverage the interviewee's physical and verbal behavior while avoiding denials to reach a truthful confession. Interviewers develop their own style after years of practicing, learning a variety of styles, and putting their personality into the interview.

The interviewer's needs

Experienced interviewers learn to keep their own biases and feelings in check during an investigation. Investigators who try to fulfill egocentric, personal, or childish needs during an interview may become frustrated, which may lead them to act out personal tensions and misuse their authority. The potential for destructiveness goes with a position of authority. Given authority, some individuals become destructive in ways and at times that are not helpful to society or to their own goals in an investigation.

When the self-image and self-esteem of interview participants are at stake, pressure can be overwhelming. Overstimulation of the body's autonomic nervous system, which governs involuntary actions, routinely adds to distress, particularly when there is no way to vent built-up pressure. When the investigation becomes intense—stressful enough to cause emotional involvement—proficient interviewers try to remain detached.

Deception

Deception and lying have many different meanings once you cross-cultural borders. These cultural differences determine whether deception or some level of truth telling is acceptable. Because of these differences, it is not possible to establish a universal motive for one's deceptive behavior. Here, for the purpose of the investigative interview, we review deceptive behavior in North America and how to identify verbal and nonverbal signs of deception.

Before we explore deception, let's establish some criteria for credibility. The credibility of interviewees is based on their truthfulness and believability, and it is related to their observation skills and accuracy in reporting. Here are some possible tests of interviewee credibility:

1. Was the interviewee present and aware during the incident? Presence includes more than being there physically.
2. If questions relate to a timeline, are their statements consistent? By asking the interviewee to repeat or recall the order of events at different times during the interview, you can observe and watch for inconsistencies.
3. How well developed are the interviewee's powers of observation?
4. Can the interviewee relate the facts briefly, correctly, and clearly, without showing signs of emotional disturbance?
5. Does the interviewer's nonverbal behavior signal deception? There are some common physical signs that might indicate deception, but these same physical gestures may be stress related.

In an interview the interviewee is deceptive when he or she makes a false statement with the intention to deceive the interviewer. Deception is generally thought to be the intentional act of concealing or distorting the truth for the purpose of misleading.

As investigators, we need not only to watch for inconsistencies in a story but also to pay close attention to how the story is told. If the person is deceptive, there will be a variety of signals, both physically and in the words spoken. You will need to remember that the liar is also trying to read the investigator, telling her story in the way she thinks will get the best result for her. She is also trying to manage her body language, voice tone, and style. Trained investigators will have to assess all the indicators, both verbal and nonverbal.

Convincing liars are often self-assured and cunning. They can be difficult to identify because their comments are never too strong, too defensive, or out of context. Their motivation to lie is rarely based on anger or hostility; that would weaken the basis of their confidence. If they are trying to help someone by lying, they will be at ease, and their comments will sound natural. Because they have rationalized their lying, they maintain both confidence and peace of mind, suffering no question of conscience. Conscience is the internal sense of what is right and wrong that governs a person's thoughts and actions, urging him or her to do the right thing. Conscience is expressed through behavior.

Verbal signs

Listening is one of the most important skills you will need to develop. I use the term *develop* because almost everyone can improve their listening skills. Listening is critical if you want to determine whether an interviewee is being truthful or deceptive. The interviewee might not be showing signs of stress through nonverbal signs. You will have to determine whether the information you are getting is, in fact, the truth or a lie. Sometimes the deceptive interviewee will provide too many details, or sometimes not enough.

A lack of clear thinking can signal deception and evasiveness. When interviewees express themselves in a calculated, dissociated, or awkward manner rather than in a smooth, flowing way, something, somewhere, is not altogether right. The deceptive tend to assert that they don't remember, whereas truthful interviewees tend not to say this. A person who wants to hide relevant information must make a conscious effort to keep the truth submerged. That effort requires contemplation, intention, and planning, all of which may happen in a brief moment, followed by a "memory lapse." The deceptive answer is more evasive than the truthful. The interviewee may attempt to distract the interviewer with inappropriate friendliness, compliments, or seductive behavior. They may present a complex, tangled, or confused explanation in response to your question, or they may try to dodge the question altogether. Their answers are general in nature and broad in content. Their apparent desire is to say as little as possible while hiding in their self-made emotional shelter. They may think that if they are silent and motionless, no one will guess they are hiding the truth. They seem to take comfort in their lack of spontaneity, and they think they are safe and secure as they try not to be noticed. If interviewees have to invent an answer that is a lie, they might spend more time searching for the right phrase to fit into their story.

Remember that the higher the consequences, the more pressure the person will be under.

With this kind of pressure, there are likely to be physical cues. For most people, lying is stressful, so you might try taking a break in between questions, which causes some discomfort, or changing the subject, which may cause the person to adjust or change his nonverbal cues.

When interviewees begin with the words "To be honest," "To tell the truth," "Frankly," or "Honestly," they most likely do not intend to be frank or honest. Interviewees who express objections rather than denials when questioned are probably not being completely truthful. Interviewees who were later shown to be lying have said the following:

- "I have plenty of money in the bank. I would have no reason to take that money."
- "I'm not the kind of person who would think of doing that."
- "I don't go around doing those kinds of things."
- "I couldn't do something like that."

The objections tend to be true, at least in part. The suspect who utters the first objection may indeed have money in the bank, but that response is not a clear denial of having stolen. Honest denials are straightforward and crystal clear: "No, I didn't steal the money."

After answering a question dishonestly, some interviewees immediately look searchingly at your eyes and face for any nonverbal signs of your skepticism. This subconscious, questioning, wide-open look lasts only a fraction of a moment. While deceptive interviewees pretend to ponder questions, they may engage in some physical action that betrays their desire to escape from the interview, mentally if not physically. This uneasiness may manifest itself as they shuffle their feet, cross their legs, or cover their eyes. They often avoid eye contact by looking around the room or at the floor, frequently picking real or imagined lint from their clothes. In addition, they blink more often than truthful interviewees.

Experienced investigators know that they can't rely on false clues or signs of deception such as eye behavior. Twenty-three out of 24 peer-reviewed studies published in scientific journals reporting on experiments on eye behavior as an indicator of lying have rejected this hypothesis.[1] No

---

[1] C. F. Bond, A. Omar, A. Mahmoud, and R. N. Bonser, "Lie Detection Across Cultures," *Journal of Nonverbal Behavior* 14 (1990): 189–204.

scientific evidence exists to suggest that eye behavior or gaze aversion can reliably gauge truthfulness. Some people say that gaze aversion is a sure sign of lying, and others such as fidgety feet or hands are the key indicators. Still others believe that analysis of voice stress or body posture provides benchmarks. Research has tested all of these indicators and found them only weakly associated with deception.[2]

They may appear calm but in a forced way. Although they smile and look composed, the deceptive often seem physically restrained. Their movements are often overly controlled and repetitive, lacking complexity and variety, not spontaneous and free moving. Interviewees who engage in rehearsed gestures, without putting their bodies into motion in a smooth, convincing manner, signal their intent to deceive. They present a false image of themselves and hope that you will accept it without question.

Nonverbal signs

Investigators can improve their ability to detect deception by becoming more aware of nonverbal cues. Gestures, mannerisms, facial expressions, and other forms of nonverbal communication are learned throughout life; they reveal underlying personality traits, subconscious attitudes, intentions, and conflicts. The more you know about nonverbal communication, the better an interviewer you will be. Your observation of the interviewee's unintentional nonverbal cues can help you make decisions about his or her truthfulness. When interviewees twist the truth, they leave clues in their facial expressions and bodily movements. Their expressions and body language may convey internal struggles as they try to cover the outward signs of lying. A mere twitch or an effort to control such a barely perceptible movement is described as a *microexpression.* Also described as a slight, unique little expression, a microexpression happens in one-fifth of a second[3]—so fast that the person can't modify or conceal it.

Microexpressions express one of the seven universal emotions,[4] which are as follows:

- happiness
- surprise
- contempt
- sadness

---

[2] B. M. DePaulo, J. J. Lindsay, B. E. Malone, L. Muhlenbruck, K. Charlton, and H. Cooper, "Cues to Deception," *Psychological Bulletin* 129, no. 1 (2003): 74–118.

[3] "The Effects of the Duration of Expressions on the Recognition of Micro Expressions," *Journal of Zhejiang University,* Science B, Vol. 13, Issue 3, pp. 221–230, March 1, 2012.

[4] Daniel Benjamin Smith, "Dr. Cal Lightman's Seven Universal Micro-Expressions," March 12, 2010.

- fear
- disgust
- anger

Something more than a nonverbal cue indicates deception. If you look at the behavioral cues when a person is truthful and determine a baseline, you can more clearly see nonverbal cues when that person is lying. Establishing a baseline will help you observe when the person's behavior, mannerisms, and physical signs change as he moves between truthful statements and false ones. The key to detecting false statements is to look for these deviations in behavior.

Body language and body physical signs

Table 12.1 presents some potential meanings of body movements that could indicate an interviewee's state of mind.[5]

Refusal to cooperate

At times, your efforts to gain the interviewee's cooperation will be unsuccessful. Interviewees might refuse to become involved in an investigation because they fear callous or indifferent treatment from legal authorities, fear of reprisal from the guilty party or others, inconvenience and financial loss, and confusion over legal proceedings. To some interviewees, court appearances entail an unnecessary burden on their time and energy. Whatever the interviewee's reason for not being cooperative, it is the skillful investigator that can build rapport with the person to get him to talk about things he was prepared not to discuss.

Physiological signs

It is not unusual for the deceptive person to exhibit symptoms of physical shock while answering questions. These symptoms include lightheadedness and numbness in the extremities due to reduced blood circulation. These physiological symptoms may be a response to the interviewee's feeling of being trapped and not knowing what to do. When they're lying, interviewees may also exhibit physiological cues such as burping, sweating, crying, and appearing to be in a state of turmoil. Truthful individuals

---

[5] Louis A. Tyska, CPP, and Lawrence J. Fennelly, *Investigations: 150 Things You Should Know*, Chapter 8.

TABLE 12.1   The use of microexpressions and body movements versus state of mind.

Body movement	Possible meaning
Lowering the eyebrows	Concentrating or anger
Raised eyebrows	Surprise or anticipation
Widening eyes	High interest or fear
Removing glasses	Withdrawal
Closing nostrils with fingers	Contempt
Index finger alongside nose	Suspicion
Lowering chin and looking up	Coy or shy
Picking face or biting nails	Unsure, negative feelings
Fingering collar of shirt	Nervous, desire to escape
Hand over heart or middle of chest	Honesty
Playing unconsciously with ring	Possible conflict
Wiping under nose with finger	Aggression
Fingers formed in steeple shape	Superiority
Mouth falls open	Boredom or unsure of self
Flared nostrils	Aggression, critical attitude
Tongue flicking teeth	Sexually aggressive
Biting lips	Self-depreciation
Hands held behind head	Confident, superiority
Male running fingers through his hair	Uncertainty
Female playing with her hair	Flirtation
Folding hands deep in lap	Defense against rejection
Self-scratching, picking, squeezing	Aggression, hostility
Woman exposing palm to man	Flirtation
Rubbing objects	Reassurance, sensuousness
Fist clenching or pounding	Aggression
Hand covering face	Protection, concealment
Covering eyes with hand	Fear or shame

generally do not undergo such stress when questioned, particularly when the interviewer remains calm and restrained.

Psychological motives for deception

Interviewees are deceptive for a variety of motives, frequently multiple motives. For some the interview is an exercise in survival. The truth might result in consequences that would cause the interviewee shame, embarrassment, and punishment. How interviewees evaluate the hazards in any given interview is up to the individual being questioned and depends on what they have to hide. For other people the interview is a game. The punishment and shame associated with getting caught are not as important as matching wits with the investigator. They make it their challenge to outsmart the interviewer. Much more could be said regarding the psychological motives behind deception, but in one form or another, these motives are woven among the interviewee's efforts to satisfy basic human needs.

The pathological liar

Pathological liars habitually tell lies so exaggerated or bizarre that they are suggestive of mental disorder. They fabricate when it would be simpler and more convenient to tell the truth. Their stories are often complex rationalizations leading to self-vindication. Most likely, pathological liars have been fabricating stories since childhood, so they might be so good at lying that they actually believe those lies. As interviewees, pathological liars are quite convincing when they say they did not just say what they actually did say. Most have the ability to refute your recall and notes pertaining to their comments. When faced with what they said only moments before, they will say something like, "Oh, no, I didn't say that!" This is when you have a reality check with yourself to see if you have lost your grip on the here and now. You know that you know what they said, but you check your notes to be sure. This is not the time to enter into an I-said-you-said game with the interviewee. Be strong and restrain your inclination to do battle, because you will lose in the end. After all, if you want information you can use, you can't win such a battle and expect friendly cooperation.

The psychopathic personality

The psychopathic personality develops along asocial and amoral lines and cannot adjust to society's standards. The psychopath is supremely selfish, living only for immediate gratification and without regard for the consequences. Normal individuals often sacrifice for the possibilities of the future and show a willingness to defer certain gratifications. The psychopath is always able to differentiate between right and wrong and usually is well acquainted with the requirements of society and religion, but he is absolutely unwilling to be governed by these laws. In fact, he may say that they do not concern him. The only interest he has in laws is to see that he is not caught when he violates them and, if he is caught, to try to secure, by some trick, a minimum punishment. Thus one of the symptoms of being a psychopath is a complete selfishness that manifests itself in every act of the person. The only one the psychopath thinks of—in fact, the only individual that he completely loves—is himself, and he is surprisingly hardened to the rest of the world, including the members of his own family.

There is no satisfactory treatment for a psychopathic personality. Psychiatrists have so far been unable to do any good once the person's psychopathic behavior pattern has been established. Neither a long term in prison nor restraint in a psychiatric hospital can affect the conduct of psychopaths. Appearing self-assured, psychopaths are often cunning and convincing liars. Their motivation is to outsmart the investigator.

Rationalization

Interviewees, like all of us, act in accordance with their own individual, rational, reasoning powers. They protect themselves with rationalizations when they hold hidden images; thus they use rationalization to justify their behavior.

Everyone wants to feel capable, normal, and worthwhile compared with others. Few people are self-confident enough to be completely indifferent to insults and criticisms. People maintain their self-image by conforming to social pressure, which can produce feelings of conflict and guilt when group behavior contradicts the dictates of their own conscience. Hence, interviewees will rationalize their actions, not wanting to expose themselves. By accepting their rationalizations, you can help interviewees feel more confident and lessen their feelings of self-doubt. As a result, you might be more likely to gain their cooperation.

You can encourage interviewees to cooperate through active listening, building rapport, asking the right questions, and being prepared. Try to eliminate negative aspects of the situation that might show signs of disgust or disappointment to reduce the interviewee's reluctance to cooperate. You might suggest that the interviewee's action (or lack of action) is not so unique after all and that many people would take the same action if they found themselves in those circumstances. Although you are diminishing the significance of her acts, you are not changing the interviewee's overall responsibility for her actions nor overlooking the effect her actions had on others. Your goal is always to allow for the free flow of accurate information.

You might need to help some interviewees rationalize their cooperation with the investigation. Cooperation may cause them to lose face if it cannot be justified. If low self-esteem is the price of assisting with an investigation, some interviewees will refuse.

Projection

Humans try to appear reasonable to themselves and to others by doing what is proper and acceptable. Some people use the defense mechanism of projection to shift onto others the responsibilities that they themselves have not adequately handled. When they cannot live up to expectations, they blame other people or the situation itself for their behavior. They use projection to make their behavior understandable and socially acceptable. Thus it is always someone else's fault. Often, interviewees project their blame onto others in their effort to save face.

Skilled interviewers use deductive logic when reaching a conclusion about the interviewee's truthfulness. When interviewing, you will need to consider the subject's verbal and nonverbal behavior equally. The interviewer's tactics are based on generalizations accumulated from personal experience.

Concluding that there has been deception

Concluding that your interviewee was truthful or deceptive will be based on all parts of the interview, verbal and nonverbal, and the personal experience of the interviewer. The interviewer will weigh the totality of the interview and look for a baseline to help indicate truthfulness or deception.

13

Communication for the investigation manager and key management skills

Introduction

Security professionals throughout the security industry are responsible for managing investigations. Whether it is a complex loss investigation, interviewing unwanted visitors or simply taking a report for a customer accident, these are all investigations that require monitoring to ensure completeness. After all, a poorly completed accident report could cost a company a significant amount, should it lead to litigation. It is because of this often-concealed responsibility that security supervisors and managers should be capable of adequately managing investigations.

Key management skills

Communication

The skill of communication is somewhat vague, particularly in the context of being a manager or a supervisor. Security departments essentially have several different customers, including organizational management, employees, vendors, customers, and any member of the public that may have a legitimate reason to be on the premises. Concise communication is necessary in three separate contexts to lay the foundation for successful information transfer within an organization. First, communication with the security staff or other personnel responsible for submitting documentation cannot be underrated, as it is these individuals that you must count on to accomplish the mission you are supervising. Second, communication with organizational management can be a tricky endeavor often because security must distribute information to more than one department.

Finally, communication with organization members, and in this case, through committee, or when responding to a complaint, can make or break the overall security program. A quick look at these aspects may provide insight as to how they are approached and handled in respect to investigations. Whenever disseminating information to persons or groups outside the security department, it can be helpful to utilize an information dissemination checklist to aid in organizing data, clarifying issues involved, and preventing the release of information or sources that could hinder future security operations.

Departmental

Within the security department, information should be shared fairly readily. Even so, there is a certain level of formality that must be maintained. Where that level exists is truly a departmental or organizational matter. Moving information from one shift to another can become a monumental task, which can be overcome with a pass-on book, a simple desk log, or a formal email process, if operations management software is not available. Oncoming members can verify that a note has been read by initialing the information. Simple desk logs can be useful in reviewing activity levels, and officers can also use this as a reference; these logs may be handwritten or a hard copy printout of the activity stored in an operations database.

Personnel concerns

Assigning investigators

Investigators are often assigned to investigations merely by being the first to answer the phone or arrive at a scene. Needless to say, this is certainly not the optimal method for matching skills to problems, but it may be the most reasonable under the circumstances. Ideally in an environment with limited manpower, investigators should be equally capable to handle any investigation. This may very well be the case but keep in mind that there can be factors within an investigation that warrant the attention of a person with a specific interest. When an individual is an investigator or dons the investigation "cap," it is their imagination, creativity, and most of all their curiosity that ensures a successful outcome. Consequently, officers that are only concerned with the "what" and not the "why" may not be strong investigators and should be encouraged to be more inquisitive.

In a perfect world a supervisor would have all the resources and a specialized investigator for any situation, but as a general rule, this is not the case. Supervisors must be able to remove or add investigators to an investigation without overlooking the impact on those individuals involved. To avoid conflicts resulting from reassigning investigators, supervisors should consider possibilities such as using partnering or specializing/centralizing some activities. It may be very difficult to maintain partner teams in an environment with normally limited resources, but it is possible for a supervisor to assign a secondary or investigative partner on a case-by-case basis. This allows the flexibility to place skills where they are best suited while avoiding problems caused by removing individuals from an investigation. This can also create an even distribution of extra work should an investigator leave the organization. With a fixed partner team, the termination of one partner leaves that individual's entire caseload on the partner, which could become quite burdensome if these should require court appearances or liaison with outside organizations. For those organizations not equipped with case management software, having investigators maintain an individual case log, it becomes rather easy to redistribute a departing investigators' case. Case logs should be designed to reflect the aspect of investigations that are choke points within your investigative process.

Another option available to supervisors is the designation of longer-term activities to one individual. For instance, if your organization has a problem with vandalism or more specifically "tagging," it may be more efficient to assign one officer to handle all these investigations. This does not mean that other officers cannot conduct the initial inquiry and photograph the evidence, but it does imply that the designated individual should track this activity and conduct liaison with the appropriate outside agencies. This is a useful method for lateral promotions that give senior officers more responsibility and experience. This also assists in developing a complete and standardized reporting system for a particular type of activity.

Motivating/tracking/evaluating investigators

The backbone of a good investigation is not generally exciting high-profile work but rather laborious surveillance and endless document review. This can cause an investigator to cut corners or to become more cursory in their work. An ironhanded supervisor can impede investigations by stifling the necessary initiative within investigators, yet a passive supervisor would indirectly cause investigations to falter or become weaker. Motivational methods can be directly tied to supervisory tracking and evaluation efforts of investigators; however, the supervisor must know each member of their team and what motivates them as individuals. Efforts to motivate the individual separately from the team, when necessary, can strengthen the investigator's connection to the team. Below are some useful tools to encourage, track, and evaluate an investigative team.

There are, however, a limitless number of ways to motivate, and a supervisor must use some creativity and sound judgment when developing these efforts:

1. *Develop a monthly or quarterly review/counseling program.* These need not be long counseling sessions but merely a 15–20 min session for each agent at the beginning or end of each month. The supervisor can write a few objectives and points of improvement for the investigator to reach within the month and identify topics that the agent will receive training on in that month. The agent in turn can write concerns or suggestions about the points listed and any comments about the department's operations. This not only provides useful documentation to support an annual review but also gives the individual a feel for their overall performance. For the supervisor this can offer valuable insight into the attitudes of the department and likely avenues for future motivation and improvement. It should also be noted that supervisors must be prepared to receive some fairly harsh criticism from their staff and that such criticism must be acted on but not retaliated against. If the staff is willing to write their criticism, then they are concerned about their workplace and are not simply "punching the clock." This is positive and can be harnessed.

2. *Hold well-defined meetings regularly.* Keep these as short as possible by using a standard naming system that helps to identify the purpose. Names such as solution meetings, planning meetings, and organizational affairs meetings can create the right mind-set prior to attendance. Limit the agenda to one or two topics in a meeting and strive to keep these under 30 min in length. Never forget that meetings should ultimately increase productivity and not become a barrier. If necessary, designate an individual to act as a facilitator to prevent the meeting from being sidetracked.

3. *Allow the staff some say in general operations.* Foster an open environment that encourages suggestions that can streamline operations. Don't be afraid of using some of these ideas. By incorporating everyone's ideas, the staff gains a feeling of ownership of the department, and consequently their interest and concern will increase further.

4. *Develop a lesson learned journal.* This can consist of a list of all cases with short entries describing the circumstances. Also included are actions that should not be repeated (hence lessons learned) as well as compliments for activities that were handled exceptionally and that agent's name. This provides a lasting acknowledgment of an investigator's achievements.

5. *Various charts can be used to show progress and organize activity.* Flowcharts can be used to graphically guide investigations and as a

reminder as to who is responsible for finding different information? Load charts can be a quick reference to show the number and length of investigations for which each officer is responsible. The example makes it plain that Smith is dealing with far fewer investigations than his peers are and this can be a tool in motivating Smith. Smith may not realize how much less he is doing and such a graphic representation is undeniable. This can be replaced by a Gant chart if project management software is routinely used. The primary difference is the accuracy of the information as more precise data would typically be entered into project management software. To help level the work load and to ensure that mundane tasks are not too mundane, internal audit activities can be developed by a supervisor. These audits can be a natural extension of patrol or other activity that aids in enforcing or monitoring protection standards, perhaps monitoring the use of safety equipment by line employees or searching back areas for concealed merchandize.

Initiating and prioritizing investigations

Introduction

Investigations are initiated for many reasons and in diverse circumstances; however, the supervisor in charge of investigations is often directly responsible for those generated by exception reports, audits, or unique incidents. These investigations must be prioritized and worked into the department schedule. The investigation supervisor or the one managing investigations should seek to have a staff investigator handle much of the so-called "legwork" so as not to cause a slighting of supervisory duties. This in no way implies that the supervisor can simply pass off the work he or she just does not feel like doing, but instead offers training and experience opportunities for other investigators. Supervisors can use all investigations in which they are directly involved as an opportunity to mentor another experienced investigator.

Once an investigation has been initiated, lead sheets, which for practical purposes can be noted in your computer, and should be created for each lead that is discovered. These can then be systematically researched or divided up among agents for follow-up. These lead sheets should contain basic information about the investigation (incident number, type of incident, date, etc.) and the lead itself. Similar leads can be grouped into the same sheet, as they will most likely be researched at the same time. Any information that is discovered from the lead should be briefly noted on the lead sheet since any evidence (receipts, photographs, vouchers, etc.) would most likely be kept separate from the lead sheet itself. Completely researched leads that provide no further leads can then be returned to the primary investigator or the case file, while any further leads can be noted on the original sheet before a new sheet is created and researched. Lead sheets are of unquestionable value when an investigation is paused or stopped, especially if the primary investigator leaves the organization during this time. In addition, this type of documentation allows the supervisor to quickly review investigations to determine the level of effort and effectiveness of an investigator.

Prioritizing investigations should not occupy more than a few minutes of a supervisor's time, but these decisions can have a great effect on the security department, the parent organization, and the public's opinion of the organization. Careful consideration must be given to high-profile incidents or when senior executives are implicated in wrong doing. Failing to properly judge the amount of emotion behind an investigation or the opinions of organizational staff, management, and the public could cause serious embarrassment to the parent organization.

Factors for prioritizing investigations include but are not limited to

- Emotionally charged issues (i.e., workplace violence, hate crimes, stalking, and active shooter).
- High-profile incidents (media or prominent figure involved).
- Organizational management interest.
- Total investigative resources available.
- Total protection obligations.
- Likeliness that activity investigated will cease quickly.
- Number and quality of leads.
- Solve-ability factors considered and reviewed.
- Was there a witness?

Can the suspect be

- Named.
- Located.
- Described.
- Otherwise identified.
- Can a suspect vehicle be identified?
- Is stolen property traceable?
- Is a clear suspect MO (modus operandi) present?
- Is there significant physical evidence present?
- Is there a positive report concerning physical evidence by a trained technician?
- Is it reasonable to conclude that the case may be solved by normal effort?
- Was there clearly limited opportunity for anyone but the suspect to have committed the crime?

Investigative priority is a frequently changing situation with investigations being set aside for periods of time when necessary. A word of caution, avoid unnecessary shuffling of investigations. If an investigation is nearly complete, there is little reason to drop it simply because of an artificial priority system.

Investigative follow-up

The investigation supervisor is directly responsible for ensuring the completeness of case files and all documentation included within and therefore must take several actions during and after an investigation. The supervisor must monitor progress, coach investigators, and be prepared to summarize the investigation to management on its completion. This is a tall order but is essential to building departmental credibility with organizational management and outside agencies. As discussed previously, progress reporting can occur in several different ways and being an inherent part of the coaching process. It is important to identify an investigator's improper actions as quickly as possible to prevent them from occurring again and to recognize proper actions in an equally timely fashion. One coaching method includes three steps on identifying the incorrect action. First a positive activity is recognized and encouraged, followed by the incorrect actions being verbalized to the individual and the correct way explained or demonstrated. The positive reinforcement can be placed at the end, but it illustrates one way to correct behavior while avoiding an unconcerned presentation of the supervisor's interest. As the investigator is coached through the investigation, the progress can be easily monitored. It is with more experienced investigators who may not seek assistance often that progress must be monitored through other techniques.

Another extremely important tool for coaching investigators is to play "devil's advocate." So long as the investigators know that you are not attacking them personally or questioning their character in a real sense, this can be very useful and often quite fun. Simply question all aspects of the investigator's report and try to put yourself in the shoes of a defense attorney. By attempting to find holes in the report or case and picking at them, it becomes possible to search for other information and aid the investigator in remembering the important aspects of the investigation.

At the right time, this can be very enjoyable for all involved and is also useful in offering newer investigators a feel for questions they may be confronted with in the future. The operating terms here are informal and impersonal. In all ways prevent the investigators from feeling that their peers are personally attacking them. In addition to ensuring that parts of a case file are complete, take the time to make sure the case file contains all the appropriate parts. Develop checklists that aid in keeping files complete from start to finish. Checklists should seek to eliminate relevant problems through prevention rather than merely identifying the existence of a problem after the fact. For example, begin with the completeness of the prepared case file to ensure that all necessary forms are present at the start, which also serves as a reminder of the requirements of the various parts of the case file. Again, try to keep paperwork to a minimum, as it should contribute to the overall productivity rather than creating extraneous work. When using an electronic database for reporting many of these, actions and requirements may be automated. Once the investigator has completed the case file, the supervisor/manager can write a summary of the case in the lessons learned journal. Later, this can be used as an executive summary in memos forwarded to organizational management. The summary should be extremely brief, identifying unique aspects of the case and actions taken, and the current disposition.

Below is an example of such a summary

Review of alarm access reports identified access activity at the satellite location outside of normal business hours. Subsequent surveillance and investigation identified a total of approximately $5000 in potential loss through property theft, and identified newly hired manager John Smith's code as the one used for access. During the interview, Smith admitted to the theft of property totaling $25,000 from the satellite location and $2300 in fraudulent invoices for undelivered services. Smith agreed to pay restitution in full and criminal charges have been filed. Total loss in this case is approximately $17,300, and a new exception report has been developed to aid in a more timely identification of similar loss opportunities.

After the case file is completed, the supervisor must review further aspects of the case, such as evidence preservation, and conduct one last review of all the paperwork. Proper preservation of evidence can prevent uncomfortable courtroom situations. The local prosecutor's office should be contacted and preservation practices reviewed. Any time evidence may be maintained outside of a police evidence operation, it is likely that some questions will be raised about chain of custody and access. A little extra time spent on this matter may lend considerable credibility to one's department in the future. Moreover, it is important for the supervisor to review all cases with investigators prior to their court appearances. The investigators should do the same for the supervisor on the days of his or her appearances. The fact that court appearances can occur months or even years after an investigation is completed makes this review and drilling of great importance. This is just another application of the old adage, "… a gallon of sweat in training is better than a pint of blood in battle." Keep this in mind when an investigator grumbles about the extra effort.

Information/intelligence

Investigative supervisors are expected to have volumes of current information literally at their fingertips at any given time. They need to have a firm understanding of local and regional trends that could affect their organization. Collecting and maintaining information can be a very useful tool with little extra effort in the long run. Using a card filing system like the one mentioned earlier, it is possible to track activity in the vicinity of the organization, which quite possibly becomes the source of a lead in a later incident. When using an electronic database trend, reporting capabilities are considerably easier than with paper-based intelligence. Information can be located from a variety of open sources such as newspapers, phone books, crisscross directories, and the World Wide Web. Newspapers often have a section on police-reported incidents in the area. This can be of tremendous value in recognizing activity trends in the immediate area. When one is at a court appearance, it only makes sense to listen to the other cases being heard, and if any are for activities related to your organization, then make note of this. It is possible that a robbery could occur in a mall parking lot while the tenant stores remained unaware of this activity. If your organization were located in or around the area, this information might be useful in determining staffing needs and informing employees. As with any information collection and storage function, it is important to regularly purge the records to maintain just those that will be useful. Any information provided by an individual, whether solicited or not, must be carefully reviewed to determine credibility.

The following questions represent the minimum scrutiny any provided information should receive:

- Why did this event happen?
- At this particular time?
- At this location?
- Why is this information being provided to us?
- Presented in this fashion with this slant?
- Why does or doesn't this information stand up when compared to all other information available?
- Why or how will someone or some group benefit by others believing this information?

Conclusion

Always keep in mind that information that is received or developed may be false or incorrectly organized. This may be intentional or not; however, the result is the same. Investigators must seek to corroborate any information to ensure its accuracy.

15

The rules of evidence

Introduction

Whether the investigator is a police detective, a loss prevention officer of a large corporation, or a private investigator hired to look into a particular incident, he or she must operate within predefined parameters in conducting an investigation and collecting evidence. Police investigators must work within federal and state laws intended to protect society from unreasonable police behavior. In addition, they work within the bureaucracy and operating procedures of their respective agencies. Private investigators have a wider choice of investigative methods because there are fewer laws governing their actions. A company's internal investigators may take investigative liberties that might seem unreasonable, but their actions do not affect society generally. Still, their behavior is limited and controlled by company policy and the fear of possible civil suits. Company control of an investigator's behavior generally cannot influence the inquiry to such an extent that it causes the investigator to violate personal ethics and professional responsibilities. If this happens, there is a question of integrity.

Regardless of whether an offense is investigated by public or private detectives, the evidence needed to prosecute the case is the same. If a piece of evidence is to be of value to a company (or, for that matter, to society), the methods used to collect and preserve it must meet the highest standards imposed by the courts. This is true even when the collected evidence serves only to justify an employee's dismissal rather than prosecution in court. The case may turn ugly if the fired employee sues the company for wrongful termination and the company must produce the evidence on which it based the termination. If evidence collection and preservation fall short of acceptable standards, the company may be in deep trouble financially. In the public sector, of course, if a police investigator does not properly collect and preserve evidence, the prosecution's case may dissolve, allowing the guilty party to go free.

Testimonial evidence

Obviously the main topic of this book is the collection of testimonial evidence through investigative interviewing. Most, if not all, of the offenses cataloged in the FBI's *Uniform Crime Report* require investigative interviewing of victims, witnesses, and suspects. Most of the evidence presented during the prosecution of Part I and Part II offenses was obtained in an interview or interrogation.

There are legal means available to assist both public and private investigators in searching out all forms of evidence that will reveal the truth. Subpoenas, for example, help investigators collect evidence without resorting to illegal methods.

As this book points out, the investigator's major job is to persuade the interviewee to cooperate long enough to reveal truthful information about the crime under investigation. To this end, investigators of all kinds must cultivate professional attitudes and techniques that promote communication and cooperation. Most interviewees will acquiesce to requests for information, but they need encouragement from the investigator. There is always some resistance to an investigator's inquiries. Some people believe that the degree of resistance depends on the nature of the offense under investigation. My thought is that the degree of resistance is a reflection of the interviewee's personality, the interviewer's attitude, and the qualities the interviewer brings to bear on the interview.

Are people more likely to refuse to cooperate with a private investigation than with a police investigation? Certainly, people perceive less of a threat if then investigation is private instead of law enforcement. Most consider losing a job to be less damaging than being fined or going to jail. Employees are expected to cooperate in reasonable inquiries undertaken by company management. The refusal to cooperate in an investigation is often regarded by management as insubordination and sufficient cause for dismissal. But it does not prove that the employee is guilty.

Occasionally the greater threat of a police investigation works to obscure rather than reveal the truth. Because of the fear that a police interview can inspire, interviewees feel pressured to provide answers that they sense the investigator wants—and thus lead the police to a wrongful arrest. It can be difficult for police investigators to discover the truth while simultaneously protecting the rights of the alleged victims and the accused. There is a need for comprehensive training in interviewing at the beginning and throughout a police officer's career.

Evidence gathering and transporting

However, you elect to identify evidence you must mark or tag as well as transport it for safekeeping. For the collection of evidence to be acceptable in the various courts, it must conform to the rules of evidence. Whatever method is selected—either numbering, lettering, or some other combination thereof—a log must be kept. Listed in the succeeding text are some suggested or recommended methods of transporting evidence:

- Documentation disks and tapes are to be placed in cellophane bags without folds. Mark the exterior of the bag with details of place, time, date, conditions, and any other pertinent data.
- Hairs, fibers, soil, fingernails, and residue are to be first placed in bond paper and then cellophane bags with appropriate marks.
- Garments with blood or other liquids should be first allowed to dry naturally and then placed within individual cellophane bags and marked.
- Liquids, oils, and grease are to be left in containers within which they were found. If they are not in a container, place them in specimens or clean glass bottles.
- Glass or glass-like substances are to be lain on strips of cardboard and layers built up. If available, place on clay on a flat surface or on a clay bed. Twist cap the specimens with paper. Never allow the glass to touch or clang together.
- Knives or scissors should be lain flat on a surface that can be penetrated by holds to tie the object in question down.
- Weapons should be placed in a box. A gun should be secured with a trigger lock and the box locked and secured.
- Lead slugs or casings should be placed in paper without touching and twisted like saltwater taffy.
- Paint, paint chips, or flecks are to be collected along with the sample of the paint to be matched (known as the *control*) marked accordingly and placed in a cellophane bag.
- Food/beverage substances are to be kept in the containers in which they are found.
- Substances/liquids that may evaporate quickly must be tightly sealed.

When tagging evidence, there are seven basic items to be noted. These are as follows:

1. The crime(s).
2. Name and address of the victim or the accused.

3. Date of the crime.
4. Place of the crime.
5. Brief description of the article, where it was found, and what part in relation to the crime.
6. Who you represent or are affiliated with?
7. Your name.

Physical evidence

Rules involving physical evidence

There are four basic rules surrounding physical evidence[1]:

1. Get all evidence that can have any bearing on the case.
2. Mark it.
3. Properly wrap, package, or preserve to protect the evidence from contamination or destruction.
4. Establish a chain or continuity between the discovery of the evidence and its subsequent presentation.

Get all evidence that can have any bearing on the case. The emphasis belongs on the word all.

Put another way and get everything that can have a bearing on the case. If everything really boils down to enormous quantities, such as a freight carload of goods, take a sampling as evidence, treat it as evidence, photograph the rest, and simply recover the balance and return it to its proper place. The strategy of getting everything simply ensures that nothing is overlooked or left behind, because once the investigator leaves the scene, unless specific arrangements have been made to preserve that scene, evidence left will be lost, often, forever. If not literally lost, evidence recovered from an unsecured crime scene during a later search can also be figuratively lost by being excluded from use because the investigator cannot assure the court or hearing officer that the evidence was either there at the time of the first search or remained in an unaltered state until found during the second search. Remember that, at least in the area of evidence collection, too much is better than too little. From that overabundance, one can pick and choose what should be presented in a hearing or in court.

Mark it. The marking of evidence should ideally occur when and where it was discovered, within reason, of course. That is to say, if a crowbar was left on the ground beside the forcibly entered boxcar, the investigator is not obliged to stop in his or her tracks and mark the crowbar right then

---

[1] The Process of Investigation, Elsevier, 4th ed. 2015, Charles A. Sennewald and John K. Tsukayama.

and there, but it should be marked prior to its removal back to the office. Minimally the marking should be the initials of the investigator and the date. If possible the case number is included. This marking must not in any way affect the evidentiary value of the object or damage or deface or take away from the value of the object.

Avoiding such damage may require some care. In one shoplifting case an expensive ladies' hand bag had been recovered as evidence. It was lined with a light, melon-colored silk fabric. The investigator noted her initials and date with blue ballpoint pen on that lining, rendering the handbag a total loss. Proper identification of the evidence is simply a matter of using some imagination when applying the markings.

If it is not possible to mark on the items, then attach a label and mark on that. If the item is too small to mark on or to attach a label to, put it in a small container, seal the container, and mark on it. Again, if possible, photograph or videotape the small item to minimize the need to open the sealed container for a gross visual (as opposed to a microscopic) examination. Marking serves the obvious purpose of making it possible to positively identify the object later, during an administrative or judicial hearing.

The investigator may be asked, "Is this the shirt you say you found in Mr. Martin's locker?"

The investigator responds, "Yes, sir."

"Are you positive this is the shirt, and not one like it?"

"I'm positive it is the shirt."

"Absolutely positive?"

"Yes, sir."

"How can you be so positive?"

"When I found this shirt in Mr. Martin's locker, I took my pen and placed my initials and the date right here inside the washing instructions tag in the tail of the shirt. Here it is, right here."

Properly wrap, package, or preserve to protect the evidence from contamination. If the evidence is of a fragile nature, such as glass or a plaster of Paris cast, or if the evidence is easily destroyed, such as a plastic or latent fingerprint, great care should be taken to ensure that when the package is reopened the evidence is not destroyed. Common sense gives direction here. If there is a question, seek advice.

Establish a chain of continuity between the discovery of the evidence and its subsequent presentation. Accounting for the uninterrupted control of the evidence is referred to as the "chain of custody" or the "chain of evidence." The so-called "chain" is the inked documentation of each person's possession of that evidence by name, time, and date. The shorter the chain (or the fewer the people who handle it), the better. Ideally the chain would be only one person, the one who discovered, collected, marked, packaged, carried, and locked the evidence in the vault and subsequently retrieved it from the vault and carried it to the hearing. The inked documentation (to avoid erasures) should be on the outer container or package as well as noted in the investigation file itself.

The evidence storage must be completely secure to prevent the evidence from being altered, damaged, or stolen. Even well-respected law enforcement agencies have found themselves ruing their failure to properly restrict access to evidence storage. The O.J. Simpson vehicle evidence lot fiasco will be long remembered as a classic example of this kind of failure. Ensuring the evidence storage integrity keeps the careful investigator from being forced to explain to the judge and jury why such poorly protected evidence should be relied upon.

Definitions and purpose of evidence

1. That[2] is legally submitted to a competent tribunal as a means of ascertaining the truth of any alleged matter of fact under investigation before it.
2. Anything that a suspect leaf at a crime scene or takes from the scene or that may be otherwise connected with the crime.

Terminology

"Physical," "real," "tangible," "laboratory," and "latent" are all adjectives to describe the types of evidence that the laboratory examines.

Purpose of physical evidence
1. Aids in the solution of the case because it can do the following:
    a. Develop modus operandi (M.O.'s) or show similar M.O.'s.
    b. Develop or identify suspects.
    c. Prove or disprove an alibi.
    d. Connect or eliminate suspects.
    e. Identify loot or contraband.
    f. Provide leads.
2. Proves an element of the offense, for example:
    a. Safe insulation, glass, or building materials on suspect's clothing may prove entry.
    b. Stomach contents, bullets, residue at scene of fire, semen, blood, and tool marks may all prove elements of certain offenses.

---

[2] Investigations: 150 Things You Should Know, Elsevier Publisher, 2nd ed. 2018, Fennelly, L.J., CPOI, CSSM and Marianna Perry, CPP, CPOI.

   c. Safe insulation on tools may be enough to prove violation of possession of burglary tools statutes.

3. Proves theory of a case, for example:

   a. Footprints may show how many were at scene.

   b. Auto paint on clothing may show that a person was hit by car instead of otherwise injured.

The rules of evidence

Rules[3] of evidence govern the presentation of evidence at a trial in much the same way that the rules of a game govern the conduct of the players and, continuing with this analogy, the judge acts as the impartial referee or umpire. Evidence consists of legal proofs presented to the court in the form of witnesses, records, documents, objects, and other means, for the purpose of influencing the opinions of the judge or jury toward the case of the prosecution or the defense. The four kinds of evidence are as follows:

1. Real evidence: Real evidence refers to objects of any kind (weapons, clothing, fingerprints, and so on). Real evidence must be the original evidence, the original objects. Reasonable facsimiles such as photographs, reproductions, or duplicates that are necessitated by practical considerations may also be introduced as real evidence.

2. Testimonial evidence: Testimonial evidence is the statements of competent, sworn witnesses. All **real evidence must be accompanied by testimonial evidence**.

3. Direct evidence: Direct evidence refers to the observations of eyewitnesses.

4. Circumstantial evidence: Circumstantial evidence comprises any information that tends to prove or disprove a point at issue. Circumstantial evidence proves a subsidiary fact from which the existence of the ultimate fact in the criminal trial—the guilt or innocence of the accused—may be inferred.

To be accepted by the court, evidence must be relevant, competent, and material. Relevant evidence directly pertains to the issues in question. That is, evidence is relevant not only when it tends to prove or disprove a fact at issue but also when it establishes facts from which further inferences can be drawn.

Whether the defendant "did it" is not relevant to his or her successful prosecution. What is relevant—the only thing that is relevant is the prosecution's ability to produce admissible evidence to prove the defendant's guilt beyond a reasonable doubt. Sometimes, this is problematic, especially when dealing with the human factor.

---

[3] Territo L, Halsted JB, Bromley ML. Crime and justice in America: a human perspective, 5th ed. 1998, Boston: Butterworth-Heinemann. http://www.bh.com.

Evidence: Types of examinations

DNA examinations

DNA testing provides a basis for positive identification, but is it not expected to become a suitable technology for validating identification in security settings. DNA analysis would be inappropriate in situations where a nearly immediate determination must be made as to whether a person seeking entry to a particular area or seeking to conduct a particular transaction is, in fact, authorized to do so. The chemical analysis required to make a DNA comparison takes weeks, not minutes. DNA testing is increasingly used to determine paternity, and, in forensic settings, it has been most prolifically and successful used to identify or exonerate a suspect.

Deoxyribonucleic acid (DNA) is analyzed in body fluids and body fluid stains recovered from physical evidence in violent crimes. DNA analysis is conducted utilizing the restriction fragment length polymorphism (RFLP) method or other appropriate DNA methods. Evidence consists of known liquid and dried blood samples, portions of rape kit swabs, and extracts and body fluid stained cuttings from homicide, sexual assault, and serious aggravated assault cases. The results of DNA analysis on a questioned body fluid stain are compared visually and by computer image analysis to the results of DNA analysis on known blood samples as a means of potentially identifying or excluding an individual as the source of a questioned stain. As such, this technique, like fingerprinting, is capable of directly associating a victim of a violent crime with the subject or the subject with the crime scene. The implementation of this technique in the laboratory represents a significant advance in forensic serology.

Toxicological examination

A toxicological examination looks for the presence of drugs and/or poisons in biological tissues and fluids. The toxicological findings show whether the victim of a crime died or became ill as the result of drug or poison ingestion or whether the involved persons were under the influence of drugs at the time of the matter under investigation.

Digital evidence

Evidence from an electronic source, such as text messages, audio, or video files, files from servers or stored data. With the trend of the Internet-empowered devices such as watches, smart speakers, baby monitors, toys, medical devices, and other smart devices, there are many sources of digital evidence. Vehicles with an electronic audio system, toll passes, and in-car cameras also store evidence. While some devices store data on the device itself, others act as sensors that transmit data back to a smartphone application, cloud service provider, or other remote location.[4] Warrants may be required to collect any digital evidence; however, this may be challenging for law enforcement. With a recent Supreme Court case highlighting the Fourth Amendment, *United States* v. *Jones*,[5] the government obtained a search warrant to install a GPS on a vehicle for 28 days, which led to an indictment of Jones. Because the vehicle was parked at the residence of Jones, it was protected under the fourth amendment.

Other challenges are the large amount of storage on electronic devices, the ability to remotely delete all data, in corporate investigations in which the company owns digital data, they have the right to collect this evidence.

Examinations for informational purposes

1. Some of the kinds of information that can result from metallurgical examinations of metals or metallic objects in various physical conditions:
   a. Broken and/or mechanically damaged (deformed) metal pieces or parts.
   b. Cause of the failure or damage, that is, stress exceeding the strength or yield limit of the metal, material defect, manufacturing defect, corrosion cracking, excessive service usage (fatigue), etc.
   c. The magnitude of the force or load that caused the failure.
   d. The possible means by which the force or load was transmitted to the metal and the direction in which it was transmitted.
   e. Burned, heated, or melted metal.
   f. Temperature to which the metal was exposed.
   g. Nature of the heat source that damaged the metal.
   h. Whether the metal was involved in an electrical short-circuit situation.
   i. Rusted or corroded metal.
   j. Length of time the metal has been subjected to the environment that caused the rust or corrosion requires that the investigator submit information concerning the environmental conditions surrounding the item when it was recovered.
   k. Nature of the corrosive environment.
   l. Cut or severed metal.
   m. Method by which the metal was severed—sawing, shearing, milling, turning, arc cutting, flame cutting (oxyacetylene torch or "burning bar"), etc.
   n. Length of time to make the cut.

---

[4] www.merelation.com/.

[5] https://www.law.cornell.edu/supremecourt/text/10-1259.

o. Relative skill of the individual who made the cut.
p. Metal fragments.
q. Method by which the fragments were formed.
r. If fragments had been formed by high-velocity forces, it may
   possibly determine if an explosive has been detonated and the
   magnitude of the detonation velocity.
s. Possible identification of the item that was the source of the
   fragments. In bombings, timing mechanisms can often be
   identified as to type, manufacturer, and model; determinations
   are sometimes possible as to the time displayed by the mechanism
   when the explosive detonated and as to the relative length of time
   the mechanism was functioning prior to the explosion.
t. Nonfunctioning watches, clocks, times, and other mechanisms.
u. Condition responsible for causing the mechanism to stop or
   malfunction.
v. Whether the time displayed by a timing mechanism represents
   a.m. or p.m. (usually calendar-type timing mechanisms only).
w. Items unidentified as to use or source.
x. Possible identification of use for which the item was designed,
   formed, or manufactured, based on the construction of and the
   type of metal in the item.
y. Possible identification of the manufacturer and of specific
   fabricating equipment utilized to form the item.
z. Identification of possible sources of the item if an unusual metal or
   alloy is involved.

Narcotics

Illicit drug records are examined to determine the type of drugs being distributed, gross sales, gross and/or net weights or quantities, number of persons involved, organizational structure, and other pertinent
information.

Prostitution

Prostitution records are analyzed to determine the scope of the business, including the number of employees, their roles, gross and net revenues, and other financial and organizational information.

Material to be furnished to the laboratory

1. Cryptographic and mathematical.
2. Any work papers available.

3. Identity of foreign languages that might be involved.
4. Information as to what the intent of the document might be.
5. Complete background information on the case.
6. Special training a subject may have had.
7. Books, code books, cipher machines, pads, tables, programmable calculators, etc. in the subject's possession.
8. Other clandestine business records.
9. Reports/numbers wagering slips.
10. Summaries of wagering slips or tallies including adding machine tapes used to calculate wagering or to summarize writers' accounts. Charting of wagers systematically done to determine the volume of wagering on various events.
11. Accounting and financial records or "bottom sheets" showing numerous accounts (sometimes encrypted), amounts, and/or commissions paid to writers.
12. Related paraphernalia—sports schedules or lines sheets, sports records materials, dream books, cut cards, parlay manuals, conversion charts, scratch sheets, racing forms, computer printouts and related materials, etc.
13. Semidestroyed material such as charred, shredded, torn, or wet water-soluble paper.
14. Transcripts of pertinent legally obtained telephone conversations.
15. Cards, dice, carnival paraphernalia such as "razzle dazzle" charts, and similar types of gambling material.
16. Electronic and electromechanical gambling devices including slot machines, bingo-type pinball machines, and video display devices.
17. Other devices or evidence, when pertinent, such as "cheese bones" and clandestine signaling devices.
18. Any other suspect papers indicating clandestine business operations.

PART 3

Specific investigations and skills

Creating the report

Introduction

Very often reports are official documents that detail how evidence was collected and preserved during an investigation. Hence, they are an important part of the chain of custody.

The technique of report writing can be learned by anyone who possesses two basic qualities: fundamental communication skills and a trained ability to observe. To be a competent investigator, you must write reports clearly so that everyone who reads them will know what you did and why. Often the report is needed long after the crime and must be interpreted by many people unfamiliar with the crime. Interviewers must write the report so that the prosecutor and courts can fully understand what took place.

Clear expression is not difficult to achieve, but it does take practice. Always write just the facts when you are taking notes or writing your report. A statement is the literal reproduction of the actual words spoken by the interviewee. Be a creative listener, use skillful phrases, and ask questions politely. First listen, and then write notes. Be supportive and encouraging.

There are five basic steps in writing a report as listed below:

1. Gather the facts (investigate, interview, and interrogate). What are you going to tell us?
2. Take notes and record the facts as soon as possible.
3. Organize the facts; create an outline and bullet points.
4. Write the report—just the facts. Decide how many words you want to write for each part of the report.
5. Edit and revise your report.

Good notes are a prerequisite for a good report, and they share many of the characteristics of a good report. When you're taking notes, organize your information, and then report it in chronologically arranged paragraphs. Keep your writing straightforward and simple.

Characteristics of a well-written report

A well-written report indicates that you have done your job and that you recognize your responsibilities to your client, corporation, or community. A well-written report reflects positively on your education, your competence, and your professionalism and it communicates better than a poorly prepared report.

Well-written reports share the following characteristics:

- *Factual.* Facts make up the backbone of all reports. A fact is a statement that can be verified and known as a certainty. *Black's Law Dictionary* defines a fact as a thing done, an action performed or an incident transpiring, an event or circumstance; and an actual occurrence. Present your facts, draw your conclusion, and stipulate which is which. A well-written report does not contain unidentified opinions.
- *Accurate.* Just as there are rules for spelling, capitalization, and punctuation, there are rules for word choice. Ensure accuracy by being specific in your language and by choosing the most appropriate words for each situation. Avoid jargon, which creates confusion.
- *Objective.* A good report is fair and impartial. Subjective writing might be more colorful than objective writing, but it has no place in a report. You can ensure objectivity in your reports by including all relevant facts and by avoiding words with emotional overtones. Specific types of crime require different information, but you will frequently need certain general information. You will want to include the *who, what, when,* and *where* questions that should be answered by factual statements. The *how* and *why* statements may require inferences on your part. When this is the case and especially when addressing the question of motive, clearly label your opinions. Avoid personal opinions.
- *Complete.* A report should give as full an account as possible. To avoid slanting your report, record all possible motives reported to you, no matter how implausible they may seem.
- *Concise.* The information you choose to include should be worded as concisely as possible; no one wants to read a wordy report. You can reduce wordiness two ways: (1) leave out unnecessary information and (2) use as few words as possible to record the necessary facts. Avoid vague phrases such as "a long time ago" or "sometime in the winter." You need to create a detailed report, and these phrases do not provide such detail.
- *Clear.* Clarity, one of the most important characteristics of a well-written report.
- *Mechanically correct.* Be sure to use correct spelling, capitalization, and punctuation in your report. A report riddled with errors in these areas gives a poor impression of its writer and the writer's actions.

- *Written in standard English.* When you translate your ideas into words, follow the rules for correct writing. Use the past tense, complete sentences, and good grammar. Keep your sentences short and language simple and concise. Do not use jargon or texting phrases that are not complete sentences.
- *Legible.* An illegible report gives a poor impression of the writer and a distorted explanation of who said what. Reread and edit your report, or even better, have another person proofread your report for accuracy and grammatical errors.
- *On time.* A report that is submitted late reflects negatively on the report writer.

Make your reports, like all your other communications, as clear and direct as possible. The following suggestions will help ensure that your reports can be easily understood:

- Use the first person. That is, write *I* instead of *the investigator* or *the interviewer.* First-person writing is recommended for law enforcement reports because it is direct.
- Write in past tense throughout your report.
- Write in active voice. For example, say, "I asked Jane Smith ..." rather than "Jane Smith was asked ...." The active voice clearly indicates who performed the action.
- Be objective.
- Correctly modify details to be included.
- When using pronouns, be sure it is clear to whom they refer.
- Don't use police lingo.
- Don't use slang.
- Use parallelism. That is, use the same type of structure for similar parts of a sentence.
- Choose your words carefully. Avoid legal, technical, unfamiliar, and slang words.
- Include specific, concrete facts and details.
- Keep descriptive words and phrases as close as possible to the words they describe. Use correct grammar.
- Use diagrams and sketches to clarify a complex description.
- Quality reports are always typed, using paragraphs, past tense, and first person. Remember that all reports are a permanent written record of your case.

Investigation report writing guideline sheet

Over the years, we have written hundreds of reports, they must address the who, the where, the when, the why, and the how. We don't want this to be an English class like in school. But these concepts carry on to your everyday life as an investigator. Currently, we have just finished typing a nine-page report, knowing in 2–3 years we will be in court.

An effective investigation report:

- It should be easy to read and follow.
- It must be detailed enough so that someone unfamiliar with the case can understand what has happened and cover all facts.
- Documents the findings and facts of an investigation.
- Demonstrates that all allegations were addressed.
- Includes recommendations and a follow-up of corrective action taken.
- Is clearly written, without grammatical, spelling, and factual errors.

What goes into a report:
Every investigation report should include the following sections:

- How and when the incident occurred.
- Date that the complaint was made/brought to the employer.
- Date that the investigation started.
- Names and information for those who conducted the investigation.
- A summary of the investigation process used.
- A summary of the allegations investigated Documentation of Interviews.
- List of the people interviewed, their titles and contact information.
- The location of each interview.
- List of anyone who refused to be interviewed or couldn't be interviewed and why.
- List of any follow-up interviews that occurred and the interview details.

Evidence

- Complete list of the evidence collected and reviewed allegations and findings.
- Allegations investigated and responses.
- Facts of the event(s) that occurred.
- Factual discrepancies uncovered.
- Reasons why or why not someone's statements are considered to be truthful.

Internal controls and investigations

By definition, internal theft is the theft of property committed by individuals who are employed in some way by a corporation/client, etc. The best defense for this is background checks, preemployment screening, internal controls, and auditing. Some other techniques for preventing internal theft are as follows:

- Background checks to identify and eliminate future internal problems.
- Internal controls, ID badges, sign-in sheets, and separation of common space from internal space.
- Audits and accountability for detecting and uncovering loses and problems. A common method of internal controls to defect fraud through financial transactions.
- A story policy signed off by all employees. If you steel anything, prosecution to the full extent of the law and termination.

It should be noted that internal theft is the hardest of all crimes to deal with, to solve, and to obtain a conviction.

You need to have strong security controls, processes, and procedures in place that minimize opportunity for unethical business conduct.

In a retail environment the number one most desirable item is cash and/or theft from a safe followed by as follows:

- fraudulent refunds
- fraudulent returns (different from refunds)
- fraudulent voids
- fraudulent suspension
- fraud credit card transactions
- sweet hearting
- merchandize

Internal theft is a crime committed by person or persons known within your community, for example, employees, executives, vendors, contractors, janitors, and security personnel. Over the years, unusual crimes occur within a variety of security disciplines, and security managers are called to address the issue.

Consider these five objectives:

1. Procedure to address internal theft.
2. Perform an overall crime analysis study.
3. Bring in a consultant if the company does not have trained personnel.
4. Improve your physical security and controls.
5. Have a security assessment of your business operations performed.

Consider these six controls:

1. Conduct background checks of all personnel, categorize by position.
2. Establish adequate policy and procedures.
3. Conduct audits.
4. Reduce risk factors.
5. Conduct proper investigations.
6. Determine process to recover losses.

Apprehension of the thief can be obtained by the following:

1. Undercover investigators.
2. Covert video security surveillance system (CCTV) setup.
3. Employee awareness and orientation.

Fact No. 1: 25% of all employees will steal from their employer if opportunity presents itself.

Fact No. 2: 30% of all businesses fail due to internal theft.

Fact No. 3: Employee deviance leads to more dishonesty, deterioration of productivity, and customer dissatisfaction.

Fact No. 4: Employee awareness programs are vital to reducing loss in any type of company.

Fact No. 5: There are several ways of detecting employee dishonesty:

- Co-worker tip off
- Hot line number for anonymous callers to report
- Security audit
- Job sharing
- Required vacations
- Shopping services
- Electronic surveillance

If you are an investigator working for a corporation, security firm, retail organization, insurance company, or private client, you will likely find yourself conducting interviews for the purpose of securing a confession to a criminal offense. Our role often starts with preliminary research, moves into an investigation, and finally leads into an interview for the purpose of obtaining a statement or confession. I have spent much of the past 42 years conducting corporate investigations into fraud, embezzlement, drug use, theft, and other wrongdoings. These investigations have taken anywhere from hours to more than 6 months, working with human resources, audit, facility management, and other department managers within the corporate structure. You will need to exercise patience in conducting internal investigation cases; however, it has been my experience that once an employee is successfully (i.e., not being caught) stealing or committing fraud, they continue to do so. The manner in which they commit the crime may change, but their greed doesn't subside.

Depending on the state laws and company laws, you may need several conclusive videos in which the criminal act is being committed prior to conducting your interview.

There are many things to consider when you're conducting internal investigations:

- What was the source that provided initial information and under what terms? (i.e., informant, whistleblower, coconspirator, witness, etc.)
- Determine who might be allowed into the knowledge of an ongoing investigation.
- Who will you want to interview and what information might they have?
- Determine whether the allegations fall under criminal conduct or an internal discipline matter.
- Address any conflicts of interest by anyone connected to the investigation.
- Be prepared to document everything related to this case.
- Who in the company needs to be notified of the investigation? (i.e., human resources, legal department, auditing, and financial department)
- What evidence will you need to gather to prosecute this case?
- Know and follow all relevant company policies.
- Consider all laws that might apply.

While trying to understand the complexities of internal investigations, let's look at internal theft, dishonest employees, danger signals, and keys to reducing theft.

The remaining text in this chapter is reprinted, with permission, from Chapter 13, "Internal Theft Controls and Personnel Issues," from *Introduction to Security*, ninth edition (https://www.elsevier.com/books/introduction-to-security/fischer/978-0-12-385057-7).

Introduction

It is sad but true that virtually every company will suffer losses from internal theft—and these losses can be enormous. Early in this new century, even the large corporate giants such as Enron, WorldCom, and Martha

Stewart have been affected by internal corruption that reached the highest levels of the organization. In addition, the name Bernie Madoff will long be associated with perhaps the greatest customer and company theft of all times. In its 2018 Report to the Nations, the Association of Certified Fraud Examiners[1] report that 50% of corruption cases were detected by a tip and that internal control weakness were responsible for nearly half of the known fraud cases. This report estimates that organizations lose 5% of their annual revenues to fraud, which if the 5% were applied, the 2017 estimated gross world product of USD 79.6 trillion, or nearly USD 4 trillion[2] estimated that fraud (employee theft) cost the world business community $2.9 trillion, or 5% of the estimated gross world product, in 2009. Although this figure is startling, it must be remembered that there is no accurate way to calculate the extent of fraud. In 2002 security reported that in the retail business alone, 1 in every 27 employees is apprehended for theft from an employer. Internal theft in the retail business outstrips the loss from shoplifting by approximately 7.9 times.

According to the National Retail Federation (NRF), in strategic collaboration with Dr. Richard Hollinger of the University of Florida, the risk landscape is changing. While conducting their 2019 security survey, which provides insights about internal and external retail crime, overwhelmingly respondents report an increase in the overlap between loss prevention and cyber issues.[3]

What is honesty?

Before considering the issue of dishonest employees, it is helpful to understand the concept of honesty, which is difficult to define. Webster says that honesty is "fairness and straightforwardness of conduct, speech, etc.; integrity; truthfulness; freedom; freedom from fraud." In simple terms, honesty is respect for others and for their property. The concept, however, is relative. According to Charles Carson, "Security must be based on a controlled degree of relative honesty" because no one fulfills the ideal of total honesty. Carson explores relative honesty by asking the following questions:

1. If an error is made in your favor in computing the price of something you buy, do you report it?
2. If a cashier gives you too much change, do you return it?

---

[1] https://www.acfe.com/report-to-the-nations/2018/default.aspx.
[2] https://www.dol.gov/agencies/ofccp/executive-order-11246/ca-11246.
[3] https://www.dol.gov/agencies/oasam/regulatory/statutes/title-vi-civil-rights-act-of-1.

3. If you found a purse containing money and the owner's identification, would you return the money to the owner if the amount was $1? $10? $100? $1000?

Honesty is a controllable variable, and how much control is necessary depends on the degree of honesty of each individual. The individual's honesty can be evaluated by assessing the degree of two types of honesty: moral and conditioned. *Moral honesty* is a feeling of responsibility and respect that develops during an individual's formative years; this type of honesty is subconscious. *Conditioned honesty* results from fearing the consequences of being caught; it is a product of reasoning. If an honest act is made without a conscious decision, it is because of moral honesty, but if the act is based on the conscious consideration of consequences, the act results from conditioned honesty.

It is vital to understand these principles because the role of security is to hire employees who have good moral honesty and to condition employees to greater honesty. The major concern is that the job should not tempt an employee into dishonesty.

Carson summarizes his views in the following principles:

- No one is completely honest.
- Honesty is a variable that can be influenced for better or worse.
- Temptation is the father of dishonesty.
- Greed, not need, triggers temptation.

Unfortunately, there is no sure way by which potentially dishonest employees can be recognized. Proper screening procedures can eliminate applicants with unsavory pasts or those who seem unstable and therefore possibly untrustworthy. There are even tests that purport to measure an applicant's honesty index. But tests and employee screening can only indicate potential difficulties. They can screen out the most obvious risks, but they can never truly vouch for the performance of any prospective employee under circumstances of new employment or under changes that may come about in life apart from the job.

The need to carefully screen employees has continued to increase. In today's market, there are many individuals who belong to what has been called the "I Deserve It!" generation. According to a study by the Josephson Institute for the Advanced Study of Ethics, cheating, stealing, and lying by high school students have continued an upward trend, with youth 18 and younger five times more likely than people over age 50 to hold the belief that lying and cheating are necessary to succeed. The 2008 report showed that 64% of US high school students cheated on an exam, 42% lied to save money, and 30% stole something from a store. The institute, which conducts nonpartisan ethics programs for the Internal Revenue Service, the Pentagon, and several major media organizations and educators, states that their findings show evidence that a willingness to cheat has become the norm. The 2008 study found that young people believe that ethics and character are important but are cynical about whether a person can be ethical and still succeed.

The dishonest employee

Because there is no fail-safe technique for recognizing the potentially dishonest employee on sight, it is important to try to gain some insight into the reasons that employees may steal. If some rule of thumb could be developed that will help identify the patterns of the potential thief, it would provide some warning for an alert manager.

There is no simple answer to the question of why previously honest people suddenly start to steal from their employers. The mental and emotional processes that lead to this change are complex, and motivation may come from any number of sources.

Some employees steal because of resentment over real or imagined injustice that they blame on management indifference or malevolence. Some feel that they must maintain status and steal to augment their incomes because of financial problems. Some may steal simply to tide themselves over in a genuine emergency. They rationalize the theft by assuring themselves that they will return the money after the current problem is solved. Some simply want to indulge themselves, and many, strangely enough, steal to help others. Alternatively, employees may steal because no one cares, because no one is looking, or because the absence of inadequacy of theft controls eliminates the fear of being caught. Still others may steal simply for excitement.

The fraud triangle

A simplified answer to the question of why employees steal is depicted in the fraud triangle. According to this concept, theft occurs when three elements are present:

1. incentive or motive
2. attitude/rationalization or desire
3. opportunity

In simple terms, incentive or motive is a reason to steal. Motives might be the resentment of an employee who feels underpaid or the vengefulness of an employee who has been passed over for promotion. Attitude or desire builds on motive by imagining the satisfaction or gratification that would come from a potential action: "Taking a stereo system would make me feel good, because I always wanted a good stereo system." Opportunity is the absence of barriers that prevent someone from taking an item. Desire and motive are beyond the scope of the loss prevention manager; opportunity, however, is the responsibility of security.

A high percentage of employee thefts begin with opportunities that are regularly presented to them. If security systems are lax or supervision is indifferent, the temptation to steal items that are improperly secured or unaccountable may be too much to resist by any but the most resolute employee.

Many experts agree that the fear of discovery is the most important deterrent to internal theft. When the potential for discovery is eliminated, theft is bound to follow. Threats of dismissal or prosecution of any employee found stealing are never as effective as the belief that any theft will be discovered by management supervision.

Danger signs

The root causes of theft are many and varied, but certain signs can indicate that a hazard exists. The conspicuous consumer presents perhaps the most easily identified risk. Employees who habitually or suddenly acquire expensive cars and/or clothes and who generally seem to live beyond their means should be watched. Such persons are visibly extravagant and appear indifferent to the value of money. Even though such employees may not be stealing to support expensive tastes, they are likely to run into financial difficulties through reckless spending. Employees may then be tempted to look beyond their salary checks for ways to support an extravagant lifestyle.

Employees who show a pattern of financial irresponsibility are also a potential risk. Many people are incapable of handling their money. They may do their job with great skill and efficiency, but they are in constant difficulty in their private lives. These people are not necessarily compulsive spenders, nor do they necessarily have expensive tastes. (They probably live quite modestly, since they have never been able to manage their affairs effectively enough to live otherwise.) They are simply people who are unable to come to grips with their own economic realities. Garnishments or inquiries by creditors may identify such employees. If there seems a reason to make one, a credit check might reveal the tangled state of affairs.

Employees caught in a genuine financial squeeze are also possible problems. If they have been hit with financial demands from illnesses in the family or heavy tax liens, they may find the pressures too great to bear. If such a situation comes to the attention of management, counseling is in order. Many companies maintain funds that are designated to make low-interest loans in such cases. Alternatively, some arrangement might be worked out through a credit union. In any event, employees in such extremities need help fast. They should get that help, both as a humane response to their needs and as a means of protecting company assets.

In addition to these general categories, there are specific danger signals that should be noted:

- Gambling on or off premises.
- Excessive drinking or signs of other drug use.
- Obvious extravagance.
- Persistent borrowing.
- Requests for advances.
- Bouncing personal checks or problems with creditors.

What employees steal

The employee thief will take anything that may be useful or that has resale value. The thief can get at the company funds in many ways—directly or indirectly—through collusion with vendors, collusion with outside thieves or hijackers, fake invoices, receipting for goods never received, falsifying inventories, payroll padding, false certification of overtime, padded expense accounts, computer record manipulation, overcharging, undercharging, or simply by gaining access to a cash box or company goods.

This is only a sample of the kinds of attacks that can be made on company assets using the systems set up for the operation of the business. It is in these areas that the greatest losses can occur because they are frequently based on a systematic looting of the goods and services in which the company deals and the attendant operational cash flow.

Significant losses do occur, however, in other, sometimes unexpected, areas. Furnishings frequently disappear. In some firms with indifferent traffic control procedures, this kind of theft can be a very real problem. Desks, chairs, computers and other office equipment; paintings; and rugs all can be carried away by the enterprising employee thief.

Office supplies can be another problem if they are not properly supervised. Beyond the anticipated attrition in pencils, paper clips, notepads, and rubber bands, sometimes these materials are stolen in case lots. Many firms that buy their supplies at discount are in fact receiving stolen property. The market in stolen office supplies is a brisk one and is becoming more so as the prices for this merchandize soar.

The office equipment market is another active one, and the inside thief is quick to respond to its needs. Computers always bring a good price, as does equipment used to support high-tech offices.

Personal property is also vulnerable. Office thieves do not make fine distinctions between company property and that of their fellow workers. The company has a very real stake in this kind of theft because personal tragedy and decline in morale follow in its wake.

Although security management or loss prevention managers cannot assume responsibility for losses of this nature because they are not in a position to know about the property involved or to control its handling (and they should so inform all employees), they should make every effort to apprise all employees of the threat. They should further note from time to time the degree of carelessness the staff displays in handling personal property and send out reminders of the potential dangers of loss.

Methods of theft

According to the Better Business Bureau, nearly 30% of all business failure is due to employee theft. In addition, a 2014 report by the Association of Certified Fraud Examiners estimates that 5% of total revenue losses for most companies are from employee fraud of some type. Therefore there is a very real need to examine the shapes that dishonesty frequently takes. There is no way to describe every kind of theft, but some examples may serve to give an idea of the dimensions of the problem:

1. Payroll and personnel employees collaborating to falsify records by the use of nonexistent employees or by retaining terminated employees on the payroll.
2. Padding overtime reports and kicking back part of the extra unearned pay to the authorizing supervisor.
3. Pocketing unclaimed wages.
4. Splitting increased payroll that has been raised on signed, blank checks for use in the authorized signer's absence.
5. Maintenance personnel and contract servicepeople in collusion to steal and sell office equipment.
6. Receiving clerks and truck drivers in collusion on falsification of merchandize count (extra unaccounted merchandize is fenced).
7. Purchasing agents in collusion with vendors to falsify purchase and payment documents (purchasing agent issues authorization for payment on goods never shipped after forging receipts of shipment).
8. Purchasing agent in collusion with vendor to pay inflated price.
9. Mailroom and supply personnel packing and mailing merchandize to themselves for resale.
10. Accounts payable personnel paying fictitious bills to an account set up for their own use.
11. Taking incoming cash without crediting the customer's account.
12. Paying creditors twice and pocketing the second check.
13. Appropriating checks made out to cash.
14. Raising the amount on checks after voucher approval or raising the amount on vouchers after their approval.
15. Pocketing small amounts from incoming payments and applying later payments on other accounts to cover shortages.
16. Removal of equipment or merchandize with the trash.
17. Invoicing goods below regular price and getting a kickback from the purchaser.

18. Manipulating accounting software packages to credit personal accounts with electronic account overages.
19. Issuing (and cashing) checks on returned merchandize not actually returned.
20. Forging checks, destroying them when they are returned with the statement from the bank, and changing cash account records accordingly.
21. Appropriating credit card, electronic bank account, and other electronic data.

The contagion of theft

Theft of any kind is a contagious disorder. Petty, relatively innocent pilferage by a few employees spreads through a facility. As more people participate, others will follow until even the most rigid breakdown and join in. Pilferage becomes acceptable—even respectable. It gains general social acceptance that is reinforced by almost total peer participation. Few people make independent ethical judgments under such circumstances. In this microcosm the act of petty pilferage is no longer viewed as unacceptable conduct. It has become not a permissible sin but instead a right.

The docks of New York City were once an example of this progression. Forgetting for the moment the depredations of organized crime and the climate of dishonesty that characterized that operation for so many years, even longshoremen not involved in organized theft had worked out a system all their own. For every so many cases of whiskey unloaded, for example, one case went to the men. Little or no attempt was made to conceal this pilferage. It was a tradition, a right. When efforts were made to curtail the practice, labor difficulties arose. It soon became evident that certain pilferage would have to be accepted as an unwritten part of the union contract under the existing circumstances.

This is not a unique situation. The progression from limited pilferage through its acceptance as normal conduct to the status of an unwritten right has been repeated time and again. The problem is that it does not stop there. Ultimately, pilferage becomes serious theft, and then the real trouble starts. Even before pilferage expands into larger operations, it presents a difficult problem to any business. Even where the amount of goods taken by any one individual is small, the aggregate can represent a significant expense. With the costs of materials, manufacture, administration, and distribution rising as they are, there is simply no room for added, avoidable expenses in today's competitive markets. The business that can operate the most efficiently and offer quality goods at the lowest prices because of the efficiency of its operation will have a huge advantage in the marketplace. When so many companies are fighting for their economic lives, there is simply no room for waste—and pilferage is just that.

Moral obligation to control theft

When we consider that internal theft accounts for at least twice the loss from external theft (i.e., from burglars, armed robbers, and shoplifters combined), we must be impressed with the scope of the problem facing today's businesspeople. Businesses have a financial obligation to stockholders to earn a profit on their investments. Fortunately, steps can be taken to control internal theft. Setting up a program of education and control that is vigorously administered and supervised can cut losses to relatively insignificant amounts. Creating a culture of integrity and honesty is the most successful way to control losses. Setting the right culture can be done through a complete and thorough hiring process, messages while in orientation, mandated annual training, security visibility, and risk audits.

It is also important to observe that management has a moral obligation to its employees to protect their integrity by taking every possible step to avoid presenting open opportunities for pilferage and theft that would tempt even the most honest people to take advantage of the opportunity for gain by theft.

This is not to suggest that each company should assume a paternal role toward its employees and undertake their responsibilities for them. It is to suggest strongly that the company should keep its house sufficiently to avoid enticing employees to acts that could result in great personal tragedy and in damage to the company.

Employment history and reference checking

The key to reducing internal theft is the quality of employees employed by the facility. The problem, however, will not be eliminated during the hiring process, no matter how carefully and expertly selection is made. Systems of theft prevention and programs of employee motivation are ongoing efforts that must recognize that elements of availability, susceptibility, and opportunity are dynamic factors in a constant state of flux. The initial approach to the problem, however, starts at the beginning—in the very process of selecting personnel to work in the facility. During this process a knowledgeable screener who is aware of what to look for in the employment application or résumé can develop an enormous amount of vital information about the prospective employee. Some answers are not as obvious as they once were, and the ability to perceive and evaluate what appears on the application or résumé is more important than ever as applications become more restrictive in what they can ask.

The increased focus on screening and background checks over the past decade is a direct result of the following:

- A rise in lawsuits from negligent hiring.
- An increase in child abuse reporting and abductions, which have resulted in new laws that require criminal background checks for anyone who works with children, including volunteers.
- September 11, 2001, resulted in heightened security and required identity verification.
- The Enron scandal increased scrutiny of corporate executives, officers, and directors.
- Increasing use of inflated and fraudulent résumés and applications.
- New federal and state laws requiring background checks for certain jobs, for example, armored car employees.
- The information age added to the increase in checks because information is now available through many computer databases.

Privacy legislation coupled with fair employment laws drastically limit what can be asked on employment application forms. The following federal legislation relates directly to hiring and dealing with employees:

- Title VII of the Civil Rights Act of 1964.
- Pregnancy Discrimination Act of 1978.
- Executive Order 11246 (Affirmative Action).
- Age Discrimination in Employment Act of 1967.
- National Labor Relations Act.
- Rehabilitation Act of 1973.
- Vietnam Era Veterans' Readjustment Assistance Act of 1974.
- Fair Labor Standards Act of 1938 (Wage and Hour Law).
- Federal Wage Garnishment Law.
- Occupational Safety and Health Act of 1970.
- Immigration Reform and Control Act of 1986.
- Employee Polygraph Protection Act of 1988.
- Consolidated Omnibus Reconciliation Act of 1985 (COBRA).
- Worker Adjustment and Retraining Notification Act (Plant Closing Law).
- EEOC Sexual Harassment Guidelines.
- Americans with Disabilities Act of 1990 (for a more complete list, see Table 17.1).
- Family Educational Rights and Privacy Act (FERPA).
- Bankruptcy Act.
- Fair Credit Reporting Act (FCRA).
- Equal Pay Act 1963.
- Privacy Act of 1976.

TABLE 17.1 Who is protected and who is affected? Federally covered employers and protected classes.

Legislation	Race/color	National	Origin/ancestry	Sex	Religion	Age	Disabled	Union	Covered employers
Title VII Civil Rights Act	X	X	X	X					Employers with 15 + EEs; unions, employment agencies
Equal Pay Act (EPA) as amended			X						Minimum wage law coverage ("administrative employees" not exempted)
Age Discrimination in Employment Act (ADEA)[a]						X	40 +		20 + EEs (unions with 25 + members), employment agencies
Age Discrimination Act of 1975 (ADA)[b]						X			Receives federal money
Executive Order 11,246.11141[b]	X	X		X	X	X			All federal contractors and subcontractors
Title VI Civil Rights Act[b]	X	X		X	X				Federally assisted program or activity—public schools and colleges also covered by Title IX
Rehabilitation Act of 1973[b]							X		Receives federal money: federal contractor, $2500 +
National Labor Relations Act (NLRA)	X	X		X	X	X		X	ER in interstate commerce
Civil Rights Act of 1866	X								All employers

Continued

TABLE 17.1 Who is protected and who is affected? Federally covered employers and protected classes—cont'd

Legislation	Race/color	National	Origin/ancestry	Sex	Religion	Age	Disabled	Union	Covered employers
Civil Rights Act of 1871	X	X			X				Private employers usually not covered
Revenue Sharing Act of 1972	X	X			X	X	X	X	State and local governments that receive federal revenue sharing funds
Education Amendments of 1972 Title IX					X				Educational institutions receiving federal financial assistance
Vietnam Era Vets Readjustment Act—1974								X	Government contractors—$10,000 +
Pregnancy Discrimination Act of 1978					X				All employers 15 + EEs
Fair Labor Standards Act	Induces minimum wage law and equal pay act with DOL complex method of coverage								

Rehabilitation Act of 1973[b]	X	Receives federal money: federal contractor, $2500 +
Americans with Disabilities Act of 1990	X	Covers employers with 15 or more employees
Federal Privacy Act of 1976		Federal agencies only
Freedom of Information Act		Federal agencies only
Family Educational Rights and Privacy Act		Schools, colleges, and universities, federally assisted
Immigration Reform Act of 1986		All employers

[a] https://www.eeoc.gov/statutes/age-discrimination-employment-act-1967.

[b] Applies to federal agencies, contractors, or assisted programs only. A mandatory retirement eliminated except in special circumstances.

DOL, Department of Labor; EE, employee; EEOC, Equal Employment Opportunity Commission; ER, employer; INS, Immigration and Naturalization Service; NLRB, National Labor Relations Board; OFCCP, Office of Federal Contract Compliance Programs.

In some respects, these regulations had a streamlining effect, eliminating irrelevant questions and confining questions exclusively to those matters relating to the job applied for. The subtler kinds of discrimination on the basis of age, sex, and national origin have been largely eliminated from the employment process. In making these changes to protect the applicant, state and federal laws have created new dilemmas for employers and their security staffs.

Various federal and state laws prohibit criminal justice agencies (police departments, courts, and correctional institutions) from providing information on certain criminal cases to noncriminal justice agencies (e.g., private security firms or human resource departments). The Fair Credit Reporting Act requires that a job applicant must give written consent to any credit bureau inquiry.

All states have some type of privacy legislation meeting the guidelines set forth in the Federal Privacy Act of 1976. The most controversial portion of the Act states "that information shall only be used for law enforcement and criminal justice and other lawful purposes." The crux of the issue is the way that "other lawful purposes" is defined. Does this meaning include human resource departments and private security operations? The verdict is mixed. Human resources, security, and loss prevention operations must be aware of the interpretation of the privacy legislation in each state in which they operate. Recent legislation regarding the Department of Homeland Security has allowed for greater access of government agencies and private security firms to criminal histories, financial records, and medical records.

Understandably, there is some confusion regarding the rules governing employment screening. In spite of such confusion, the preemployment inquiry remains one of the most useful security tools employers can use to shortstop employee dishonesty and profit drains. Security management should consult with legal counsel to determine which laws relate to their locality and establish firm and precise policies regarding employment applications and hiring practices. An employer should be as familiar as possible with the federal Fair Credit Reporting Act (FCRA), which governs what employers must do when contracting record checks with third parties.

Generally speaking, look for and be wary of applicants who do the following:

- Show signs of instability in personal relations.
- Lack job stability; a job hopper does not make a good job candidate.
- Show a declining salary history or are taking a cut in pay from the previous job.
- Show unexplained gaps in employment history.
- Are clearly overqualified.

- Are unable to recall or are hazy about names of supervisors in the recent past or who forget their address in the recent past.

In general, all or some of the following information might be included in a background check:

- driving records
- vehicle registration
- credit reports
- criminal records
- Social Security number
- educational records
- court records
- workers' compensation
- bankruptcy
- character references
- neighbor interviews
- medical records
- property ownership
- military records
- state licensing
- drug tests
- past employment
- personal references
- arrest records
- sex offense lists

If the job applied for is one that involves handling funds, it is advisable to get the applicant's consent to make a financial inquiry through a credit bureau. Be wary if such an inquiry turns up a history of irresponsibility in financial affairs, such as living beyond one's means.

Application forms should ask for a chronological listing of all previous employers to provide a list of firms to be contacted for information on the applicant and to show continuity of career. Any gaps could indicate a jail term that was "overlooked" in filling out the application. When checking with previous employers, verify dates on which employment started and terminated.

References submitted by the applicant must be contacted, but they are apt to be biased. After all, since the person being investigated submitted these references' names, they are not likely to be negative or hostile. It is important to contact someone—Preferably an immediate supervisor—At each previous job. Such contact should be made by phone or in person.

The usual and easiest system of contact is now by email, but this leaves much to be desired. The relative impersonality of these forms of communication, especially one in which a form or evaluation is to be filled out, can lead to generic and essentially uncommunicative answers.

Because many companies as a matter of policy, stated or implied, are reluctant to give someone a bad reference except in the most extreme circumstances, a reply will sometimes be misleading.

On the other hand, phone or personal contacts may become considerably more discursive and provide shadings in the tone of voice that can be important. Even when no further information is forthcoming, this method may indicate information without stating such when a more exhaustive investigation is required.

CHAPTER

18

Cargo theft investigative techniques

Introduction

Investigative techniques that can be employed to investigate cargo thefts are limited only by one's imagination. Repeated use of new techniques will enable investigators to become more proficient. Tried and true techniques will always remain in an investigator's bag of tricks. Some investigative techniques include, but are not limited, to the following.

Informants

Although informants were previously discussed as a source of information, the cultivating of informants is an important investigative technique. Informants' personalities vary, as do their motivations. An investigator must be constantly aware of informants' personality traits and motivations without losing sight of the object of the investigation. This can best be accomplished by appropriate direction and control of an informant by the investigator. Informants who come from a cargo-related background are diverse.

Undercover investigation

For many investigators, this is the most popular investigative technique. However, selection of an investigator for an undercover assignment is critical. Cargo situations demand specific needs from an investigator such as knowledge of cargo handling, suitable appearance and physical makeup, and possession of a specific mindset.

Investigations and the Art of the Interview
https://doi.org/10.1016/B978-0-12-822192-1.00019-2

Surveillance

With the increased mobility of the criminal element, surveillance techniques have expanded from the traditional vehicle and foot to include air, vessel, and hardware. Foot, vehicle, air, and vessel surveillance involve separate skills. Proficiency is acquired only through extensive participation in each type of surveillance.

Use of technical equipment

Technical aids that, when properly used, can greatly assist the investigator in his investigation include the following:

- electronic sensors and devices
- photography
- fluorescent powders
- night vision and infrared scopes
- closed-circuit television with videotape time sequences

Telephone number analysis

Internal and company-generated telephone data may be reviewed to determine patterns of activity and possible internal conspirators. A computer system is available for producing reports from toll data in which the information is sorted chronologically and numerically by telephone. This system can be extremely helpful in solidifying cargo theft conspiracy cases that have internal company involvement.

Identify "fence" operations

Cargo thefts would be greatly reduced if the thief did not have a readily available outlet to buy the merchandize. Fence operations are directly and indirectly connected with organized crime. Fencing operations vary. In many instances, they operate legitimate businesses or warehouses, but their fencing operations are carried out clandestinely. In recent years, flea markets and swap shops have become a distribution point for fences.

To identify fences, investigators work undercover and make larger and larger purchases of stolen merchandize. This technique may enable an investigation to proceed in an upward direction in an effort to identify other individuals involved in a theft organization or redistribution process.

Storefront operations

By identifying fences and making purchases, a certain amount of expertise in this area is gained. The knowledge of a fencing operation and the argot used between a thief and a fence will be of great help when a storefront project is undertaken by public or private enforcements. Storefront operations are time consuming, expensive, and extremely hazardous, but the payoffs are great when the need for such operations has been identified.

Fraudulent cargo documentation

Detecting practices involving fraudulent papers and other forms of misrepresentations that facilitate cargo thefts is a technique that should be developed. Knowledge of documents required for the importation and movement of cargo to its ultimate destination and the authenticity of those documents can disclose fraudulent practices. As soon as fraudulent documentation is used to steal cargo, the authorities should be alerted. The thieves may become aware that their method of operation has been discovered; however, prevention of future thefts is most important.

Cargo theft reporting: 14 things you should do

All reported cargo thefts should be documented. Efforts should be made to determine the extent of investigation required. Some cases of reported theft involve losses so small that investigation, or at least extensive inquiry, may not be warranted. However, investigation of pilferage of even low-value merchandize from security enclosures within bonded premises may be warranted in most cases, since such thefts indicate breakdown of strict controls set up to protect those enclosures where high-value, low-bulk cargo presents an ideal target for thieves. Records are the backbone of an investigation and any effective prevention program.

Every reported theft should be documented. A report prepared in connection with a formal investigation should completely identify the shipment of merchandize and that portion stolen. An indication of actual or estimated retail value should be included in the report. Every effort should be made to include in the report the following information concerning the merchandize:

1. Name of importing vessel, vehicle or aircraft.
2. Date and time of arrival of conveyance.
3. Foreign port of lading, if appropriate.
4. Bill of lading number or airway bill number.

5. Identify foreign shipper and/or manufacturer.
6. Identify customs broker (if applicable).
7. Name and identity of ultimate consignee.
8. Carton and/or serial numbers of stolen merchandize (and other identifying marks or numbers).
9. Estimated retail value of stolen merchandize.
10. Indicate whether stolen merchandize is imported or exported.
11. Name and identification of person discovering theft.
12. Location of apparent theft.
13. Date and time theft discovered.
14. Date theft was reported to authorities and to whom.

Identification data for individuals and vehicles who are suspect in the investigation also should be included in the report.

Cargo documentation investigations

The movement of cargo is accompanied by documentation from the time it leaves the exporter's premises until it is received by the consignee. To conduct a meaningful investigation, it is necessary to understand the paper flow and the part played by each segment of the industry. Knowledge of general procedures and local differences in these procedures will be extremely beneficial in determining where a theft may have occurred, whether fraudulent documentation was used, and if collusion took place between various elements within the industry.

Marine cargo

1. The *steamship company* (or agent) receives via mail a copy of the vessel's cargo manifest. Normally the consignee is notified 2 days prior to the ship's arrival. The carrier provides freight release to the terminal operator.
2. The *customs broker* or consignee obtains freight release, Department of Agriculture clearance, and so forth before contacting the motor carrier. The broker forward to the motor carrier an original of the domestic bill of lading and an original of the pickup order, which authorizes pick up of the cargo. It is the broker's responsibility to check the bill of lading for completeness and guarantee with the terminal operator the loading charges and demurrage.
3. The *motor carrier* secures an interchange agreement with a steamship company on containers and ascertains expiration of free time and availability of cargo for pick up before dispatching the driver for the pier. The motor carrier furnishes the driver with the original and a copy

of the pickup order before his departure for the pier. An appointment is made with the terminal operator at least 24h before pick up. Within port movements of bonded shipments (warehouse or general order) require a motor carrier to be a customhouse license holder and require the truckmen to possess customs cartman identification cards. When bonded shipments are authorized to be transported by common or private carriers, the identification cards are *not* required.

4. The *terminal operator* issues a pass to the driver at the gatehouse. The pickup order is checked for completeness and legibility by the terminal operator dispatcher. The motor carrier's credit rating for loading charges is verified and arrangements made for payment of demurrage, if any. Unless cargo has been authorized for delivery to the steamship company by customs, the terminal operator directs the driver to the pier customs office.

5. The *customs inspector* will verify the driver's papers against prelodged customs entry documents. When all customs requirements are completed, the inspector will stamp the delivery order "delivery authorized."

6. The *terminal operator* will notify the driver to load and assign a checker and loading area. The cargo is then loaded onto the vehicle by pier personnel, and the checker notes exceptions and shortages.
   It is at this point (with inbound entries only) that the joint determination between the checker, acting as the agent of the carrier, and driver, acting as the agent of the importer, presents a joint determination to the customs inspector. If there are any discrepancies, the inspector makes appropriate notations on all copies of the inbound documents, indicating that the joint determination was sub mitted. The inspector's notation does not affirm or deny the count, it only acknowledges the joint determination and the amount that is permitted. The original delivery order is retained by the terminal operator.

7. It is the *driver's* responsibility to assist in and/or supervise the loading of his vehicle. He signs the delivery order for the quantity received and exceptions and shortages that are noted and retains a copy of the delivery order. Upon departure from the pier, he surrenders the gate pass at the gatehouse. Prior to leaving the pier, the driver notifies the motor carrier dispatcher that he has picked up the cargo and is proceeding with the delivery.

Air cargo

1. Upon arrival an aircraft is given clearance by public health and commences to unload its cargo. The *airline* checks the shipment against airway bills and notifies the consignee within 24h subsequent to arrival.

2. The *customs broker* or the consignee prepares the entry. The broker forward to the inland carrier an original of the airway bill and an original of the pickup order that authorizes the cargo to be picked up.
3. The *customs officer* will review all documents and upon examination will authorize delivery of the shipment to the carrier. The customs inspector may designate a portion of the shipment to be held for appraisal.
4. The *air cargo terminal operator* will examine the pickup order presented by the motor carrier and check it for completeness. If the cargo has not been authorized for delivery by customs, the motor carrier must obtain this authorization prior to loading.
5. Upon loading of an inbound shipment, the *driver* and *airline representative* will make a joint determination and submit the results on the delivery order to customs. All imported cargo arriving in the United States, other than noncommercial merchandize carried on the person by a traveler, is temporarily in the custody of the US Customs Service until the importer or his authorized agent complies with whatever customs requirements apply. Duty-free, noncommercial importations may be cleared to the importer with little or no formality. Whenever formality is involved in the customs transaction, authorizing delivery of the merchandize to the importer is referred to as an *entry*. Basically, there are three classes of entry:
   a. transportation inbound
   b. consumption
   c. warehouse

Inbound entries

1. Immediate transportation (LT.): This type of entry is used when merchandize arrives at one port and is released on condition that it be transported inbound to another port. Upon arrival, customs once again takes temporary custody until an entry of another type is filed by the importer.
2. Transportation and exportation (T&E): This entry is used when merchandize may be merely passing through the United States to another country. The merchandize is permitted on condition that it be transported inbound out of the United States. Other entries of this type are temporary importation bond and permanent exhibition entry.

Consumption entries

1. Informal consumption entries: These entries are allowed for commercial importations under specified value limits and for noncommercial importations regardless of value.

2. Formal consumption entries: At the time a formal consumption entry is filed, the importer pays whatever duties are due on the merchandize. After the shipment is examined and authorized for delivery by customs, the importer can dispose of the merchandize as he wishes.
3. Immediate delivery procedure (1D)-pending formal or informal entries: This procedure is used to expedite the clearance of cargo. It allows up to 10 days for the payment of estimated duty and processing of the commercial entry. In addition, it permits delivery of the cargo prior to payment of estimated duties and allows subsequent filing of the entry.

Warehouse entries

The use of this type of entry allows the importer to hold his merchandize in a bonded customs warehouse ready for sale and distribution, but does not have to pay customs duty until he withdraws the merchandize from the warehouse.

Cargo: Air and marine documentation

The movement of goods by air or sea requires proper formal and informal documentation from the time it exits the shipper's facility until it is received by the consignee. To conduct an investigation, you must understand the flow of documentation in each segment of movement. Understanding general procedures and any local variances can be helpful in determining where a theft occurred, whether fraudulent documentation was used, and if collusion took place.

Marine cargo

1. The steamship authority or its agent receives a copy of the vessel's manifest either electronically or via mail or messenger. The consignees of the various shipments are usually notified at least 2 days prior to the ship's arrival. The carrier provides a freight release to the terminal operator.
2. The consignee or the customs broker obtains the freight release and such clearances as are required by law and then contacts the truckmen. The broker forward to the truckman an original of the domestic bill of lading and an original of the pickup order that authorizes the pickup of the cargo. It is the broker's responsibility to check the documentation for completeness, accuracy, and any charges required.

3. The truckman obtains an interchange agreement with the steamship company in the case of containers. They determine the availability of the cargo prior to dispatching a driver for pick up. The driver has an original and one copy of the pickup order.

4. The terminal operator issues a pass to the driver when he presents himself at the terminal. This is the first clearance location for the driver who is then to report to the US Custom office at the terminal in the case of international cargo.

5. US Customs verifies the driver's papers against prelogged US Customs entry documents. When all obligations for duties and/or charges are satisfied, Customs will authorize delivery.

6. The terminal operator will load the driver with the authorized cargo. Any notations, such as exceptions or shortages, are noted by the load checker assigned by the terminal. It is at this juncture that there is a joint determination between the checker as the agent for the carrier and the truckman as the agent for the importer or consignee, as to the accuracy of the pickup. The original delivery order remains with the terminal operator.

7. It is the truckman's responsibility to assist in and supervise the loading of his truck. He signs the delivery order for the quantity and condition of goods received. Any exceptions or violations are noted on the copy of the delivery order that he keeps. Upon departure from the terminal, the truckman surrenders the pass at exit.

Air cargo

1. Upon arrival an aircraft is given clearance by public health and commences to unload its cargo. The airline checks the shipment against airway bills and notifies the consignee within 24 h subsequent to arrival.

2. The customs broker or the consignee prepares the entry. The broker forwards to the inland carrier an original of the airway bill and an original of the pickup order that authorizes the cargo to be picked up.

3. The customs officer will review all documents and upon examination will authorize delivery of the shipment to the carrier. The customs inspector may designate a portion of the shipment to be held for appraisal.

4. The air cargo terminal operator will examine the pickup order presented by the motor carrier and check it for completeness. If the cargo has not been authorized for delivery by customs, the motor carrier must obtain this authorization prior to loading.

5. Upon loading of an inbound shipment, the driver and airline representative will make a joint determination and submit the results on the delivery order to US Customs.

Cybercrimes and investigations

Introduction

Cybercrime is a global threat, and the evidence suggests that this threat will continue to rise. Cyber crime is also one of the biggest threats to every company, everywhere in the world. It is also the fastest growing crime in the United States. Cybercrimes involve criminal offenses that are committed through Internet use or supported in some way, by computer technology. Internet use can be through a computer, smart phone, or any technology that connects to the Internet. Crimes using the Internet or computer technology resulting in fraud, identity theft, credit card fraud, stolen merchandize selling, etc. is known as ecommerce crime (ECrime). Other cyberoffenses include bullying, theft, harassment, sending sexually explicit photos, along with many more. With the increase of cybercrime, it is predicted that cybersecurity spending will dramatically rise, both for the demand of those trained in cybersecurity and the demand for products.

This chapter illustrates the challenging landscape of this type of crime, the technical knowledge needed if we are going to defend against cyberattacks and some of the challenges in trying to combat this crime. Another information technology offense is to access the computer itself through unauthorized access to tamper with the systems or programs, allowing entry into an individual's information and data. Through access, the bad actors commit fraud, theft, and more, along with the ability to gain valuable, private personal information.

The top five most popular cybercrimes are the following[1]:

1. phishing scams
2. identify theft scams
3. online harassment
4. cyberstalking
5. invasion of privacy

---

[1] https://www.enigmasoftware.com/top-5-popular-cybercrimes-how-easily-prevent-them/.

173

On February 11, 2020 the FBI released their Internet Crime Complaint Center 2019 Internet Crime Report. There were 467,361 complaints, with reported losses in excess of 3.5 billion.[2] They reported phishing, nonpayment/nondelivery, and extortion as the top three scams.

The cost associated with cybercrime encompasses a wide array of costs such as the cost of lost data, loss of currency, theft of personal information (PI), theft of financial information, cost associated with personal health information (PHI), cost to repair and replace data, fraud, and the loss of reputation. There are other costs, these are just a few. We are witnessing an evolution of cybercrime, in part due to the IoT (Internet of Things) and the increase of smart phones, smart watches, cameras, implantable medical devices (i.e., pacemakers), and Bluetooth devices (i.e., headsets, speakers).

Who should be investigating?

Cyberinvestigations require specific skills and training. If an investigation rises to the level for law enforcement, it is critical that proper procedures are followed. If not, you risk more than violating the civil rights of the bad actors. If you engage in anything illegal, you can also be charged with a crime, regardless of any advice the company's corporate counsel's might give. Just as security management doesn't like to be called into an investigation after another department has messed it up, rather than report it to security initially, neither does law enforcement appreciate being called in after company security or the IT department tried to investigate but realized they needed law enforcement. This is why it's important to know when to report the crime and follow the legal process. Following a rigorous process with the intent of collecting evidence that holds up in court is the number one goal. Both the evidence collection and the evidence preservation will determine the outcome. Cybercrimes should be handled by law enforcement or authorities trained to do so or by experts.

Electronic evidence

As stated in the preceding text, preserving evidence is critical. When it comes to electronic evidence and the legal process, both sides share information with each other. The Electronic Discovery Reference Model (EDRM) is a framework that outlines standards for the recovery and

---

[2] https://www.fbi.gov/news/pressrel/press-releases/
fbi-releases-the-internet-crime-complaint-center-2019-internet-crime-report.

discovery of digital data. The Electronic Discovery Reference Model involves eight steps for electronically stored information[3]:

- information management
- identification
- preservation
- collection
- review
- analysis
- production
- presentation

For evidence to be considered admissible in court, it must meet three basic requirements; it is relevant, material, and competent.

Challenges

There are many challenges involved when working cybercrimes, such as: the dollar threshold for federal investigations, local law enforcement funding, training and dedicated staff, interstate crimes, and complicated legal challenges anytime criminal activity encompasses international investigations. Currently in 2020, the United States is inadequately prepared to handle the amount of cybercrimes, suitable investigations, and recover any level of losses. Another challenge is that cybercrime laws vary from state to state and law enforcement is struggling to catch up with the laws and legislature. This is a huge problem and one that is getting worse all over the world. Although police departments are putting together special units to handle cybercrimes, they also have to train officers to become more technical. This crime is so massive to tackle, with not only the issue of passing new legislation but also the lack of trained manpower to combat this crime.

Fighting cybercrime is in the interest of national security because it targets computer systems. Additionally, government computers contain critical data such as political, economic, and critical infrastructure information.

Agencies that have extensive experience in cybercrime are the FBI, Secret Service, NSA, and the Air Force Office of Special Investigations (AFOSI). The Secret Service has always been the leader in financial crimes that many cybercrimes fall under. Whether the FBI or Secret Service will chose to investigate or prosecute depends on the threat level, which is what the amount of damage the case has. An example of a high level

---

[3] https://searchcompliance.techtarget.com/definition/EDRM-electronic-discovery-reference-model.

threat might involve organized crime and terrorism. Both the FBI and Secret Service have established extensive partnerships with private Businesses.

Traditional skills and acquiring technical skills

If you have been an investigator but you haven't investigated cybercrimes, you will want to bring in a trained cybercrime investigator. The investigative skills that you have, such as persistence, passion, inquisitive, and driven, are all great soft skills that can be used in the majority of investigations. Cyberinvestigations are not one of those. Investigating cybercrimes will require you to have an understanding of cybersecurity, be knowledgeable of the law in regard to cybercrimes, and understand the methodology used in the preservation of evidence.

In addition to being experienced in forensics, intrusion detection, malware analysis, basics of programming, risk analysis and mitigation, cloud security, offensive training (black hat), and security analysis, experts have a well-rounded skill set in the field of cyber security. Gaining knowledge in this field is more than a degree, boot camps, or taking cyber courses. Hands on and practice, along with certifications, can leverage the types of cyber investigations you work. Boot camps are 5–6 days in a row, long hours and very intense. All boot camps and trainings are not alike; it will be important to do your research and vet the ones you are interested in. Having experience in data analytics will also be very helpful. Consider the methodology you have used in other areas of security, some will be familiar to you. When conducting investigations involving cybercrimes, you will be evaluating information from a variety of sources and integrating them into a logical outcome to create a conclusion. Intelligence is a product that assembles trustworthy information for the authorities to determine the complexity, criminality, and the level of threat. How successful the cyber investigation is will often be determined by many variables, but it is clearly related to the information you have collected and the intelligence you have gathered.

Earlier in Chapter 7, we discussed preparation and how critical it is. In cyberinvestigations, it is also critical to the success. In the preparation, intelligence is an important element in identifying a bad actor.

Cybertalent in demand

If you are interested in the cyberinvestigations field, you are in luck because there is a huge market for cybertalent. The number of unfilled cybersecurity jobs is expected to grow by 350%, from 1 million positions in

2013 to 3.5 million in 2021.[4] Positions range from intelligence to operations and from security operations to security services. This includes such positions as analysts, forensics, incident response, threat assessments, technical policy, artificial intelligence (AI), compliance, and auditing and more. If you have a good comprehension of cybersecurity, knowledge of the law, and analytical skills, your skills will be in demand.

Privacy legislation

An additional obstacle when investigation a cybercrime is the privacy laws that are being instituted throughout the world. The General Data Protection Regulation (GDPR) is a regulation in the European Union (EU) and European Economic Area (EEA), containing legal requirements on privacy and data protection. The GDPR also addresses transfer of personal data outside of the EU. This regulation is aimed at giving individual control over their personal data. The GDPR has also set a standard for strict data privacy legislation all over the world. Several states in the United States are adopting similar regulations such as Illinois, Nevada, California, Maine, New York, Oregon, Texas, and Washington. These states have enacted legislation effective in the last 6 months, with Maine's Act being effective July 1, 2020.

The California Consumer Privacy Act (CCPA) of 2018, taking effect January 2020, implemented several similar privacy initiatives as the GDPR outlines. It gives California residents unmatched data privacy rights. This affects companies in California, whether or not they are physically located in California. These laws are important to be aware of because of the information and data we collect during investigations and how we share and use this information.

As more US states undoubtably will be looking to implement data privacy laws and privacy legislation, we must be keenly aware of these laws. From a compliance standpoint, these privacy laws will require changes in business processes and corporate awareness.

---

[4] https://cybersecurityventures.com/jobs/.

Investigations using open source intelligence (OSINT)

Open source intelligence (OSINT) refers to intelligence that you collect from any public source. OSINT is a *must* tool that all investigators should be very skilled at. *Open* refers to any public source that is open and available rather than hidden or secret sources. OSINT includes a variety of resources such as: newspapers, ecommerce sites, social media sites, public data, professional association data, or any other internet data. Collecting information from Facebook, Twitter, and other social websites might be easy, but it will take additional skill to sift the truth from fiction. You should use caution when conducting your searches. As investigators, you will want to know how to find information but also how to gain the intelligence from the information. Understanding and knowing what constitutes being ethical is first and foremost. Chapter 3 gives an overview of ethics in reference to open source intelligence gathering. The chapter discusses how your searches may be visible to users of some social media sites.

Getting started

First point, you will want to set up an email account just to use in investigations. Second is in relation to the first point; this new separate email will help to safeguard your anonymity (we discuss more details further in this chapter). Be sure to read the social media sites as some sites do not allow fake accounts. My third suggestion is never believe anything you see or hear unless you vet the information, so do your due diligence. Another rule is to stay relevant by knowing what is changing on the Internet. Because sites are changing often, you will need to know what is current and the rules of conducting OSINT on the various sites. More suggestions are to learn how to use geolocation so you can understand clues within photos and establish where the photo was taken. This helps against claims when pictures/media is presented as evidence.

Research tools

Research is an extremely significant tool in the current Internet era. Whether you are researching information on due diligence, workplace investigations, background investigations, or searching for someone, never underestimate what research can do for you. It is also a critical part of the preparation process for interviews.

Every investigator has their favorite websites and ways to research. This is a technique you will develop over time and your choice and options of available websites will evolve. I have utilized many different companies to run backgrounds, skip tracing, locate people, businesses, due diligence and investigating fraud cases.

I used Autotrack for many years, and in the past 10 years, I've used TLOxp. Both companies provided a good service for the price, had options for membership and the format, which included an overview which was very helpful to pick out the specific areas you want, which saves time. Besides looking at the format, you'll want to look for the option to customized. You can often request a trial period or a demo from various companies to find the right fit for your needs.

These are all factors that you should consider when contracting a company for records, both public and proprietary. Although you can gather information via use of OSINT, TLOxp has tools and technology that you may not have access to. You will also want to evaluate the membership qualifications and pricing options. Some companies charge an annual or monthly fee (subscription fee), while others might have options for pay per request. As my need for this service was intermittent due to a variety of cases, not all requiring such backgrounds, I found that paying for individual reports was the best option for me. These online investigative companies can provide such information, not inclusive: public and private records, neighbors, past locations, assets (not guaranteed to show all assets), family members and helps with identity authentication.

They *do not* provide financial information unless the owners of this information have signed documents requesting financial information specifically. One example might be a housing rental agreement calling out specifically for financial background, therefore signed by the tenant application.

In the United States, information that contains financial information is regulated by federal regulation such as the Gramm-Leach-Bliley Act and the Fair Credit Reporting Act, as further discussed in this chapter. I have found these reports, which I call preliminary, are very helpful because while they do not provide financial information, they do, however, report on public information containing both bankruptcies and liens, both of which will give some insight as to whether you or your client will want to spend additional money to investigate deeper. These reports also aid in fraud prevention and detection, analyzing millions of records at a time. Because these types of backgrounds are relatively inexpensive, it is the first step that I take when taking on a new case because the report helps identify the direction in which I will suggest my client invest in. If your client is a company, the company you use may depend on what your client uses or has access to. Some firms already have license agreements with an investigative system such as "CLEAR," which is an online investigative service by Thomas Reuters.[1]

Some require their clients to be attorneys, licensed investigators, reporters, or law enforcement. The company you chose will likely need to verify your private investigators state license, some will require you have additional security for the location that you keep any background records, or if you are with a law enforcement agency, the name of the agency.

They may also require you to reside in a particular country. You will have to do some research to determine what company will serve your needs best, along with your qualifications to access the company's database. Tools such as TLOxp are governed by the Gramm-Leach-Bliley (GLB) Act and the Driver's Privacy Protection Act (DPPA) and cannot be used for Federal Fair Credit Reporting Act (FCRA) purposes. FCRA prohibits purposes related to credit, insurance, employment, or other financial information.[2]

There are many Internet tools that investigators use. Here are a few:

- *Zaba Search* is a free people-finder website. A private investigator can search for public information using an individual's basic information.
- There are so many if you are looking at family history searches.
  A few are:
  - https://www.findagrave.com/
  - https://www.myheritage.com/search-records
  - https://www.ancestry.com
- *Internet Achieve* is a nonprofit digital library offering free universal access to books, games, software applications, movies, music, and billions of archived web pages.
- Searching for a URL is easy and is public information. The records will show who the registered owner is, their contact information, status, dates, name servers, and IP addresses and locations.
  - http://whois.domaintools.com/
- *Public Record Retriever Network* (PRRN) is where you can go to access government records for local, state, or federal courts, including recorders offices for name searches. You can also request copies of documents. PRRN members are often hired to assist with the

---

[1] https://legal.thomsonreuters.com/en/products/clear-investigation-software.

[2] https://www.transunion.com/client-support/compliance-notifications.

preemployment screening, investigations, lending, litigation, or legal compliance.[3]

- *E-investigator* is a comprehensive site that provides a multitude of resources for private. Investigators and law enforcement officers and reference guides.
- *Pacer* (Public Access to Court Electronic Records) is one of my favorite sites as you can search in either "read only" (view) mode or "E-File" as an attorney or nonattorney. For view mode, it allows you to read only, but you can still print. If you want to electronically file documents, you will need to go to the E-File option. The charge is only $0.10 per page. They have a free training site and a user manual. I use this to find bankruptcies. They cap the total amount so the information is great along with the price.
  - https://www.pacer.gov/
- To search for information across the globe (153 contracting states) using the *World Intellectual Property Organization*, you can find information on topics such as copyright, artificial intelligence policy, including trademarks, global brand, and patents.
  - http://www.wipo.int/pct/en/pct_contracting_states.html
- For US Patents and Trademarks, giving you policy information on copyrights, trademarks, patents, enforcement, trade secrets, along with resources including attorneys, inventors, researchers, and patent and trademark practitioners. Also a wealth of information when you have a due diligence or trademark case.
  - https://www.uspto.gov/trademarks-application-process/search-trademark-database
- ISP (Internet Service Provider) is a list of Internet service providers, providing their legal contact and instructions on how to get a subpoenas, court orders, and search warrants.
  - https://www.search.org/resources/isp-list/
- Been Verified is a website that provides criminal histories on people and career history and addresses.
- Another free government site in the United States is the US Securities and Exchange Commission which uses EDGAR, the Electronic Data Gathering, Analysis, and Retrieval system.
  - https://www.sec.gov/edgar.shtml
  This provides information on companies filing with the SEC (Security and Exchange Commission). This database contains millions of companies and individual filings, and benefits investors, and more. Access to EDGAR is free as it is a public database. You can examine a company's financial records and the filings they made. The Office of Investor Education and Advocacy developed a guide to help new users.
  - https://www.sec.gov/oiea/Article/edgarguide.html

---

[3] http://prrn.us/.

- *Dogpile.com* is a metasearch engine that searches other search engines. This can save you time and be very useful if you are looking for images, videos, news, shopping, or simple going to the web. This is just one option among the many choices.
  - https://www.dogpile.com/
- Some specific sites to search mobile phones, car history, employment history, investigator tools, or people search tools are:
  - www.mobilephoneno.com
  - www.carfax.com/entry.cfx
  - www.theworknumber.com
  - www.pimall.com
  - http://find.intelius.com/index.php
- You can also research any company site web pages and the County Clerk of Court Public Information.
  - https://archive.org/
  - https://www.zoominfo.com/
  - https://epic.org/privacy/choicepoint/
  - https://www.lexisnexis.com/en-us/gateway.page

There are also search engines called metasearch engines. These search other search engines and get the best of various engines.

These are just a few as it would take an entire book to list all the available websites that can be useful to an investigator. Social networking sites are also very helpful in preparing for interviews. Information on these sites can help you determine deception, formulate questions, or determine background of a subject.

Remember that when searching, expect anything. It may be an easy find or you may have to think outside the box. **Trust but verify** all information and practice due diligence when researching open source intelligence. There are many ways to search a name, besides the exact name. You should keep in mind that the specific search engine that you are using also have their own rules.

One example is: one of the most commonly used email providers ignores periods and capitalization in usernames. You will want to understand the rules of the various sites to understand how to search within them. I will use Google as an example on learning to search. If you are new at searching on Google, you can go to http://www.googleguide.com/ for an online learning tool and reference guide. You will learn how to set your searches at 100 results instead of the 10, set by default, when and how to use the "*" feature to narrow results, common phrases, and more useful tools. Google also allows you to search images, news, maps, products, and many more options. You can also add Google alerts if you want them to automatically alert you when there are new results for a search you submitted. Google maps is great for driving directions; however, another tool within Google maps that I use often is the "my map," when I want to narrow in on a geographical location.

This also has a distance measurement tool that is helpful when needing exact measurements between distances. This provides critical, detailed information for documentation to include in the case file.

There are many different search techniques such as: adding quotations around specific words, the order that your keywords are written in, using all uppercase or lowercase, and inserting an asterisk (*) instead of the entire word or phrase. For many reasons, ethics being the critical one, you always want to know the site you are going to and the site that you are currently. Know what you are clicking before you go to any site because your computer can be tracked so every site you visit that visit is tracked. Also good to remember is that free site are not always safe sites. Many virus's attack through free sites and free apps, such as free music sites, pornography sites, and other free sites. Have you ever wondered why they are "free?" Your computers operating systems and the browsers that you use will also influence your searches. This is why you want to search for the same information on various browsers.

Search engines

Common Internet search engines in the United States are Google, Microsoft Edge, and Bing. Other search engines include:

- DuckDuckGo, which doesn't collect, store, or pass on any personal information about its users. It is free from ad targeting.
- Startpage has strict privacy controls.
- Baidu is the popular search engine in Asia.
- Yandex is popular in Russia and other countries.

If you want to search quickly, try using a search engine like www.dogpile.com or www.beaucoup.com, which compiles results from various search engines but gives you one report.

Be sure to look more in depth than Google, Firefox, or the websites I've listed. Always verify your information with another source. To repeat my previous comment, always practice due diligence. Be diligent with the information you enter because as you've probably heard the phrase, if you put garbage in, you will get garbage out.

Social network sites

There are many sites that are social sites that connect people like the well-known Facebook site. Others are Twitter, Instagram, Tumblr, Google +, LinkedIn, and Snapchat, to name a few. There are also dating sites, hobby groups, school groups, or others defined by your friends, hobbies, or interests. Some are free, others are paid membership like dating sites. If you don't already have an email address that you use for searches, go to Gmail and create one now that you can use to register with the social network sites making searching private.

Social network is a valuable tool used in so many ways through both the investigative and interview process; therefore investigators should be paying attention to social media. You can learn a lot about the case, the subject, and the witnesses. There are many reports about social media use, one report finding that 45% of the population has a daily active social media account, and according to Oberlo, Facebook is the market leader.[4] It also reports that 90% of millennials have social media accounts, 77.5% of Gen Xers have them, while baby boomers make up a smaller, and 48.2% have a social media account. This information will be valuable as you have cases and will determine what information you can retrieve in person or through open source.

From Facebook, you can retrieve information such as the history and timeline from photos. You can also determine places visited or current location. Everyone has the ability to set up their own privacy controls, but not everyone takes advantage of doing this. Facebook is frequently used for workers compensation cases and loss prevention departments because of the type of information posted. If you have an email address but you don't have a face and want one, enter the email in the search bar within Facebook.

Twitter has both public and protected tweets. With public tweets, all members' status and updates are visible so anyone can see your twitter updates. These updates can also be indexed by search engines. With protected tweets, people request to follow a user and must be approved to see the protected tweets. When tweets are protected, they don't appear in searches.

Social network sites can be instrumental when profiling a person of interest. Due to privacy settings, there may be limits of what you can retrieve. You should check the privacy settings for the social network sites you use. Knowing the privacy settings will allow you to understand what your limitations will be. With each post you make, you leave your digital footprint behind that is then owned by the site.

There are also unique social networks that exist throughout the world that you may have never heard of because the site may be unique to that country or culture.

Here are a few social network sites across the globe:

- *QZone*, this is a social network site in China created in 2005. It allows users to keep diaries and write blogs have photos, videos, and music. This site lets the users customize their background, providing other preferences.

---

[4] https://www.oberlo.com/blog/social-media-marketing-statistics.

- *VK*, formerly VKontakte, meaning "in touch" in Russia, is the largest European social network and is the dominant site rather than Facebook in Russia. It is very similar to Facebook when it comes to building their profile, photos, and adding their friends.

Browsing anonymously

While good investigators use open source intelligence to collect information and data, they also need more in-depth search tools. If you want to do some digging and searching for your investigation but you don't want to be seen, then using an anonymous search engine might be an option to consider. For searching online, with some amount of privacy, try browsing in *private/incognito* mode. These private browsers *do not guarantee* that you won't be tracked, but they offer some level of privacy. Some browsers have this feature. Firefox calls it private browsing, while chrome calls it incognito. While some say they don't save your browser history, I recommend still using caution.

You can also go back and forth between private and public browsing. If you are using a Windows machine, simple press Ctrl, Shift, and n, and if you are on a Mac, press the Command, Shift, and n keys at one time. Browsing will be the same on private browsing, as you normally would enter a site. Surfing the web and hiding your identity is easy by using a virtual private network, known as a VPN. If you have a VPN, then you don't need to go to a private browser because everything you do on the VPN is secure. You can chose wherever in the world you want to be. If you are in New York and chose South Africa, any site you go to will have your IP listed as being in South Africa. Your choice can be different each time you use your VPN. This service is relatively inexpensive. I personally prefer "Private Internet access"; however, there are many options.[5] Search engines like DuckDuckGO does not track you and lets you be in control of your information. If you have never used it, there are instructions on sites such as Facebook, YouTube, and others.

The dark web

It is important to offer you an optional tool in investigations; therefore, I will provide limited information about the dark web. For a more private way to search, there are special browsers that are designed with the purpose of not collecting any user data. While there are several, Tor, Epic, and

---

[5] https://www.privateinternetaccess.com/.

Brave are the most effective.[6] All provide free downloads to Windows or Mac systems. These sites block ads, hide your IP address, and delete your browsing history as a few of the ways they keep your identity hidden.

The dark web is where I might search if I am investigating a specific fraud case such as stolen credit card account numbers, iPhones, iPads, bank account numbers, or a particular item stolen. (I also search on other sites such as craigslist and eBay.) It is not a site that I would sent to others unless they are searching for something and the dark web is a likely place to find it. The Tor is more than a private Internet browser, it is a specialized software browser. This part of the Internet is not indexed by search engines. You may or may not want to go to this site, or even know about it, because it goes deep into the very dark parts of the Internet. The main characteristic of the Tor is its anonymity, which attracts bad actors; hence, it is a hotbed for criminal activity.

To access the Tor, you simply type Tor-Download into your browser. Additional investigative tools:

- Review Internet media postings
- Review potential catalog print publications
- Physical surveillance of public property

If forensic review under legal authority (if company-owned property), refer to company policy

- Review of E-mails (provided you stay within legal and ethical boundaries)
- Search of temporary Internet files
- Cookies
- Favorites
- History
- Unallocated space
- OLK directory
- Outlook PST files
- Registry activity

Privacy legislation

With the growing concern over privacy, it's important to discuss the impact of maintaining control of privacy and the impact on investigators that collect, use, and safeguard this personal data. Because privacy legislation will affect the information you collect from the states that you work

---

[6] https://www.computerworld.com/article/3299429/get-serious-about-privacy-with-epic-brave-tor-browsers.html.

or collect information in, it will be your responsibility to know, understand, and comply with applicable state or federal regulations. Personal identifying information (PII), also known as sensitive personal information (SPI), is any data that are unique to a specific person like a social security number, social insurance number, driver's license number, or a passport. Personal, sensitive information is protected across the globe by various regulations and jurisdictional laws. In Europe (EU), personal data are much broader as indicated in the General Data Protection Regulation (GDPR), which took effect in May 2018. This regulation affects investigators because most of the information collected during an internal investigation is covered in the GDPR. Investigators in the EU that are conducting internal investigations that use the data of EU employees should keep in mind the overall GDPR requirements and national laws relating to the GDPR.[7] Even corporations outside the EU need to know and comply with this regulation if there is any connection to the EU, including storing EU data outside of the EU. GDPR affects investigations and whether the investigator is with a corporation, forensics, or law enforcement agency, any review of personal information must be acceptable under this regulation. If data are to be transferred to the United States, participating corporations offers a way to transfer data via the *EU/US Privacy Shield.*

Similarly states across the United States are also broadening their privacy and transparency regulations. California enacted the first state privacy bill, Consumer Privacy Act (CCPA) that takes effect January 2020. Although the CCPA's purpose is to control what personal information a business can collect, disclose, and sell from their consumers, California's definition of PII is much more broad than other states in the United States. Other states in the United States that are revising their disclosure of personal information collected and safeguarding personal information are Nevada[8] and Massachusetts.[9] Vermont requires businesses that collect personal information of consumers, register annually with the Secretary of State.[10]

---

[7] https://www.dlapiper.com/en/us/insights/publications/2018/07/global-anticorruption-newsletter/the-gdpr-impact-investigations/.

[8] https://www.leg.state.nv.us/NRS/NRS-603A.html.

[9] https://www.mass.gov/regulations/201-CMR-1700-standards-for-the-protection-of-personal-information-of-ma-residents.

[10] https://legislature.vermont.gov/statutes/section/09/062/02447.

United Nations Trade and Development

According to the United Nations Conference on Trade and Development (UNCTAD), there are approximately 107 countries that have put in place legislature to secure the protection of data and privacy.[11] The UNCTAD is now mapping cyberlaws in a variety of fields, one of them being data protection/privacy, within their 194 member states. They consider whether a country already adopted such legislation or if a draft is pending.[12] There are other states and new legislation being drafted, and it is imperative that you understand the laws in your jurisdiction and how they apply to the data you collect, share, and store.

Your personal style

The most valuable tool to develop is your own personal style and rapport—developing the ability to form a relationship, almost an intimate one, with your subject. This might not be necessary for witnesses or all interviewees, but if you are interviewing a subject that you need a confession from, you will need to form a close, almost intimate relationship. Doing so will require you to be empathetic without being judgmental or accusatory. You need that person to open up to you. As valuable as OSINT is, it doesn't replace what a face-to-face interview or investigating in person can give you.

---

[11] https://unctad.org/en/Pages/DTL/STI_and_ICTs/ICT4D-Legislation/eCom-Data-Protection-Laws.aspx.
[12] https://unctad.org/en/Pages/DTL/STI_and_ICTs/ICT4D-Legislation/eCom-Global-Legislation.aspx.

Fraud investigations

Introduction

White-collar crime is generally synonymous with a broad range of frauds committed by business and other professionals. Perpetrators use deceit, cheating, scams, and, most troubling, the violation of trust. Many fraudsters appear as everyday honest (of course they are not honest) people that you would expect to believe. Many of those who commit white-collar crimes commit these crimes while they are working. While the primary motivator for fraud may be financial, it has other devastating effects associated to it such as productivity and company reputation. Most agree that fraud is generally nonviolent in nature; however, fraud is not a victimless crime. Just as a violent crime is devasting to a victim, so are the victims of fraud schemes/white-collar schemes. Being a victim can be devastating and has been linked to an increased risk of depression and suicide.[1] Fraud is on the rise and currently costs American businesses an estimated $652 billion each year,[2] and this doesn't give the billions lost in indirect costs.

Over the past 40 years, I have investigated crimes such as corporate embezzlement, health care fraud, retail fraud, the Nigerian fraud ring, financial fraud, and other fraud schemes. All have had serious implications to businesses, our wallets, our criminal justice system, and our social values. There are devastating effects on businesses, and frankly everyone should be concerned because ultimately we all pay the cost of this crime through increased costs, taxes, licenses, insurance, travel, health care, and everyday costs. Most disturbing is the fact that fraud is under reported, and little is done to prevent or punish the bad actors. Fraud is an economic crime that most of society seems to be unenthusiastic, apathetic, and disinterested in preventing or detecting. Society dictates the controls we put on fraud crime, the implications and the punishment. Furthermore,

---

[1] https://www.mielerymsza.com/blog/2018/10/effects-of-white-collar-crime-on-society/.
[2] https://www.allbusiness.com/the-true-cost-of-fraud-direct-costs-2-5222152-1.html.

recovering losses is extremely low. Those companies that take proactive measures and reward ethical performance tend to have fewer cases of criminal activity.

Whistleblowers protection

Many businesses have set up hotline phone numbers to encourage reporting of suspicious activity. When someone does make a report, it should be a priority to protect any such whistleblower. As investigators, ethics and integrity are paramount and complete confidentiality including information about and from the whistleblower is critical. Every business needs a whistleblower, whether or not the information is valid, you are still obligated to investigate, protect all information and verify. Remember to, *trust but verify*. There are whistleblower protections such as the Whistleblower Protection Act (WPA) for federal employees who report an illegal act, waste of funds, and abuse of authority and more. There is also the Whistleblower Protection Enhancement Act (WPEA) that Congress passed in 2012 to help federal employees report fraud, waste, and abuse. Occupational Safety and Health Administration (OSHA) also has a whistleblower protection program. These agencies also have antiretaliation programs in place for the whistleblower's protection. Most recent is the amended Securities and Exchange Act of 1934 that was referred to the Senate on July 10, 2019 and is known as the Whistleblower Protection Reform Act of 2019. This further defines whistleblower incentives and protections as well as extending the antiretaliation protections afforded to whistleblowers. Fraud investigators have a great appreciation for whistleblowers that are courageous enough to identify fraudsters. Sometimes the whistleblower is ignored and forced to remain silent; however, as professional investigators, we should have the experience and knowledge to understand the ramifications of such ignorance. Many whistleblowers who have come forward with exposing billions of dollars, reported fraudulent activity many times before an investigation was started.

One such whistleblower is Howard Wilkinson, a former employee of Danske Bank. Mr. Wilkinson, now considered an international hero, risked his career to expose, what may be, the largest money laundering scheme in history. His exposure of this money-laundering scheme was courageous and is an example of ethical behavior. Mr. Wilkinson first reported on irregularities internally 5 years earlier; however, the bank failed to act on his report of the billion dollar money-laundering scheme from Russia to Western banks.[3] Important to address in this chapter is the relentless efforts that Mr. Wilkinson's went to address his concerns along

---

[3] https://www.kkc.com/whistleblower/howard-wilkinson/.

with investigative reports into financial documents supporting these concerns. He first went to three Danske employees, all bank management employees only to get a promise of follow-up along with excuses about so-called mistakes. After a year a senior bank official informed Wilkinson that this particular client was no longer a client. However, in addition to that disclosure, the senior official mentioned other intriguing comments such as that client had been a "so-called" relative of Vladimir Putin, which now caught more of Wilkinson's attention. Months later, Wilkinson again sent emails, describing his findings, to four Danske officials including the chief risk officer, group chief auditor, the head of AML, and the head of the Baltic Banking division.[4] This all lead to Mr. Wilkinson's investigating several of the most profitable LLP clients, determining they too were false and appeared similar to the first client he reported, including that all shared the same UK address. Wilkinson then sends another report to the auditor that he initially reported this, with no resolve. It was apparent to Wilkinson that the bank was not going to address this matter. In total, Wilkinson reviewed 16 LLP's, 15 with the same address and fake accounts. Wilkinson made two more whistleblowing reports to lawyers and board members after which time, he resigned. After all of these reports to Danske, the Danish Financial Supervisory Authority (FSA) began investigating these matters. This case is so fascinating because of the persistence of Wilkinson to report this fraudulent activity to management, the disregard and protection of Wilkinson, the blatant, deliberate failure by the bank to act and so many of Danske's controls were ineffective. When the law firm Danske hired released its report, the CEO, Thomas F. Borgen, resigned. Other fall-outs include the Copenhagen International financial crimes unit brought charges against Danske, preliminary charges against Danske's former CEO Thomas F. Borgen and nine other Danske bank officials, including searching their homes. Estonian regulators also forced closure of the operations at Danske's Estonia location.[5]

Mr. Wilkinson never intended on being publicly identified; however, his identity was illegally disclosed by Dankse Bank employees in September of 2018. Mr. Wilkinson later testified in front of the Danish Parliament and the European Parliament that he was disheartened and saddened with Denmark's lack of whistleblower protection. This story was on CBS's 60 min show[6]: *How the Danske Bank money-laundering scheme involving $230 billion unraveled.*[7] Mr. Wilkinson is being awarded the Cliff Robertson Sentinel Award "For Choosing Truth over Self," by ACFE at

---

[4] Fraud Magazine, March April 2020, page 36–44 by Dick Carozza "The Smoke Detector."
[5] ibid.
[6] https://www.kkc.com/whistleblower/howard-wilkinson/.
[7] https://www.cbsnews.com/video/how-the-danske-bank-money-laundering-scheme-involving-230-billion-unraveled-60-minutes-2019-05-19/.

their 31st Annual Conference this summer (June 2020). He will be speaking about his experience with this case at this conference. The Cliff Robertson award was started for Cliff Robertson in 2003. Robertson was an Academy Award-Winning Actor who uncovered that a powerful Hollywood producer creating fraudulent royalty checks by forging signatures from the intended recipients. After this powerful Hollywood producer threatened Robertson that if he reported him, Robertson would never again work. Robertson was indeed blacklisted in the industry for years.[8]

Corporate executives need to observe how agencies, specifically the DOJ and the Securities and Exchange Commission, both prosecute and enforce laws and regulations. An anticorruption agency is a specialized law enforcement agency that fights political corruption and other corruption activities. Some of these agencies are constitutional where others are individual statutes. Countries across the globe have anticorruption agencies. A few examples are: Australia has the Independent Commission Against Corruption in the New South Wales, the Crime and Corruption Commission in Queensland, the Independent Commissioner Against Corruption in South Australia, the Corruption and Crime Commission in Western Australia, the Anticorruption in South Korea, and in the United Kingdom, the Serious Fraud Office. In the United States, we have agencies such as the Foreign Corrupt Practices Act, along with the Office of the Comptroller of the Currency (OCC). The OCC regulates and puts controls in place to deter and detect money laundering, terrorist financing, and other criminal acts and misuse of our nation's financial institutions.[9] The Banks Secrecy Act (BSA)/ AML maintains compliance with the OCC through formal and informal enforcement action.

While investigators can be both experienced or trained, specific areas of fraud, whether mortgage fraud, healthcare fraud, or organized crime fraud, have unique characteristics, requiring specific skills sets for these types of crimes. It takes training and experience to understand the elements connected specific fraud type.

As a member of the Association of Certified Fraud Examiners (ACFE) since its inception, it is said that if you are an accountant, investigator, lawyer, and criminologist, you will make the perfect fraud investigator. Although these are the perfect skills needed, it is a rare combination to find all of these in many fraud investigators. Since earning my CFE in 1994, I have witnessed a larger percentage of accountants each year for the skills that accountants have. I will discuss further into this chapter.

Covered in this chapter are some specific cases to describe some of the unique characteristics of fraud, internal and external, along with the

---

[8] ibid.

[9] https://www.occ.treas.gov/topics/supervision-and-examination/bsa/index-bsa.html.

3. Specific investigations and skills

significance of whistleblowers. Also described are specific skill-sets beyond the required investigative skills, for these unique types of fraud crimes.

Nigerian fraud ring

My first experience investigating fraud was back in the early 1980s. This case was while working for a national car rental company who owned their own brand of credit cards. The loss and impact for the company I worked was huge because this fraudulent scheme allowed them to fraudulently obtain credit cards, ultimately using the fraudulent credit cards to fraudulently rent vehicles, often stealing the vehicle. The loss could be $30,000–$50,000 per vehicle. This fraud scheme was known as the Nigerian fraud ring. I want to clearly state that this was a particular fraud ring and because they originated out of Nigeria, they were labeled as the Nigerian fraud ring. This label is not intended as a representation of Nigerians. This group of Nigerians came to the United States with the intent purpose of defrauding people and businesses. One of their many schemes was to obtain credit cards through fraudulent means. The group would apply for a credit card using someone's credit history, social security number, and other personal identification but having the credit card sent to their PO Box or another fraudulent address. This was the case that made me realized that, as much as I wanted to solve these crimes and arrest those involved, many law enforcement agencies didn't or couldn't help. This was in large part, due to lack of training at local departments, time, and the element of white-collar crime instead of a violent crime. While this particular case had me spending 3–4 weeks at a time in Miami, I was fortunate enough to find a Miami-Dade (known back in the 1980s as Metro-Dade) police officer, along with an attorney at the State Attorney General's office, to work with me. Several of the lessons they taught me were the following: as there were so many homicides, fraud is not the number one priority and also, because many types of fraudulent crime of this nature crosses city, county, and state lines where local law enforcement agencies are both understaffed and they do not have the funds available for this level of involvement. Another impactful trip the state attorney general took me was to the coast line to discuss how the natural elements influence criminal activity and the possibility of searching every means of transportation to stop criminal activity that could never be done. I was both disappointed and disheartened when realizing the magnitude and sophistication of these crimes and the complexity of solving them or even recovering our losses.

The Nigerian fraudsters are also known for a broad range of fraud scams, some involving check fraud schemes, money laundering, romance schemes, business email schemes, and more. More recently, Ikechuwku "Ike" Amadi, a dual Canadian and Nigerian citizen, was a member of the Nigerian-based criminal ring known as the Black Axe Group. The FBI investigated this group for over 6 years, starting with them defrauding a small Georgia law firm out of almost $100,000 and continuing with a complex international fraud scheme to include losses of over $10 million dollars. I point out some of these cases to show the effort, time spent, and cost that are involved. Skill investigators for fraud schemes should have the following:

- partnerships with local and federal law enforcement agencies
- communications skills
- open source investigation skills (refer to Chapter 20, Open source investigations)
- compliance laws
- knowledge of credit card policies and laws
- knowledge of intricate fraud schemes
- ability to retrieve records
- field investigation experience
- ability to travel
- interviewing skills
- written skills for comprehensive reports
- ability to have dialog with government agencies
- knowledge of background investigations
- patience due to lengthy investigation process

Organized retail crime investigations

My intent in this section is to provide an snapshot of what organized retail crime is, some of their schemes and challenges investigating this group, and the additional training investigators will need to investigate these criminal entities. They can be groups of two or more or gangs that participate in illegally obtaining retail merchandize through theft or fraud. Their intent is to steal significant quantities for profit. A wide variety of fraud schemes are orchestrated by organized crime groups. The schemes encompass a wide range of crimes, anywhere from an uncomplicated theft of merchandize to very intricate schemes involving refunds, gift cards, and even fraudulent credit cards.

Loss prevention officers that worked for me were responsible for shoplifting arrests, otherwise known as external theft cases; they were not qualified nor trained to investigate internal fraud, embezzlement, or organized crime. Loss prevention officers are typically hourly employees that may or may not be experienced or may even be contract officers. Due to a variety of elements, some complex, and intricate, investigating organized criminal activity requires additional skills and training because organized crime groups are sophisticated, educated, and often have well-planned thefts. While some of these groups often operate locally or even regionally, other known groups operate on an international level. Organized retail crime

(ORC) rings are responsible for many billions of dollars in losses every year, and they can have devastating effects on businesses, ultimately the cost that shoppers pay. While investigating theft for a major retailer, ORC groups stole by using booster bags or repackaging while others were stealing, then fencing their stolen merchandize.

For those interested in investigating organized crime, there are multitudes of new positions today that are specific to organized crime investigations. Organized retail crime investigators work alongside their asset protection partners while having specific skills in ORC investigations. Communication skills are extremely important because you will need to build and maintain partnerships with law enforcement, other security agencies and retail business partners. Ideally the perfect organized retail crime investigator has skills consistent with a criminologist, investigator, attorney, analyst, and effectively communicate with people.

Skills necessary for such positions are as follows:

- advanced written skills for detailed documentation
- communication skills
- knowing the tools indicative of organized crime rings
- ability to identify steps and methodology of organized crime
- data analytics
- understanding of the legal process
- provide awareness training
- evidence recovery for successful prosecution
- ability to deliver action plans
- partner with leadership teams
- open source investigation skills (refer to Chapter 20, Open source investigations)
- lead and manage ORC teams
- ability to coordinate aggressive blitz operations
- coordinate with prosecution teams

Organized retail crime is just one of the many criminal activities that organized crime focuses on.

Organized criminal rings are also active in:

- prostitution
- illegal drugs
- human trafficking
- child pornography
- illegal firearms
- illegal arts and cultural items
- fake/knock off goods of name brands

Investigating these require a high level of open source investigations and coordinating with local and federal law enforcement. The Federal

Bureau of Investigation (FBI) has a loss threshold, which means that each office has a budget limitation for which they can't investigate a loss of less than a particular amount. Most of their offices set this threshold at $100,000 for white-collar crimes while a few offices set their threshold at $500,000. This threshold is due to the fact that a white collar crime case can easily cost the agency and ultimately taxpayers over $200,000. While the FBI's investigative jurisdiction extends to more than 200 categories of federal crimes, their white-collar crime program is their largest of all their criminal programs. Some of their targets are public corruption, human trafficking, health care fraud, election criminal violations, telemarking fraud, and more. One of the FBI's priorities is to continue the investigation of corporate fraud. Corporate fraud does enormous damage to the US economy with substantial losses to investors. The FBI's focuses their efforts on crimes that involve accounting schemes, self-dealing by corporate executives, and obstruction of justice.[10] As stated in the first paragraph in this section, these corporate fraud crimes are perpetrated by deceiving employees, investors, auditors, and others at the corporation. The FBI works closely with the US Securities and Exchange Commission (SEC), Commodity Future Trading Commission (CFTC), other regulatory agencies and law enforcement agencies. Corporate investigators that work on these types of cases might work in jobs like: Antimoney laundering (AML) investigators, certified fraud examiners, financial investigators, and compliance related positions.

Skills for money laundering positions and financial crime positions may include the following:

- excellent writer to prepare investigative and security action reports (SAR)
- ability to read financial/profit and loss reports
- understanding of corporate policies and control environment
- ability to triage investigation cases
- experience in antiterrorist financing
- experience in antimoney laundering
- experience in fraud
- experience in intelligence
- strong analytical skills
- ability to work with local, federal law enforcement
- understanding of due diligence
- training in risk management
- understanding of trading
- ability to use a variety of technical tools
- ability to work effectively with a team
- know compliance regulations and laws

---

[10]https://www.fbi.gov/investigate/white-collar-crime.

Internal fraud

Internal fraud is committed by an employee or employees within your organization. These can be theft of money, fraudulent payments, asset misappropriation, fraudulent financial statements, theft of assets, theft of corporate internal documents, skimming, and more. It can also be the misuse of company property or company funds.

In the world of retail, internal fraud might involve the misuse of credit card information, chargeback schemes, cash receipt schemes, gift card schemes, write off schemes, inventory manipulation, returns without receipt, altered register receipts, and many more. In my experience, employees start with one scheme, but over time, they experiment with other ways in making more money faster and less evident. It was very prevalent to arrest an employee after they devised many different schemes. We may have focused in on one particular scheme, only to find out the many things they did when we interviewed them. Interviewing employees was something I mastered and 100% of the time, ended with a full confession and statements. I rarely had to go to court because I focused on the evidence involving data analytics, often video evidence and other evidence that made prosecution easy. As discussed in Chapter 10, Interviewing techniques, every investigator will have their own style. Mine included often asking the associate to help me understand discrepancies and that I needed their help in solving losses for company financials. They rarely realized that they would be terminated, held accountable, and charged with fraud. They were usually willing to help resolve an audit issue. This was one technique that I combined with others over the years as your techniques will also evolve. I found that treating the employee respectfully was also a key in obtaining the confession. I encourage you to practice interviewing and learn different styles so you can find the style that best fits your personality, one that allows the criminal to want to fully cooperate.

Even those companies that have internal investigators may have to consider hiring outside investigators for certain cases. Consider that different cases require different skills and often require the skills of an investigator from the outside. Companies need to access whether their internal investigator has the skills and experience for a particular case, if they have the time to focus on this particular case, or if there may be a conflict of interest due to whom or what is being investigated.

Internal partnerships

The most valuable information my experience has taught me is, you can't succeed as an internal investigator without your internal partnerships. Building relationships with your internal partners is critical if you want a career as a corporate investigator. There have been investigations that internal audit worked on for 6 months to over a year before coming to me with their findings. You will find that auditors uncover irregularities sometimes without knowing what their results actually mean because they often see their reports and data without seeing the entire picture and other elements of a case. In an embezzlement case committed by a franchise who rented vehicles under the car rental company I worked, it was internal audit that alerted me. This franchise would submit their paperwork (seven pages to every rental agreement at that time), but instead of submitting one rental agreement to the corporate office, they would have rented another six vehicles by using the other six pages of the original agreement, ultimately embezzling the money from the other six rentals but only reporting one rental. These are times that internal auditors can discover irregularities that we wouldn't know until they bring them to us. I have found the most success by working with auditors and other internal partners.

Partnerships that you may consider working with are those on the leadership team, human resources, and legal counsel. Many cases have initially been brought to me in general conversations with a manager, about something they told me about one of their employees, without really understanding what the comment would ultimately mean, because we didn't advertise internal investigations (unless they had a reason to know about it). One such case is a particular cash register had a fraud charge on a different credit card holder account every Sunday. One event lead me to run data analysis against credit card abnormalities by register, and this could have taken many months; however, the manager that oversaw that department told me about one of his employees that told every Monday off. While talking to some other employees on a casual basis, one mentioned his custody battle and the need for money. All of the pieces led to a very specific investigation and the installation of an overhead camera, which lead to an arrest after a couple of months. The significant part was the information given to me by the manager without understanding the information. This happens often through the relationships you make with internal partners. Being included in leadership team meetings helps build those relationships.

Skills for building relationships are as follows:

- integrity
- ethical
- proving unbiased
- being professional
- communication skills
- data analytics
- ability to follow through
- proven history of confidentiality

- manage thoroughness of undercover projects
- multitask
- patience as internal operations take time

External fraud

External fraud is *fraud that is* committed by outsiders of the organization. Social engineering is one of the five most likely used schemes that fraudsters use to deceive and manipulate their victims. The priority for businesses today is to protect their assets against data breach and cybercrimes (see Chapter 19, Cybercrimes and investigations). Because this crime targets individuals directly, there is no antivirus or protection from this. The perpetrator uses social engineering by impersonating your coworker, client, or vendor. The benefit for them is ultimately money but they can also obtain personal information, credit card information, and sensitive company information.

External fraud not only may be investigated by corporate investigators but also is contracted to agencies specializing in external fraud. The skills required will be directly related to the type of criminal activity. While some skills may overlap, some will be very skill specific such as money-laundering investigations, and organized crime.

The increase of white-collar crime

White-collar crime is on the rise, and there may be several factors for this, several tie directly into the fact that our population is aging. Health care fraud is a white-collar crime, which is on the rise based on the misrepresentation or deception made with the intention of benefiting a recipient of healthcare. The fraud and abuse may involve billing, kickbacks, medical testing, billing for services not provided, and more. Another crime increasing with the increased aging population is technically related.

Another crime on the increase is the fraud exploitation of the elderly. Because fraud involves deceit, they target credit cards and other ways to obtain money through electronic way. This is similar to financial fraud except it is termed financial exploitation because they abuse their relationship of trust.

Because white-collar crime is nonviolent and fits the professional worker, the fact that our population is aging increases the likelihood of the perpetrator being older. It is likely that this crime will continue to increase in the future.

Investigators will need skills to investigate healthcare fraud, financial fraud, cybercrimes, and more.

As time increases, skills in technology and open source investigations will become more valuable.

Workplace violence and harassment investigations

The subject matter of workplace investigation is very broad as it encompasses any investigation in the workplace, for example, harassment, sexual harassment, violence, theft, and generally speaking, anything the company wants investigated. In this chapter, we will look at internal investigations and some of the nuances of each depending on the type of investigation. The company's policy should dictate how investigations are handled and by whom. In many companies, human resources may receive an initial complaint and handle it depending on the nature of the complaint. If there is a loss to the company and may involve an issue of noncompliance with laws, often the responsibility of the investigation may be with human resources. If a company has a security department, security may be called in to assist with human resources, or security may take the lead. Most often, company policy will dictate the roles and responsibilities of departments and their staff. The size of the company will also determine roles and responsibilities; larger companies are more likely to have specific procedures when it involves workplace violence prevention, mitigation and intervention, sexual harassment, fraud and embezzlement. Not every incident will lead to an investigation; however, your company's policy should dictate what leads to an investigation.

This chapter does not cover fraud investigations as that is found in a separate chapter. Policy may call for a threat assessment to be completed first or it could call for a threat assessment, a perpetrators history evaluation, and a threat assessment team meeting. Deciding on an investigation is based on factual information you have from the person who first reported the behavior and all of the information you gather to justify opening a case. Investigating these matters properly can protect your company but how the behavior is investigated can also negatively affect your company's reputation. Regardless of how a complaint comes in, a prompt and thorough investigation is imperative.

A formal investigation has these elements:

- is prompt
- initiated with clear strategy
- viewed as credible by stakeholders
- investigators are experienced
- identify persons to be interviewed
- confidential
- well documented
- clear scope
- well organized
- provides protection and support for the victim
- conducted in a way to protect the accused
- investigation conducted using clearly defined policy
- protects the organization from liability

The investigator must be:

- credible
- nonbiased/objective
- experienced
- have great interview skills that facilitate others to share information
- be well prepared
- an excellent note taker
- a good communicator
- anticipate the unknown (witnesses, questions, etc.)

Internal investigations are identified through various ways, for example, fraud may be identified through an internal audit, a security review, shortage in some form, or a manager or coworker. Sexual harassment is often identified through a specific complaint from a victim or witness. Workplace violence may be identified through a manager or coworker, but there is also a chance of needing to response in short notice.

As all experienced investigators will tell you, cases are often started from an initial complaint; however, once the investigation and interviews are underway, aspects of a case and the scope can change.

Investigations need to follow policy to ensure consistency. This will be important; should the company be taken to court for any legal action, they can show that policies were consistent throughout the investigation, fair and with integrity. Again, you will want to determine if there are conflicts of interest or parties too close to the investigation, it may justify hiring a third party to conduct this investigation.

Investigators must have the skill to write clear and relevant notes as this is extremely important for future litigation.

In cases of reported sexual harassment, your policy will want to be clear on protecting the victim (and the accused), which may require your company hiring an outside third party to protect the confidentiality of the case. If you chose not to go outside of your company, you risk exposure and unforeseen events that arise from the perpetrator's knowledge of the complaint. I have been involved with as many as four ongoing workplace violence cases per week, involving many different situations. Some common themes I have noticed: there tends to be a higher risk in environments such as call centers, workplaces with high turnover, and a higher volume of hourly employees along with a largely female population of workers. If you have a high level director, such as a Global Director sexually harassing one of his subordinates, it not only affects that victim but also will affect the department, his authority and respect, and the work product from the department.

While an investigation is in progress, steps need to be in place to ensure:

- The victim is protected from harassment, fear of losing job.
- The perpetrator does not sexually harass another employee.
- The perpetrator does not do harm to the company while employed.
- The victim is provided support through counseling or working with HR.

It is important to remember that while someone is being harassed in the workplace, their work suffers, and they under added stress and put many additional hours in to document everything. No one except those who have gone through harassment and understands the work involved in continuous documentation of the perpetrator's actions.

Having a policy for handling cases such as sexual harassment and workplace violence should include a clear process identifying policy that will dictate exact order or workflow:

- Behavior witnessed and determine level of threat (policy spells out levels).
- Notification to legal, human resources, and policy/governance director.
- Determine action plan.
- Incident management documentation (you may have a data tool for this).
- Implementation of the plan (if you have one).
- Threat assessment should be part of your plan.
- Determine impact.
- Recommend action.

Workplace violence and investigations

It is important to understand workplace violence so that you can better investigate this complicated and dangerous threat. The following are the risks, OSHA's role, formulating a threat assessment team that you will be a part of, education and the workplace violence policy. All that you should have a clear understanding of all of these for a comprehensive overview of this threat. Many of you may be a company investigator, human resources, or an OSHA investigator or an investigator on a legal team. Because perpetrators of workplace violence are not predictable, no one can guarantee whether they will commit an act of violence because they have planned something or if they will be impulsive and react to someone or something.

Because there is no Federal Workplace Violence Standard, we must rely on standards such as OSHA, NIOSH, ASIS/SHRM, and other professional standards.

The National Institute of Occupational Safety and Health (NIOSH) defines Workplace Violence as violent acts (including physical assaults and threats of assaults), directed toward persons at work. Examples of threats can be expressions of intent to cause harm, including verbal threats, threatening body language, and written threats.[1]

Bullying includes such actions as threats, making threats, spreading rumors, attacking someone verbally or physically, or criticizing or excluding another based on their religion, sexual orientation, or group.

Workplace harassment is a form of discrimination and violated Title VII of the Civil Rights Act of 1964, along with other federal regulations. Workplace harassment is very common and victims can be unsure of what constitutes harassment. Workers also are not clear on what they should and can do. Often this goes unreported and can become a bigger issue.

Although said repeatedly that companies need to have a workplace violence program, we should say more firmly that companies **must have a** *well-defined* **program** in place, one that the CEO endorses is approved by legal, and one that lets their employees know that employee safety is priority #1. We must teach our leaders how to prevent a workplace violence incident, identifying potential problems, and steps in communicating a problem to minimize losses and mitigate the event when it occurs, because it will. There is no magic solution to stopping the violence because the perpetrator will not be as obvious as you think. They may not give us the warning signals we are trained to spot or they might give several indications but to various people. What I propose that needs to be done is: mitigate the risk while mitigating losses through training, planning, preparation, and taking proactive action. I am not talking about the same old, security approach of reacting to a problem. I am talking about being proactive.

---

[1] https://www.cdc.gov/niosh/docs/2002-101/default.html#What%20is%20workplace%20violence?

OSHA

OSHA defines workplace violence as violence or a threat of violence against workers. It can occur at or outside the workplace and can range from threats and verbal abuse to physical assaults and homicide. Homicide is one of the leading causes of job related deaths.

Workplace violence is such a threat and serious enough that OSHA issued a directive on workplace violence on September 8, 2011.[2] This "directive" outlines enforcement procedures for OSHA field officers to help them investigate employers for alleged workplace violence. OSHA's general duty clause requires employers to maintain a workplace that is free from recognized hazards that cause or are likely to cause death or serious physical harm. OSHA can cite and fine employers for failing to provide workers with adequate safeguards against workplace violence after an investigation. This directive doesn't require OSHA to respond to each complaint or incident related to workplace violence but it does help provide guidance for field officers to help determine whether an investigation should be pursued and if a citation is appropriate. This directive is an initiative on OSHA's part to examine the issues surrounding workplace violence. Although OSHA issued guidelines for preventing workplace violence for health care and social service workers in 1996 and late-night retailers and tax drivers in 1998, few citations were ever publicized after these guidelines were put in place. In recent years, there has been a heightened interest in the subject of workplace violence and OSHA has fined and cited employers on the basis that death or physical harm was likely to result from hazards that the employer knew or should have known about. Violence in the workplace has had devastating effects on businesses, both financially and in lost lives. Employers have a legal and moral obligation, along with the responsibility, to provide a safe and secure work environment. Every day thousands of employees are subjected to workplace violence in one form or another. Workplace violence includes any use of physical force against or by a worker that causes or could cause physical injury, threatening behavior, harassment, veiled threats, and intimidation. It also includes anger-related incidents, rape, arson, property damage, vandalism, and theft. Incidences can occur at off-site business-related functions like conferences, trade shows, social events, or meetings, but we refer to it as workplace violence because it takes place at work.

The US Bureau of Labor Statistics reported that assaults and violent acts, including homicides, accounted for 18% of the overall fatal work injuries in 2010.[3]

---

[2] OSHA Guidelines for Preventing Workplace Violence.
[3] US Bureau of Labor Statistics, U.S. Department of Labor, 2012.

When talking about the legal responsibility or duty of employers to safeguard employees, customers, and others from preventable harm, we also need to keep in mind the employer's obligation to respect employee rights and appropriate management of these investigations. Having recognized the possibility of workplace violence is the first step in planning and mitigating such an event when it occurs.

The risk

Workplace violence needs to be seen as a RISK that requires you to implement risk-based programs such as a risk assessment. The assessment, which should be a specific workplace violence assessment, will provide you with an understanding of the likelihood of a possible workplace violence threat and recommended solutions. Until we accept and acknowledge the possibility of a violent incident occurring at our worksite, we will miss the signs of potential problems and the chance to develop solutions to avoid it.

So how do we get companies to make workplace violence a serious component of their strategic management initiative? If you are to be successful in delivering a solid workplace violence prevention program, you must have the total commitment of senior management. As stated in ASIS/ SHRM WVPI.1-2011, section 8.1 "Warning Signs and Their Significance to Incident Management":

> Inappropriate behaviors and communications by a perpetrator usually will precede a violent incident. Conduct by a perpetrator that falls short of actual violence often creates disruption and fear in and organization and drains scarce resources.

Some behaviors emerge as "warning signs" of potential violence, offering a key opportunity for the organization to prevent a progression to more serious misconduct and violence.[4] While no one can predict whether or not someone will commit violence, we must examine all of the factors, conduct a violence risk assessment, and gather all facts of the person involved including their personal history, past history of any corrective action, grievances, or past actions.

According to the US Department of Labor (dol.gov), employee anger is on the rise and are becoming a common investigation in the workplace. The DOJ suggests we train staff to recognize the levels of violence[5]:

1. Early warning signs/low
May involve bullying.

---

[4] ASIS/SHRM WVPI.1-2011 American National Standard, section 8.1.

[5] https://www.dol.gov/agencies/oasam/centers-offices/human-resources-center/ policies/workplace-violence-program.

Intimidation.
Uncooperative.
Verbally abusive.
Disrespectful.
Overly defensive or paranoid behavior.
Isolationist.
2. Moderate (some escalation)
Argues with coworkers, management, and vendors.
Doesn't obey policies or procedures.
Sexually aggressive behavior.
May disrupt/damage business equipment and computer systems.
May see themselves as victimized.
May send threatening notes to coworkers.
3. Further escalation (high)
Destruction to property.
Serious breach of security.
Signs of extreme rage.
Obsessed with war and guns violence.
Brags about or in possession of weapons.
Gets into physical fights.
Threats of suicide.

According to the Bureau of Labor Statistics Census of Fatal Occupational Injuries (CFOI) of the 5147 fatal workplace injuries that occurred in the United States in 2017, 458 were cases of intentional injury by another person.[6]

Identification of the risks

You are an investigator and why do you need to know the risks? You need to know the risks to adequately identify these throughout the investigation process. Because the process can trigger additional risks, the more you understand the risks, the more prepared you will be for steps and resources you might want to tap into.

More needs to be done by every business to address critical components and to effectively address the issue of workplace violence. We will begin by identifying the risk because you need to examine not only the risks internally but also the external variables such as domestic violence, stalking, and other forms of unknown, aggressive behavior that enters the workplace. It is impossible to understand all the psychological and physical factors that might push an individual into committing a violent or aggressive act. For this reason, workplace violence is a very complex issue, and

---

[6] https://www.osha.gov/SLTC/workplaceviolence/.

we must look at all aspects of the risk/threat spectrum and be prepared to respond to any type of violence whether it is an active shooter, suicidal employee or domestic partner. Everyone reacts differently to stress that makes it next to impossible to determine which one of the two, three, or more stressors might lead a particular person to commit a violent act.

To review all the risks, it's critical that a violence risk assessment, specifically identifying the risks associated to workplace violence, is done. Having a security risk assessment is an extremely important process in identifying security concerns and risks. Your role and responsibility may also include conducting this assessment. During the security assessment, our process is often to identify assets, identify specific events that would cause loss of assets, estimate the frequency of such losses, estimate the potential impact of such loss, and finally identify ways to mitigate such losses. When evaluating various options of mitigating loss, we need to look at how feasible the option is and the cost versus benefit. A workplace violence that needs assessment will go beyond reviewing general vulnerability to assessing the possibility of violence from internal and external sources. We want to identify threats that might pertain to a particular industry type or organization, relationships that exists between a perpetrator and an organization, or relationships that may exist between a perpetrator and a current or former employee.

Threat assessment team

As an investigator, you will likely be involved in the assessment process, which should be a methodical process reviewing past and current behaviors. You and the threat assessment team will need to determine the propensity for violent behavior and the course of action that is within the procedures. Background checks may be a necessary component of the threat assessment.

Having a workplace violence policy is not enough unless you first have the full commitment from senior management. With senior management involved, you will need a team of leaders from various units of the business, to make a plan of what will be delivered, how it will be delivered, and to whom. This team of leaders can be referred to as the "threat assessment team" and should include a variety of disciplines, or representatives, including someone from legal, human resources, security management, and EAP. If you have a union environment, a union representative should be included. The key is to have a multidisciplinary approach, drawing on the different parts of the management structure, with different perspectives and areas of knowledge. It would also be helpful to include a member of your local law enforcement. Remember to identify the personnel who will carry the primary responsibility for preventing and responding to incidents of violence. You want to provide

them with necessary resources, policies, procedures, or guidelines, which will assist them with a coordinated response. Training a threat assessment team helps to maintain lines of communication and authority and helps guide the incident management process before a threat or violent incident occurs.
Start planning:

- Contract for an impartial, complete risk assessment and specific violence assessment. This should be designed to evaluate risks from within and outside the company.
- Institute a written workplace violence policy developed by management and employee representatives. Incorporate multidiscipline to research and write this policy. Use clear examples of acceptable behavior. Use firm, clear, and concise language.
- Institute a firm harassment and zero tolerance policy.
- Communicate your organizations view on workplace violence and harassment.
- Involve every employee.
- Implement an incident reporting system.
- Prioritize training and frequency of training for new hires, existing employees.
- Train the receptionist with extra training in the areas of detection and facial recognition.
- Train front line supervisors and management.
- Nonviolent conflict resolution for all management.
- Mandate annual training to reenforce policies.
- Develop partnerships with local police and emergency departments and mutual aid agreement with another business.
- Conduct tabletop exercises, including partners.
- Monitor and adjust training as needed based on statistics of success and intervention.
- Outline and communicate the investigation process and investigate every incident.
- Offer a confidential Employee Assistance Program (EAP) allowing employees to seek help and provide support services for victims of violence.
- Have plans in place for sheltering in place along with a safe zone off site.
- Maintain copies of company diagrams and property off site.

Supervisors and managers should be have specialized training on their role in identifying and reporting ways of diffusing aggressive behavior, conflict resolution, employee relations, personal security measures, and communication skills. These are not inclusive as there are other aspects that managers should be trained.

Workplace violence assessments can indicate the following:

- risk level and escalating aggression
- past history of violence
- mental health status if possible
- know weapons
- negative employment history
- personal stressors such as divorce, death of child, and bankruptcy
- outside organization influences

Ranking and scoring as done in risk assessment will bring you to a methodical score that will give direction on the continued process and steps that may be crucial to mitigate violence.

Workplace violence prevention policy

The workplace policy must be written, using firm, clear, and concise language. It should be clearly communicated, both at new hire orientation and ongoing, that there is a "zero tolerance with regard to threats and violence." The policy should emphasize the employer's commitment in providing a safe and secure workplace environment along with a clear definition of unacceptable behavior. The policy should state the code of conduct, prohibiting all threats, violent behavior, and other behavior that might be interpreted as intent to cause physical harm.

After you have written this policy and communicated it, it will be important to require prompt reporting of suspected violations along with enforcement of the policy. The policy should also include the following:

- All reports to management will be confidential and treated with discretion.
- All reports will be promptly investigated.
- Every witness and complainant will be treated fairly and impartially while investigated.
- The investigated staff and their qualifications.
- Identify how information about potential risks of violence will be communicated to all employees if necessary.
- Investigations are void from conflicts of interest, that is, not investigated by their respective supervisor.
- HR should communicate problematic employees with security.
- Offer an Employee Assistance Program EAP program to all employees.
- The commitment for nonretaliation by an employee making any report in good faith.
- State any applicable regulatory requirements.
- Indication of discipline for policy violation.

Train to identify warning signs

As investigators (or security professional), we know that some employees may have a higher risk of behavior issues or tendencies. Training and experience are the keys to understanding what behaviors might lead to violence. In many cases, attacks are perpetrated by individuals who display some of the following characteristics; however, every attacker has different psychological characteristics so it's helpful to be aware of behavioral clues that cause someone to act out:

- Prior history of violence: Involvement in previous incidents of violence, verbal abuse, antisocial activities, and disruptive behavior.
- Domestic situations: An employee caught in a domestic dispute or family turmoil may impact the work place.
- Suspicious behavior and indicators.
- Mental disorders: Mood swings, depression, bizarre statements, paranoid behavior, overly aggressive, and unstable behavior.
- Life-changing events: Whether the employee has suddenly lost a family member, a pet, extreme medical changes, divorce, or other major life changes.
- Financial stresses such as bankruptcies, mortgage arrears, or heavy debt load.
- Obsession with another employee: May be romantic or not.
- Chemical dependence: Drugs or alcohol abuse.
- Increased interest in weapons: Ownership of guns or gun collection, other offensive weapons. They may even talk a lot about guns.
- Disgruntled employee: An employee feels the company no longer cares about them or other employees creating a sense of mistrust, recently laid off or terminated.

Education and training

We need to consider what training to provide and to whom. It also needs to be repeated periodically and updated based on changes in policies, physical elements, or risk factors. The training for employees should include understanding what workplace violence is, identification of early warning signs of workplace violence, and whom and how to report it. It is important to communicate, to all employees, that every employee needs to be responsible for a safe and secure work environment. The employees need to understand policies for access control, piggybacking, and reporting red flags. They also need to understand how important it is to notify HR of any potential domestic issues. This is important because statistics show that the perpetrator kills, on average, and 3–5 innocent bystanders.

Training for supervisors and managers should include all of the training employees receive along with training in:

- the issues of workplace violence
- their role in identification of violence
- ways to deescalation or diffusing violent behavior
- recognize behavioral clues
- conflict resolution
- communication skills
- personal security options
- EAP if available
- various cycles of anger and managing anger
- crisis management
- high-risk terminations
- security procedures
- emergency procedures relative to a violent incident

Workplace violence free

The following are some practices to implement into your security policy to help safeguard your workplace from violence. This requires that you incorporate a variety of procedures such as:

- Hiring practices that not only incorporate comprehensive background checks on new hires but also consider conducting random or annual background checks on your current workforce.
- Incorporate a zero tolerance policy.
- Establish a way for employees to report problem behavior through anonymous ways, that is, employee tip line and have ensured an immediate and useful response.
- Foster a work environment that supports the reporting of misconduct and also prohibits retaliation to those who report the conduct.
- Investigate all incidents and properly document.
- Implement procedures for investigation of misconduct ensuring they are viewed as fair.
- Implement specific workplace violence training for new hires, annual training for current employees, and specialized training for management.
- Conduct a risk assessment with a workplace violence assessment.
- Utilize your threat team and your plan.
- Incorporate a fully integrated facility security program, utilizing structural barriers, ID badges, access control, lighting, key control, locks, documentation, communications, CCTV, and environmental design.
- Utilizing the security system adequately.

- Review your termination practices, having a plan for high risk terminations.
- Liaison with local law enforcement, medical staff, hospitals, and fire department.
- Develop an emergency plan including evacuation procedures and disaster recovery plans and update both frequently.
- Develop partnerships with other like businesses.
- Evaluate and update your workplace violence policies and plans as necessary.

This list is noninclusive, and each individual business will have specific needs beyond what I have suggested.

Everyone plays a role in preventing violence through observation, communication, and reporting. No organization can afford to ignore the issue of workplace violence as lives are lost daily due to such tragedies. Make the commitment and be proactive through initiatives, planning, exercising, and mitigating.[7] Whether you are the investigator, security specialist assigned to a workplace violence incident or human resources, your commitment to thoroughly investigation, document and manage these cases will make the difference of how many lives are lost.

Concluding an investigation

Concluding an investigation should have several elements:

- Clear facts based on evidence obtained, interviews conducted, observations, etc.
- Clear and completed documentation that supports a conclusion.
- Notification of result to both the complainant and the accused.
- When closing the investigation file, verify all pertinent documents are in the file including signed statements from all, relevant documentation, and all handwritten investigative notes.

If discipline action is taken, all action should be consistent with the company's policy.

Investigate promptly, investigate with unbiased, investigate thoroughly, investigate with integrity, and investigate to provide a safe and secure workplace.

---

[7] 6th Ed. Fennelly, Handbook of Loss Prevention and Crime Prevention, Chpt 13, Workplace Violence: 2020 and beyond, Inge Sebyan Black.

23

Skills of successful investigators

Developing the art of the interview

There are hundreds of books on interviewing, interrogations, and investigations for law enforcement, but if you are in the private sector or work for a corporation, there are not as many and being a private investigator has many differences. Those differences can often work in your favor. This book is written for anyone that needs some tips, reminders or helpful considerations, when doing an interview. In the United States the one big difference for investigators in the private sector is that you are not required to read the Miranda warning (detailed in Chapter 1) before questioning a suspect. Private investigators or corporate investigators have no time restrictions on how long they can meet with their employees about company business. Private investigators (working on behalf of their client, the company) have 100% access to employees' company computers, company cell phones, or any other equipment that is owned by the company, *without* a search warrant.

If your cell phone is owned by you but you use it for company email, then it can also be seized. Most of the information security company policies are presented to the employee requiring signatures while onboarding. When starting a position, employees new hire orientation paperwork will include all the controls that the company has once you combine your personal technology with company business. My personal experience and advice is to keep them separate. If you have an option of using your company email on your personal cell phone, my advice is keep your personal cell phone for personal use only and have your business email and services on the business phone. If you use your company email on a personal device, it can be confiscated during an investigation. This is true for big corporation such as banks and retail and many smaller companies also.

Let's examine what it takes to be an investigative interviewer and some helpful tips for when the time comes to conduct that first interview. You might not be a private investigator; you could be a human resource specialist, asset protection associate, insurance investigator, loss prevention officer, security director, or owner of a business. If you take away anything from this book, the author hopes it will be an understanding of the importance of preparing for an interview and how in these times, research is infinite and critical to a successful interview.

That first interview might be the only chance you'll ever have to talk to your interviewee. As a private investigator, one shot may be all you'll get.

Investigative interviewing is definitely an art. It is an art because no two people are the same, which translates into every interviewer having unique mannerisms and techniques. Each will bring to the process of different components, including personalities, traits, and styles. Individual style will be determined by the interviewer's work experience, personal life experience, and training. There are as many variables as there are individuals. No one can tell you what to do, what to ask, or what to say. What I *can* tell you is that with training and practice, you can be a successful interviewer. Through practice, you can perfect your individual style. All of the suggestions and descriptions in this book are just that—suggestions. They represent one or two individual styles, but not yours. *Your style is unique to you.*

The most valuable tool you will develop is your personal style and rapport—developing the ability to form a relationship, almost an intimate one, with your subject. This might not be necessary for witnesses or all interviewees, but if you are interviewing a subject that you need a confession from, you will need to form a close, almost intimate relationship. Doing so will require you to be empathetic without being judgmental or accusatory. You need that person to open up to you.

In conducting internal investigations, there are as many different approaches as there are investigators. One approach that I often use and that has helped me prosecute many suspect employees is to tell them I'm interviewing them about specific losses the company has had and to request their help to resolve the discrepancies. By "employing the employee" to help you, you give them a feeling of lending assistance that often disarms them and allows them to focus on resolving the losses versus the consequences that may occur because of their confessions.

Qualifications for investigators

Investigators are often more confident and professional based on the degree of their training, qualifications, and practice. There are investigators that handle any type of investigation and there are others that specialize in one or more specific types of investigations. This may depend on their individual training, their particular place in the company, size of company, or company structure. It is not uncommon to find private investigators that specialize in particular areas.

Everyone is different and will have their own specific preferences.

Although I have actively done surveillance, I personally dislike doing them and often transferred those types of investigation to another investigator. What made this the right decision was his investment of $50,000 for specialty equipment, he had the right vehicle, and he had the temperament to do this type of surveillance. It takes a special character to do this type of work. In exchange he would give me the investigations that I specialized in because he preferred the surveillance and I preferred workplace investigations, assault, fraud, and embezzlement cases. You need to know yourself and what you are best at doing, what you are passionate about, and what you are confident in doing.

I knew that because I have a "type A" personality, I disliked sitting idle for days watching and hoping for activity. Surveillance can be extremely boring and also very complicated. Complicated with restroom breaks, following a vehicle, being alert for long periods, and sleep deprived. For operations like these to be successful, your company or your client must be fully invested into spending the appropriate amount necessary for a thorough, complete, and successful operation.

Regardless, you need to be aware of all of the challenges that come with different types of investigations.

If you have control over the type of investigations you take on, you will likely find that specific investigations are a better fit for you based on your training, experience, personality, and confidence.

Soft skills that successful investigators possess the following:

- energy
- competence
- awareness
- adaptability
- critical observation
- active listening
- understanding of human nature
- conflict resolution
- oral and written communication skills
- attention to detail

Below are additional critical skills that if you want to be a successful investigator:

- Intelligence: the ability to see the entire picture; not stuck in tunnel vision; insightfulness.
- Open minded: remain unbiased and without preconceived assumptions.
- Specialized training: analytical, cyber, insurance, fraud, or forensic training are a few.
- Perseverance: persistence, grit, and determination.

- Patience: is required because it takes time to uncover the truth and get the results you want.
- Thoroughness: missing something can derail an otherwise strong case.
- Curiosity: a need to know, being proactive, and learn from everyone.
- Sensitivity: empathy; respect for yourself and others.
- Ethical: being honest and having the courage to uncover truth despite obstacles.
- Organized: keep well-documented notes on actions and result, and resources used.
- Creative: try many options when solving a puzzle, and think outside the box.
- Tenacious: don't give up, try many different ways, use variety of research tools, and try different techniques.
- Proactive: stay current on the latest technology, threats and tactics. Continuously learner.
- Teamwork: being able to work well with a teammate or team.

Lucky or skilled

Introduction

Over the years, we both have been involved in numerous investigations. Being lucky during an investigation is something we feel needs to be acknowledged. Fred Mullins, CPP, was telling us about a stakeout he was on. Five hours at a specific site and nothing. It was 5:00 AM, and he decided to head home and go to bed. While traveling toward home on a major highway, the truck and the individuals he had been waiting for passed him on the left. Fred said, "I was lucky." But was it luck, or being in the right place at the right time? What is dedication to the assignment? Was it knowing when to leave a stakeout? Was it a skilled investigator's hunch? Was it a degree of skill and a mixture of all of the above? We do know that he completed his assignments and the individuals were arrested.

Stakeouts

Stakeouts[1] usually occur when police have a tip that a crime is likely to occur at a specific location or when crime analysis pattern identification information leads them to believe that a crime may occur at one or more potential targets. In the case of a tip, it is advisable to substitute an undercover police officer in place of a potential victim, such as a clerk or salesperson. Trained police officers are better prepared to deal with dangerous situations. In addition, police have both an ethical and legal obligation to protect innocent persons in situations where they might be harmed. In the *United States* v. *Watson*, the Supreme Court held that police do not need an arrest warrant to apprehend a suspect who commits a crime in a public place. Thus, if police actually observe a robbery of a liquor store, for example, they may take the suspect into custody as soon as it is safely possible to do.

---

[1] Leonard Territo, James B. Halsted, and Max L. Bromley, *Crime and Justice 1n America: A Human Perspective*, 5th Ed. (Boston: Butterworth-Heinemann, 1998) http://www.bh.com.

When a suspect is identified after the robbery has taken place, police need to make the arrest as soon as possible. As soon as the suspect is known, police obtain an arrest warrant for that individual. Legally the officer's actions are guided by two cases, *Payton* v. *New York* and *Steagald* v. *United States*. In *Payton* the Court held that police must, in the absence of exigent or emergency circumstances, obtain an arrest warrant for a suspect before they may enter a private residence to make a felony arrest. In *Steagald* the Court ruled that an arrest warrant does not authorize police to enter a third party's home to make a felony arrest. Thus, if police believe that a suspect can be found in a residence other than that of the suspect, they must obtain a search warrant to enter the other residence to arrest the felon.

Surveillance preparation

Study all available data relating to names, aliases, complete physical description, and identifying characteristics and mannerisms. Know who the friends, associates, and contacts are. Obtain as many photos as possible. Learn all that is available about normal activities and habits. If it can be determined, you should know the person's propensity for violence and what, if any, criminal history they have. If it can be determined, it is helpful to know if the subject or object of your efforts is sensitive to or "tail conscious."

It is important to understand fully the neighborhood in which a surveillance is conducted: who are the inhabitants, what is the style of dress, and what language or dialects are spoken? What should be your dress to match that of the locals? What types of vehicles are common to the area? Determine what vehicle license plates should be usual to the area. What the subject's driving habits? Where does he/she usually go? This is important to know in case the subject is "lost" in traffic; you can then check the known usual locations to reestablish contact. It is recommended that a reconnaissance be undertaken to learn the geography, look for suitable vantage points, obtain a feel for the traffic conditions, and learn the streets. The most embarrassing thing you can do is follow someone down a dead end street.

Always carry sufficient money to defray expenses. If you know that someone is likely to frequent expensive restaurants to meet others, be prepared. There are two suggestions that must be followed to be successful under these circumstances; it is wise to pay your check before your subject does, so you can leave quickly, and when possible, you should leave before the subject does and reposition yourself outside.

Make sure your cellphone is charged, GPS is working and you have all that you need.

Investigation—175 Things you should know

1. Be confidence.
2. Be positive.
3. Be prepared.
4. Be ready for denial.
5. Be ready for rationalizations.
6. Be empathetic.
7. Be flexible.
8. Be objective.
9. Be alert.
10. Be mentally prepared.
11. Be adversarial when necessary.
12. Be adaptable.
13. Be respectful.
14. Be patient and break the interviewee's pat story.
15. Build trust.
16. Be nonjudgmental.
17. Be creative; think outside the box.
18. Research the background of the interviewee.
19. Do online research of all details.
20. Know your purpose.
21. Control your comfort zone.
22. Tailor your demeanor.
23. Admit to mistakes.
24. Eliminate possible answers.
25. Maintain high professional standards.
26. Use the skills you've developed.
27. Have a conversation.
28. Try to develop something in common with the interviewee when necessary.
29. Assess the interviewee.
30. Stay calm.
31. Know yourself.

32. Know your biases.
33. Expect the unexpected.
34. Control the interview.
35. Properly handle confidential informants.
36. Know the respective laws.
37. Know your company policies.
38. Know the interviewee's rights.
39. Understand your limits.
40. Help subjects recall events.
41. Use props if you have them.
42. Consider the time of day for your interview.
43. Listen and avoid questions that have a yes-or-no reply.
44. Maintain confidentiality.
45. Observe, attentive, and concentrate.
46. Don't have a time frame to end the interview.
47. Confirm simple details.
48. Have necessary documents.
49. Have questions ready and be ready to take a statement.
50. Always assume there is more information.
51. Know, observe, and compare body language, movements, and signs.
52. Set baseline for nervousness by asking innocuous questions.
53. If public officer, only use Miranda when subject is not free to go.
54. Keep an open mind.
55. Don't keep time.
56. Have a private location.
57. Select the location yourself.
58. Know when to shut up and be silent.
59. Prepare the seating arrangement prior to the interview.
60. Start with small talk.
61. Use deception sparingly.
62. Consider layout of the room.
63. Set the room so your comfortable level.
64. Establish common ground.
65. Know when to stop, pause, be silent, and be direct and indirect.
66. Bring a notebook and take notes.
67. Know when to get help or call an expert.
68. Be prepared to ask tough questions.
69. Choose questions wisely.
70. Avoid third-degree questioning.
71. Ask closed questions when necessary.
72. Ask open-ended questions when needed.
73. Keep questions simple.
74. Hide your personal values.

75. Maintain a neutral stance.
76. Avoid using coercive behaviors.
77. Use active listening skills.
78. Consider the human needs of the interviewee.
79. Let the interviewee talk.
80. Develop a rapport.
81. Watch for behavioral clues such as gestures, facial expressions, and tone of voice.
82. Follow your instincts.
83. Wait till you have enough leverage before you hit that home run.
84. Know when to be aggressive.
85. Practice, practice, and practice.
86. Wear a suit and tie when it might be warranted.
87. Dress casually if it fits the interview setting and style.
88. Control personal anger.
89. Cover suspicious ness.
90. Manage your time.
91. Remember the 14th Amendment regarding due process and equal protection.
92. Remember the importance of a well-written report.
93. Use bench marking.
94. Remember your code of ethics.
95. Use professional conduct.
96. Validate information.
97. Don't get sucked into the trap of familiarity.
98. Ten items to be aware of.
99. Three types of evidence.
100. Types of investigations.
101. Seven federal acts investigators need to be aware of.
102. Miranda warnings.
103. Ten things needed to be a good investigator.
104. Surveillance equipment needed.
105. Eight things you should know about surveillance assignments.
106. Workplace violence cases.
107. White-collar crime.
108. Collection and preservation of evidence.
109. How to prepare that important report.
110. Relevant facts.
111. Sources of investigative information.
112. Stakeouts.
113. Preservation of evidence.
114. Investigation basics.
115. Investigating internal cargo theft.
116. The investigative process.

161. Criminal justice: what are the legal limits of police searches?
162. Criminal justice case law: *Terry* v. *Ohio* and criminal justice case law: *Mapp* v. *Ohio* analysis and impact.
163. Cutting and stabbing investigations: five things you should know.
164. Sketching crime scenes.
165. Sketching preparation.
166. Sketching measurement.
167. Sketches: types of crime scene.
168. Types of cases.
169. Arson cases.
170. Child abuse cases.
171. Forensics.
172. Testifying in court.
173. Gaming cases.
174. Healthcare fraud.
175. Threat assessments.

Conclusion

The investigative interview is an art because each of us makes it unique and personalized. Each of you will bring your own style, technique, and personality to each of your interviews.

It is our hope that something in this book will help you examine your own values, beliefs, ethics, and behavior and help you to be a successful interviewer. Remember to treat everyone with respect, and you will earn trust from colleagues and those you interview. Building relationships will allow for dialog.

The most powerful advice that we can give to you is to practice, practice, practice, and embrace your art.

Subject Index

Note: Page numbers followed by *f* indicate figures and *t* indicate tables.

Made in the USA
Middletown, DE
19 August 2023

36954940R00146